BILLS OF LADING AND BANKERS' DOCUMENTARY CREDITS

BILLS OF LADING AND BANKERS' DOCUMENTARY CREDITS

By

PAUL TODD, M.A., B.C.L.

Lecturer in Law
University of Wales, Cardiff

|L|L|P|

LONDON   NEW YORK   HAMBURG   HONG KONG
LLOYD'S OF LONDON PRESS LTD.
1990

Lloyd's of London Press Ltd
Legal Publishing and Conferences Division
One Singer Street, London EC2A 4LQ

USA AND CANADA
Lloyd's of London Press Inc
Suite 308, 611 Broadway
New York, NY 10012 USA

GERMANY
Lloyd's of London Press GmbH
59 Ehrenbergstrasse
2000 Hamburg 50, West Germany

SOUTH EAST ASIA
Lloyd's of London Press (Far East) Ltd
Room 1101, Hollywood Centre
233 Hollywood Road
Hong Kong

© Paul Todd, 1990

First published 1990

British Library Cataloguing in Publication Data
Todd, Paul *1954*—
Bills of lading and bankers' documentary credits.
1. England. International banking. Documentary credits.
Law
I. Title
344.20673

ISBN 1–85044–262–2

Text set 10 on 12pt Linotron 202 Times by
Promenade Graphics, Cheltenham, Glos.
Printed in Great Britain by
Bookcraft Ltd, Midsomer Norton

ACKNOWLEDGMENTS

It is impossible to write today on bankers' documentary credits without referring extensively to International Chamber of Commerce publications. I am grateful to the International Chamber of Commerce for permission to reproduce in Appendix A the entirety of the *Uniform Customs and Practice on Documentary Credits* (1983 revision), a publication to which I have also referred extensively in the text. I have also made extensive reference to other, generally available I.C.C. publications, especially *UCP 1974/1983 Revisions Compared and Explained*, I.C.C. Publication No. 411.

It is important in a book of this nature to be as up to date as possible on current banking practices, and also on topical issues. I would like therefore to extend a special gratitude to the I.C.C. Banking Commission, and in particular its Chairman, Bernard Wheble, for sending me papers which are not generally available, and providing other information which apart from being right up to date, is not available elsewhere.

PREFACE

This is a book on bankers' documentary credits, which is aimed primarily at the business, rather than the academic market. It should therefore, I hope, be comprehensible both to lawyers and to businessmen who have little or no legal background. In some cases the contractual relationships between the various parties are quite complex, as is (in other cases) the whereabouts of legal and equitable title, and where this is so, I have made free use of line diagrams.

Yet despite the book's market emphasis, I am nevertheless conscious that it shares a number of features more commonly found in more academic books. A common feature of books aimed at the business market, for example, is their tendency to state the law as if it could be reduced to a series of rules, which are rigidly defined, and about whose correctness there could be no doubt. So a black and white view of the subject is, in my view, a mistake, because there are regrettably many areas where the law is anything but clear. Unfortunately, although the English law on documentary credits is a lot clearer than it once was, there are still grey areas. Where the law remains uncertain, I have taken the view that the best course is to examine the various different points of view. No doubt this is a regrettable academic trait, but surely there is no point in pretending that certainty exists where it does not, nor in stating as categorically correct a view which later turns out to be wrong.[1]

It is also quite common for books aimed at the business market to manage without the aid of footnotes, but I am with the academics here too, and favour their use. I know that they are greatly disliked by a number of people, and of course, one can go too far: nothing is more annoying than a page which contains five lines of text and 25 of footnotes. I have tried, however, to use

---

1. Interestingly, in a recent conference at which I was one of the speakers, also aimed primarily at the business market, a criticism received from one of the delegates was that "We don't need to know both sides, we need to know what rulings exist (correct or not) so we know where to aim". I emphatically disagree with this, and see no point, for any purpose, in providing information which is wrong. He was not in the majority, and indeed another delegate took the opposite view, commenting that the treatment was too bread and butter, and that discussion of recent cases and proposals for reform were insufficiently detailed. It is impossible to please everyone, of course.

footnotes primarily to allow the text itself to flow more freely. Because the detailed arguments and counter-arguments, and the references which have to be included, and which would otherwise greatly clutter the main text, can be shunted off into the footnotes, the text itself need address itself only to the main points. I hope that I have thereby succeeded in making it more readable. On the other hand, I would also hope that those who wish to study the subject more deeply can find in the footnotes the details and additional references they need. That at least is the idea. I suspect that the real arguments against footnotes are arguments of cost, rather than desirability, but in the age when books can be typeset (as this one has been) directly from computer disk, how valid are these cost arguments in reality?

In spite of borrowing a number of features from the academic market, this book is nevertheless aimed primarily at the businessman.[2] I have tried to reflect this in the emphasis, which is certainly different from that which would be appropriate to a more academic work. By and large I have endeavoured to concentrate on modern commercial practices, and also on the *Uniform Customs and Practice on Documentary Credits*, which was adopted by the English banking community as long ago as 1962 (today some 95 per cent. of credits worldwide are subject to it). On the other hand, I have not examined in much detail the more academic aspects of the subject, although I have tried, where appropriate, to set out the relevant references in the footnotes. For the most part, these references are to the general law of contract, and in particular Treitel's excellent textbook, now in its seventh edition.

In short, the book aims to concentrate on issues which are of current topical interest to the banking community. So far as the law is concerned, I have not set out to write a polemic: my aim has been limited to an exposition of what the law is, without arguing for (or indeed against) change.[3] I am not really qualified to make comments on current banking practices, but in so far as they affect rights and liabilities, or adversely affect the bank's security, I have said so.

The title is *Bills of Lading and Bankers' Documentary Credits*, and not simply *Bankers' Documentary Credits*. There are growing pressures to replace the traditional bill of lading by newer forms of documentation, or even to do away with traditional documentation altogether.[4] The pressures by and large come from the transport community, and are by no means unequivocally in the interests of the banking community. One of the central themes of this book, therefore, is to examine the role played by the bill of lading, and the

2. The market envisaged is primarily international bankers, but also shippers, forwarding agents, shipowners, charterers, loading brokers, insurance companies, exporters and importers. There may be a small student market, in international trade courses, although the book is not primarily aimed at this market.

3. The only exception is in Chapter 7, where reforms are currently being canvassed by the Law Commission, so that the issue of reform may be seen to be very much on the agenda.

4. See section 5.7.

pros and cons of what I have called "the document revolution"[5] and the development of paperless transactions.

This is reflected in the coverage. The first chapter introduces the documentary credit, and examines the central role played by the clean shipped bill of lading. Chapter 4 examines the role of documentation in principle, and Chapter 5 the U.C.P. requirements, whether or not the credit calls for a "marine bill of lading". In particular, all the new forms of documentation, such as liner waybills and combined transport documents, as well as teletransmission or electronic data interchange, are examined, and the effect on the bank's security of using either the new documentation, or a paperless system, is fully considered. Also considered is the practice of carrying one original bill of lading on board, while the other two are negotiated (usually involving a bank).

One of the main differences between the bill of lading and almost every alternative document (apart from the ship's delivery order) is that it can provide the holder with actions against the carrier. It is true that banks as pledgees are less likely to benefit than buyers, but nevertheless the relationship between bank and carrier is intrinsic to the security afforded by the shipping documents. Chapter 7 is therefore devoted entirely to this relationship.

To some extent the timing of this book is fortuitous, since in the two and a half years which have elapsed between its conception and its completion, a number of unforeseen events have occurred. Nevertheless, its timing turns out to be opportune. The Law Commission's Working Paper No.112: "Rights to Goods in Bulk" (1989), for example, has far-reaching ramifications for banks. Perhaps of greater importance is that, in October 1989, the I.C.C. Banking Commission decided to embark on another revision of the U.C.P., which will probably be completed in around 1993. Unquestionably, further consideration will be given to questions of documentation, and a Working Group has even been set up to consider rules for an electronic trade credit, where electronic data interchange (E.D.I.) replaces (or at any rate supplements) traditional paper documentation.

Another recent development concerns the standby letter of credit, which was first brought within the provisions of the U.C.P. in 1983. Until recently, these were used mainly either as performance bonds, or to guarantee payment on, for example, the sale of a ship. Now they are coming into more general use in bulk oil sales, primarily because of the difficulties of using the traditional shipped bill of lading to secure payment under a conventional documentary credit. As use of the traditional bill of lading further declines, we can perhaps expect to see greater use of the standby letter of credit. Standby letters of credit therefore receive detailed consideration in Chapter 8.

Another advantage of writing now is that the law of the United Kingdom

---

5. See section 1.2.

on documentary credits has become much clearer in the last 10 or 15 years, as is evidenced by the fact that many of the cases referred to in this book were decided after 1975, or even 1980. Until recently, the English law on documentary credits was relatively undeveloped even on fundamental issues,[6] and until now books on documentary credits have tended to lean heavily on Commonwealth and American authorities, not so much for comparative purposes as to provide persuasive argument. While this is justifiable, indeed necessary where there is little English authority available, this fallback is no longer needed. Today, there is English authority on almost every aspect of the subject, and I have referred almost exclusively to English authorities in this book.

University of Wales   PAUL TODD
August 1990

---

6. E.g., sections 6.2 and 8.1.

CONTENTS

CONTENTS

CONTENTS

LIST OF ILLUSTRATIONS

TABLE OF CASES

References are to section numbers
A section number in **bold** *type indicates a section where the case is considered in depth*

TABLE OF CASES

TABLE OF CASES

TABLE OF CASES

TABLE OF STATUTES

References are to section numbers
*A section number in **bold** type indicates a section where the provision is set out or considered in depth*

CHAPTER 1

INTRODUCTION TO BANKERS' DOCUMENTARY CREDITS AND BILLS OF LADING

1.1 INTRODUCTION

The aim of this book is primarily to describe the law applicable to, and workings of bankers' documentary credits, as they are used in international sales and carriage of goods. Particular emphasis will however be placed on the role of the bill of lading in the documentary credit.

It will become clear as this chapter progresses that without the traditional shipped bill of lading the bankers' documentary credit could never have developed into its present form. In any international sale of goods, except perhaps between associated companies within a group, there are conflicts of interest between seller and buyer which appear at first sight to be irreconcilable. Indeed, they would probably have remained irreconcilable but for the development of the bill of lading as a document of title.

Not only does the traditional bill of lading resolve the inevitable conflicts of interest between seller and buyer in an international sale contract, but where the sale is financed by documentary credit, it also provides the bank with the security it needs confidently to be able to advance funding for the transaction.

1.2 THE DOCUMENT REVOLUTION

Recent years have seen the partial demise of the bill of lading, and its replacement in some trades by other documents. The main problem with the traditional shipped bill of lading is that in order for it to operate properly as a document of title, it is essential that delivery of the goods from the ship should only be made to the holder of an original bill of lading. It is indeed precisely because only the holder of an original bill of lading can demand the goods from the ship that it can be used as a document of title at all, since that is what enables it to be transferred instead of the goods on sales and re-sales, where obviously the goods themselves, while they remain at sea, cannot. Equally obviously, however, the bill of lading cannot perform this function

1

effectively unless it reaches the receiver before the goods themselves are delivered, and preferably before the ship arrives at the port of discharge.[1]

Today, however, the goods often arrive first, partly because of the revolution in transport methods over the last 25 years or so, speeding up the sea voyage. There are also difficulties, particularly in the carriage of oil cargoes, where the bill of lading is negotiated several times to effect successive re-sales, maybe as many as 100 or more.[2] Since each transaction takes time, sometimes the bill of lading does not arrive until months or even years after the cargo.

Another problem is that the bill of lading was developed for port-to-port shipment, and is less suitable where the carriage involves land, as well as sea elements (i.e., a combined transport operation).

It is not surprising, then, that the use of alternative documentation is increasing, partially replacing the traditional bill of lading. In particular, combined transport documents are often used for combined transport operations, and non-negotiable waybills, which can be carried aboard the vessel, are commonly used on short container routes, especially in the North Atlantic. A non-negotiable document would be inappropriate for an oil cargo, which is to be sold and re-sold many times, but shipowners commonly deliver oil cargoes without waiting for the bill of lading to catch up, relying on a bank indemnity should they deliver the cargo to the wrong person.

The overwhelming majority of bankers' documentary credits are made subject to the *Uniform Customs and Practice on Documentary Credits* (U.C.P.), published by the International Chamber of Commerce (I.C.C.).[3] When the U.C.P. was last revised in 1983, perhaps the most important change was that an entirely new approach was taken to documentation, " 'legislating' for what the transport community was, is and seems likely to be producing in the way of documentation".[4] Detailed provision has at any rate now been made for "transport documents", in cases where the traditional port-to-port bill of lading (referred to in the U.C.P. as the "marine" bill of lading) is not used. The term "transport document" includes not only the combined transport document, but also the non-negotiable sea waybill. The banking world recognises

---

1. Shipowners cannot in practice wait for bills of lading to catch up, since not only will the vessel not be earning freight, but will also be incurring port charges. There is a distinction between delivery and discharge, however. They may *discharge* the cargo into a warehouse from which it is only *delivered* to the receiver against production of an original bill of lading. There are practical difficulties in respect of some types of cargo, however, for example bulk oil aboard a large tanker, which cannot realistically be stored except in the receiver's cargo tanks.

2. In a paper given to a recent conference organised by Legal Studies and Services Ltd., "Bills of Lading: Changes to the English Law and the Commercial Implications", 2nd and 3rd April 1990, Brian Davenport Q.C. noted of oil cargoes: "The chains may be long. A banker once told me that he had seen a chain of 104 buyers".

3. See below, section 2.1.

4. Bernard Wheble, *UCP 1974/1983 Revisions Compared and Explained*, I.C.C. publication No. 411, p. 46.

that it must respond to the changes which are being forced upon it by the transport community.

In October 1989 the I.C.C. Banking Commission decided to embark on a further revision of the U.C.P., which will probably be completed in around 1993. Unquestionably, consideration will be given to widening further still the scope of the U.C.P., and a working group has even been set up to consider rules for an electronic trade credit, where electronic data interchange (E.D.I.) replaces (or at any rate supplements) traditional paper documentation.

Undoubtedly there will remain large areas of international commerce where the traditional bill of lading will continue to predominate, at any rate for the foreseeable future. The document revolution is well under way, however, and the documentary credit will no doubt have to adapt to it. The main area for concern is that none of the alternatives to the traditional shipped (or on board) bill of lading share all of its advantages, and some of the protection given to each of the parties will be lost where alternative documentation (or electronic data interchange) is used. How much of a problem will that be? That is one of the main themes of this book.[5]

1.3 PROTECTION OF THE PARTIES IN INTERNATIONAL SALES OF GOODS

1.3.1 The seller

Although the legal principles applicable to international sales of goods, deriving as they do from the general law of contract, are similar to those which apply to ordinary domestic sales of goods, international sales nevertheless differ fundamentally from ordinary domestic sales. Not only are buyer and seller dealing with each other in different countries, but they are also less likely to deal often with one another than in the case in ordinary sales of goods. Indeed, many international sale transactions are of a one-off nature (this is especially likely in the case of bulk commodity transactions).

The seller is therefore less likely to be sure of the financial standing of the buyer, and that he will be paid for the goods he dispatches, than in domestic sales. He would be taking a great risk in going to the trouble and expense of obtaining (possibly even manufacturing) and consigning goods without some assurance that he will eventually be paid for them. Also, once the goods are at sea, the seller may have some difficulty in getting them back should the buyer default on payment, and he will probably be unable to recover his goods before they have arrived in the buyer's country of business.

The obvious solution is to demand payment in advance. Of course the buyer does not wish to do this, partly for cashflow reasons, but more

5. See in particular Chapters 4 and 5.

importantly because in an international sale there is no more reason for the buyer to trust the seller to ship goods or cargo of the promised quantity and description than for the seller to trust the buyer to pay. The best that the seller can reasonably expect, therefore, is a guarantee that he will be paid by a paymaster whose integrity and solvency are not in doubt, the paymaster himself taking the risk of having to recoup the price plus commission from the buyer. The seller does not wish to commit himself to any form of performance at all under the sale contract until he has received this guarantee, and for cashflow reasons he will still wish to be paid as early as possible. In reality, however, if payment is guaranteed by a sufficiently reliable paymaster the seller may accept deferral of payment, since he may be able to use the guarantee itself as security for an advance from his own bank to cover the costs up to shipment. Realistically also, payment will not actually be made until there is clear evidence that the seller has performed his side of the bargain.

From the seller's point of view then, the most important consideration is that he is protected from the consequences of the bankruptcy of a purchaser about whose financial standing he knows nothing, or non-payment by that purchaser for any other reason. Before embarking upon the costly process of obtaining and shipping the goods he wants an assurance from a reputable bank (a "reliable and solvent paymaster"), that he will be paid. It may well be that a reputable bank can be relied upon to pay so long as the seller performs, but the seller would nevertheless prefer a legally enforceable undertaking, directly from the bank, on which he can sue if necessary.[6]

Not only is it important that the undertaking is made directly by a "reliable and solvent paymaster", but also that its validity does not depend upon the whim of the buyer. It is no good if the buyer can choose to accept or reject the goods. It is also obviously in the seller's interests that he is paid as early as possible, and certainly he would not generally favour having to wait until the goods are actually delivered in the buyer's country of business.

1.3.2 The buyer

The buyer will obviously wish to pay as late as possible. Again, this is partly for cashflow reasons, but also he will not usually be in a position to inspect the goods before he actually receives them: they are arriving on a ship from a different country, and cannot be physically inspected while at sea.

No doubt, if the seller's position as to payment is made secure, by giving him a legally enforceable action against a reputable bank, then he may be prepared to wait until the goods are delivered before being paid.[7] On the other hand, he certainly does not wish payment to depend on real or imagined dis-

---

6. One of the main difficulties of the earliest forms of credit was the lack of a clear legal basis for the relationship between the seller and the bank. The modern form of credit is somewhat different, and the correct analysis of this relationship is now clear, although by no means entirely without problems. See further section 8.1.

7. See, e.g., the credit in *Morgan* v. *Larivière*, section 8.1.7.

putes with the buyer as to whether he accepts or rejects the goods when they arrive.[8] The goods may by then be thousands of miles away, so that conducting such a dispute would be difficult in the extreme, to say nothing of the fact that it is likely to be somewhat inconvenient for them to be rejected at that stage, especially if for example they are perishable.

The buyer, on the other hand, would prefer neither to pay, nor to become liable for payment, until he has received some assurance that the seller has performed his side of the bargain. Yet as long as the cargo is at sea, its condition cannot be inspected by the buyer.

The buyer also desires payment to be delayed as long as possible, for cash-flow reasons. Ideally, he would like to be able to re-sell the goods before having to make payment, but again he has the problem that they are not physically in his possession until the cargo is delivered. Alternatively, if payment has to be made earlier, he would like to be able to use the credit to borrow in order to cover the period between having to pay for the cargo and being able to re-sell it. In short, ideally he would like to be able to use the credit to finance the transaction.

1.3.3 The bank

Given the desire of the seller to be paid as early as possible, and that of the buyer to pay as late as possible, it is likely that the bank will be required to finance the transaction. It may be that the seller will accept late payment so long as eventual payment is assured,[9] but at the very least the bank will, at an early stage, be required to give an irrevocable undertaking that it will pay. Except in the unlikely event that the buyer has put the bank in funds before this undertaking is given, the bank is necessarily taking the risk of the buyer's insolvency. Further, in the more usual situation where the seller is actually paid before the bank is reimbursed, the buyer will be required to finance the sale at least from the time that it makes payment to the seller until the time that it is itself reimbursed by its customer.

If the bank is assured of the standing and reputation of the buyer, it may be prepared to do this on an unsecured basis. The standby letter of credit, which is really simply a guarantee given against non-payment, puts the bank into this position,[10] as did the early form of negotiation credit, where the bank purchased from the seller bills of exchange drawn on the buyer, relying for reimbursement on its status as indorsee of the bill of exchange.[11] Even where the bank is an unsecured creditor, the buyer's obligation to reimburse usually depends on documents being tendered to the bank, the purpose of which is to

---

8. Another problem with the credit in *Morgan* v. *Larivière*.
9. See section 2.2 on deferred payment.
10. See further section 8.2.
11. An example of this type of credit may be found in *Borthwick* v. *Bank of New Zealand* (1900) Com. Cas. 2, a case considered for other reasons at section 4.4.10.1.

provide evidence that the seller has performed his obligations under the sale contract.

The true documentary credit differs from the above transactions in that a "document of title" is tendered to the bank, which gives the bank rights over the goods themselves as security for the advance. The bank is no longer an unsecured creditor, therefore. Because the bank now has an interest in the goods themselves, like the buyer, it therefore has an interest in ensuring that the seller has performed his obligations to ship goods under the sale contract, and it will also wish to be assured that they are adequately insured, or that it can take action against the carrier, should the goods be lost or damaged while they are at sea.

1.4 USE OF BILLS OF LADING

The document which developed to resolve the obvious conflict between the interests of buyer and seller, and to provide adequate security for the bank, was the bill of lading. There are various types of bill of lading, but the usual requirement under a documentary credit is for a clean shipped bill of lading.[12] No other document provides equivalent security to the clean shipped bill of lading, and banks should recognise that if they are prepared to accept anything less they are inevitably jeopardising their security.[13]

A shipped bill of lading is a receipt issued to the shipper by the ship's master, stating that goods as described therein have been loaded on board the vessel. The name of the vessel, and the date of shipment will also be stated. A clean shipped bill of lading will state that the cargo was loaded on board in apparent good order and condition, and will contain no clauses to qualify that statement.[14]

1.4.1 The shipped bill of lading as a document of title

For documentary credits, bills of lading only became of value when they could be sent ahead of the goods. This originally depended on the existence of a fast and reliable overland mail service. Today, airmail is commonly used. If a bill of lading is issued, the carrier must deliver only upon tender of an original bill of lading at the port of discharge. A bill of lading may be made out to a named consignee, in which case he alone may validly present it to obtain the goods from the vessel. Alternatively, it may be made negotiable. In principle, it can be made out to the bearer, in which case it can pass simply from hand to hand, but more usually a bill of lading is made out to order, usually of the shipper, in which case it is transferred by delivery and indorsement.

---

12. See further sections 5.2.1.1. and 5.2.1.2.
13. This point is elaborated upon in Chapter 4, and in particular sections 4.2 and 4.3.
14. On clauses see further sections 4.4.3 and 5.2.1.2.

Because delivery of the goods can be made only against presentation of an original bill of lading, it follows that transfer of the document can also transfer the right to take possession of the goods on discharge. It is for this reason that it is said to be a "document of title", representing the goods while they are goods at sea. It is also said to transfer constructive possession of the goods (i.e., the *right* to possess them). Clearly, then, the bill of lading can be used to sell or pledge the goods while they are at sea. The transfer of a document of title may also transfer the property in the goods should this accord with the intention of the parties.[15]

The seller can demand payment against the bill of lading, and if he is not paid can (in theory at least) retain the bill of lading and hence the right to collect the goods at discharge, or alternatively use the bill of lading to sell the goods to another buyer. He would also usually retain the property in the goods as security against non-payment, so that if the buyer went into liquidation they would not form part of the buyer's general assets. Even before the modern commercial credit was developed, this gave the seller some protection against non-payment, albeit not very adequate protection since it is by no means convenient to be put to the trouble of recovering goods from a foreign country, and there may be no ready market for goods of that description in the country of discharge.

If in a commercial credit the bank only pays against tender of a bill of lading, and only releases the bill of lading to the buyer when it is itself reimbursed, it is to some extent secured against the consequences of non-reimbursement,[16] since it can itself claim the goods at their destination, or use the bill of lading to re-sell them, thereby recouping at any rate a proportion of its losses. In addition, the bank as holder of the bill of lading may, as pledgee, obtain a possessory title to the goods: the property which the bank thereby receives forms an important part of its security should the purchaser go bankrupt before reimbursing the bank.[17]

1.4.2 The evidential value of the shipped bill of lading

The shipped bill of lading can also provide evidence that the seller has performed his side of the bargain. The buyer can inspect the bill of lading (or require the bank to do so) before payment is made for the goods, inspection of the documents providing the necessary assurance that the seller has performed. The bill of lading states that goods of the contract description were loaded, and the best assurance that the carrier can give that they were in accordance with the terms of the sale contract, when they were loaded. It is

15. See further section 3.3. The importance of requiring a document of title is further considered in section 4.3.3.
16. See further section 2.4.
17. See further sections 2.4 and 3.3.

7

not possible for the master to state that the goods were loaded in *actual* good order and condition, since he cannot know what is hidden from him, and he is not assumed to have any expertise in the quality of the merchandise. The best assurance he can give is that they were shipped in apparent good order and condition. Thus the clean shipped bill of lading provides the best indication of condition on shipment that is possible in practice.

It is usual under a commercial credit for the bank to require in addition to the bill of lading tender of a certificate of insurance, and an invoice. Payment is thus only made against the assurance that the goods were loaded in apparent good order and condition, and that if anything has subsequently befallen them, they are covered by a policy of marine insurance. It is reasonable, therefore, for payment to be made on that basis, even though the goods have not yet arrived at their destination and cannot therefore be physically inspected.

Because the bill of lading provides the protection required for all the parties, it performs a central form in today's documentary credits. As explained at the beginning of the chapter, however, the bill of lading is to some extent being replaced by other documentation, whose protection for the parties may well be less good. This particular problem is considered in detail in Chapters 4 and 5.

1.5 GENERAL PRINCIPLES OF OPERATION OF DOCUMENTARY CREDITS

This section is intended merely to outline the essentials of the bankers' documentary credit, and to explain the nature of the protection given to each of the parties. This is an introductory section, more detailed consideration of every aspect being reserved for the appropriate place later in the book.

1.5.1 The undertaking of the issuing bank

Assuming that the seller requires an irrevocable letter of credit,[18] there will be a term in the sale contract that payment is to be by irrevocable documentary credit, and the identity of the issuing bank may also be stipulated in the sale contract. The seller is the beneficiary under the credit.

It is then for the buyer to instruct the bank which is to issue the credit (i.e., the issuing bank) to open a credit in the seller's favour. Notice that the issuing bank acts as agent for the buyer, not the seller, and that the terms of the

---

18. The nature of which is described in section 2.3.1.

credit are as specified by him (the buyer). On the assumption that the bank has either already been put in funds, or is sufficiently satisfied as to the credit-worthiness of its customer (the buyer) that it is prepared to open the credit it will notify the beneficiary that it has opened an irrevocable credit in his favour, and advise him also of the terms of the credit.

By contrast with the early form of credit, under an irrevocable document-ary credit the bank makes an express undertaking directly to the beneficiary, that it will pay the price to him so long as he tenders the required shipping documents to the bank. In the traditional form of documentary credit, the shipping documents will be a shipped bill of lading, certificate of insurance for the goods, and commercial invoice.[19]

The beneficiary can therefore arrange shipment in the confidence that the bank is, in effect, guaranteeing payment for the goods, come what may, against tender of the shipping documents. Payment does not depend on the acceptance of the documents or the goods by the buyer,[20] nor on the con-tinued solvency of the buyer.

The beneficiary's security is further strengthened in that the opening of the credit is a condition precedent to his performance under the sale contract.[21] Only once he has been notified of the opening of the credit he is required to make arrangements to ship the goods, and procure the necessary bills of lad-ing. The seller ships the goods and thereby obtains the shipping documents. He forwards these to the banker, who will either pay in cash or provide a bill of exchange for the price to be drawn on the bank.[22]

So, in place of a buyer whose financial standing may well be dubious, the seller knows that he can look to a reputable bank for payment, "a reliable and solvent paymaster". Furthermore, sellers can use the credit as security to raise further capital, which may be required to ship or manufacture the goods in the first place.[23]

The bank thus takes over the risk of the buyer's insolvency, and takes upon itself the problem of eventual recovery of the money from the buyer (its cus-tomer). Its security is that the shipping documents are tendered to it, and are only released to the buyer against either payment, or (more usually) some alternative form of security.[24] Two forms of security are provided by the ship-ping documents. First, because the bill of lading is a document of title at com-mon law, its possession by the bank gives it the right to demand the goods on discharge in the event of the buyer's failure to reimburse. Secondly, if the

---

19. For variations, see Chapter 5. Early letters of credit were conceptually very different: see section 8.1.1.
20. See section 6.2.
21. See section 3.1.2.1.
22. On methods of payment, see section 2.2.
23. Indeed, this was the only reason why the seller required a documentary credit in *Maran Road Saw Mill* v. *Austin Taylor & Co. Ltd.* [1975] 1 Lloyd's Rep. 156: see further section 2.3.3.
24. See section 2.4.1.

buyer goes into liquidation before reimbursement is made, the bank may be able to claim the goods in preference to the general creditors by virtue of obtaining a special property as pledgee.[25] Gutteridge and Megrah describe the commercial credit as follows[26]:

"The bank acting on behalf of the buyer and either directly with the beneficiary, seller or other contractor, or[27] through the intervention of a bank in the seller's country,[28] assumes liability for payment of the price, in consideration, perhaps, of the security afforded by the implied pledge of the documents of title tendered in compliance with the terms of the credit or of being placed by the buyer in funds in advance or of his undertaking to reimburse, and of a commission."

It should be observed, however, that the shipping documents provide the bank with no such security unless a document of title is tendered. So far we have made the assumption that the bank obtains a shipped bill of lading, which is a document of title. This is not always the case, however, and sometimes alternative documents are stipulated, which may provide the bank with no security at all.[29]

1.5.2 Mutual benefits to both parties

The benefit to sellers of payment by irrevocable credit is clear. It should be appreciated, however, that buyers too can benefit from commercial credit sales. Once the bank has received the bills of lading it can advance to the buyer credit for their value until he is able to resell them, in the knowledge that possession of the bills of lading gives it security in the event of the buyer's default, or bankruptcy. Of course the buyer must eventually secure the bills to resell the goods, and the bank's protection is then by way of trust receipt.[30]

Thus the advantages of documentary credits are mutual. The seller can arrange shipment in the sure knowledge that he will be paid, generally by a "reliable paymaster" in his own country. The buyer can use a credit to raise funds. One consequence of this mutuality is that it is not generally open to either party unilaterally to withdraw from the credit.[31] Were the credit to be regarded as being solely for the benefit of the seller, however, he would be

---

25. Again, because the bill of lading is a document of title, its tender to the bank may also operate to transfer special property as pledgee. This will not always be the case, however: see further, section 3.3. On the relevance of the distinction between special and general property, see further section 7.1.1.
26. H.C. Gutteridge and Maurice Megrah, *The Law of Bankers' Commercial Credits* (7th ed., 1984), p. 2.
27. The word "or" does not appear in the most recent edition, but this must be a misprint since it does appear in earlier editions.
28. As, for example, in the confirmed credit: see below, section 1.5.3.
29. See further Chapter 5.
30. See section 2.4.1.
31. See further section 3.2.2.

able unilaterally to short-circuit the credit, and demand payment directly from the buyer.

1.5.3 The role of the confirming bank where credit confirmed

Although the beneficiary under an irrevocable credit is protected against the buyer's insolvency (or other default), as long as only one bank (the issuing bank) is involved, acting as agent of the buyer and probably situated in the buyer's country of business, the seller can still be faced with the possibility of having to settle disputes in a foreign country should any problem arise (for example, as to whether the documents conform to the terms of the credit).[32] So he may still be faced with the daunting prospect of litigating abroad, or at best entering a lengthy process of negotiations with a bank in a foreign jurisdiction. Quite apart from the uncertainties of litigating abroad, the expense in terms of witnesses etc., can be considerable.

It is therefore common to stipulate that an irrevocable credit, issued by a bank in the buyer's country, should also be confirmed by a bank in the seller's country of business. If the credit is confirmed the confirming bank is adding its own undertaking to that of the issuing bank. The documents are tendered to the confirming bank, and it is the confirming bank which undertakes the responsibility of paying the seller. The undertaking of the confirming bank is enforceable independently of the position taken by the issuing bank, so that the confirming bank's obligation to pay does not, for example, depend on whether it can obtain reimbursement from the issuing bank. If the issuing bank defaults the confirming bank can sue it, but cannot sue the seller for return of the money paid.[33] If the issuing bank goes into liquidation before reimbursing the issuing bank, again the confirming bank has no recourse against the seller.

The advantages to the seller are therefore that not only is he protected against the insolvency of the buyer, but also against the prospect of having to settle disputes with a foreign bank in a foreign country, with all the attendant expense and inconvenience. Any disputes now are likely to arise in the seller's own jurisdiction, and the likelihood of being faced with litigation abroad is significantly reduced. He is also protected against the insolvency of the issuing bank, but this is less likely to be a major consideration. Confirmed credits are sometimes used as a matter of course, but since an additional commission will now be involved they are very expensive, and if the issuing bank is itself reputable and reliable, and unlikely therefore to default, sellers may well be paying for a security they do not really need.

The confirmed irrevocable credit is illustrated by Figure 1.1 on page 12.

---

32. Such disputes are by no means rare. Somewhere in the region of 60 per cent. of documents presented under export letters of credit are discrepant on first presentation (I am indebted to the I.C.C. Banking Commission for this information).

33. See further section 2.3.1.

Figure 1.1 The confirmed irrevocable credit

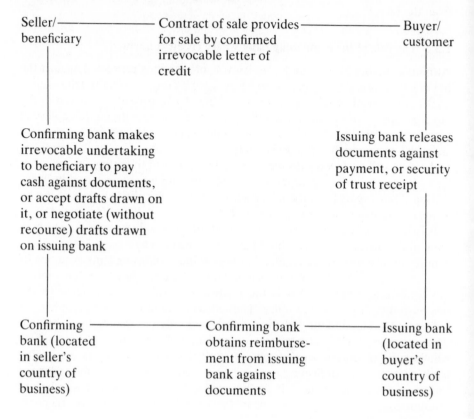

Seller/——————— Contract of sale provides ——————— Buyer/
beneficiary   for sale by confirmed   customer
                                       irrevocable letter of
                                       credit

Confirming bank makes   Issuing bank releases
irrevocable undertaking   documents against
to beneficiary to pay   payment, or security
cash against documents,   of trust receipt
or accept drafts drawn on
it, or negotiate (without
recourse) drafts drawn
on issuing bank

Confirming ——————— Confirming bank ——————— Issuing bank
bank (located   obtains reimburse-   (located in
in seller's   ment from issuing   buyer's
country of   bank against   country of
business)   documents   business)

1.6 CONTRACTUAL RELATIONSHIPS AND DOCUMENTARY CREDITS

1.6.1 The four autonomous contracts created by the credit itself

1.6.1.1 The four contracts

In *United City Merchants* v. *Royal Bank of Canada, The American Accord*,[34] Lord Diplock said that it is "trite law" that there are four autonomous contracts in an irrevocable confirmed credit[35]:

"It is trite law that there are four autonomous though interconnected contractual relationships involved: (1) the underlying contract for the sale of goods, to which the only parties are the buyer and the seller; (2) the contract between the buyer and the issuing bank under which the latter agrees to issue the credit and either itself or through a confirming bank to notify the credit to the seller and to make payments to or to the order

34. [1983] A.C. 168; [1982] 2 All E.R. 720, [1982] 2 W.L.R. 1039, [1982] 2 Lloyd's Rep 1.
35. [1983] A.C. 168, 182H–183C.

of the seller (or to pay, accept or negotiate bills of exchange drawn by the seller) against presentation of stipulated documents; and the buyer agrees to reimburse the issuing bank for payments made under the credit. For such reimbursement the stipulated documents, if they include a document of title such as a bill of lading, constitute a security available to the issuing bank; (3) if payment is to be made through a confirming bank, the contract between the issuing bank and the confirming bank authorising and requiring the latter to make such payments and to remit the stipulated documents to the issuing bank when they are received, the issuing bank in turn agreeing to reimburse the confirming bank for payments made under the credit; (4) the contract between the confirming bank and the seller under which the confirming bank undertakes to pay to the seller (or to accept or negotiate without recourse to drawer bills of exchange drawn by him) up to the amount of the credit against presentation of the stipulated documents."

The four contracts are, then, the contract of sale between buyer and seller, the contract between buyer and issuing bank, the contract between issuing and correspondent (or confirming) bank, and the contract between correspondent bank and seller (see Figure 1.2).

Figure 1.2 **The four autonomous contracts (confirmed irrevocable credit)**

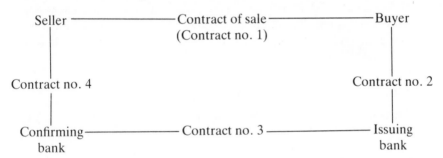

United City Merchants concerned a confirmed irrevocable credit, and Lord Diplock clearly states that the third contract only arises where the credit is confirmed: an irrevocable credit, where there is no confirming bank, consists simply of three autonomous though interconnected contractual relationships: the contract of sale, the contract between buyer and issuing bank, and the contract between issuing bank and beneficiary.

1.6.1.1.1 MULTIPLE SALES

An international sale may involve only a single seller and single buyer, in which case there is of course only one sale contract to consider. It is very common, however, particularly with bulk liquid and dry cargoes, for the goods to be resold afloat, often many times before they arrive at their destination. Furthermore, each resale may itself be financed by documentary credit.

There can also be little doubt that the reality (that there are often multiple resales) has significantly affected the development of the law.

Of course, each resale is essentially a similar type of transaction, and if financed by confirmed irrevocable credit, simply creates four more autonomous contracts. It follows that each individual sale can be considered in isolation. Nevertheless, it is worthwhile bearing in mind that the sale is often part of a larger transaction, since the law itself to some extent recognises this, and there are important decisions which are only comprehensible in this light.[36] Furthermore, any delays in processing documentation will have more serious repercussions where there are multiple resales, in particular if (as is common for bulk oil cargoes) they prevent the bill of lading reaching the ultimate receiver before the cargo itself is discharged.

1.6.1.1.2 LAYOUT OF THE BOOK

The obligations of the parties under the sale contract are set out in Chapter 3. Contract No. 4 is the only one whose nature creates any conceptual difficulty—the difficulties are discussed in Chapter 8.[37]

Chapter 6 concerns the duties of issuing and correspondent bank in relation to both customer and beneficiary, and their duties towards each other. Obviously this requires consideration of contracts 2, 3 and 4, although in an ideal world the duties owed under each of these three contracts should be the same.

1.6.1.2 Contracts autonomous but interconnected

The four contracts in figure 1.2 are autonomous in that their terms are independent of each other. So, for example, nothing in the sale contract (contract 1) can affect the terms of the credit. This is in part merely an application of the privity of contract doctrine, but were it otherwise the banks could be put into a difficult position, not necessarily being aware of the terms of the sale contract. Nor is the bank affected by subsequent variations to the sale contract, or even perhaps its subsequent repudiation by the parties to it. The bank may be entirely unaware of any such variation or repudiation, and in principle its position should not be affected by it.

It also follows that the obligation of the confirming bank to pay the beneficiary on tender of documents (contract 4), the obligation of the issuing bank to reimburse it (contract 3) and the obligation of the customer to reimburse the issuing bank (contract 2) are all independent of disputes between the parties to the sale contract (contract 1). This aspect of autonomy is enlarged upon in Chapter 6.

Where the *Uniform Customs and Practice for Documentary Commercial*

---

36. E.g., section 6.2.1.1.
37. See section 8.1.

Credits applies,[38] Article 3 preserves the autonomy of the documentary credit: "Credits, by their nature, are separate transactions from the sales or other contract(s) on which they are based and banks are in no way concerned with or bound by such contract(s), even if any reference whatsoever to such contract(s) is included in the credit." It also follows that each of the credit contracts is independent of the other. Thus in principle, the obligations of the confirming bank towards the beneficiary (contract 4) may differ from those owed to it by the issuing bank (contract 3), and those between the issuing bank and its customer (contract 2). If, for example, the terms of the credit differed from the customer's instructions, the confirming bank's relations with the beneficiary would be governed by the terms of the credit, whereas the relationship between issuing bank and customer would be governed by the customer's instructions.

It may even be that each contract is governed by the law of a different jurisdiction: certainly the courts have taken the view that the state whose law governs the credit (contract 4) is independent of the law governing the underlying transaction (contract 1, the contract of sale). This point is further elaborated in Chapter 8.[39]

The contracts are said also to be interconnected, however, and ordinarily of course, the terms of the credit (contract 4) will conform precisely with the customer's instructions (contract 2). If so, the law ought ideally to ensure that the confirming bank's obligations under contract 4 are similar in all respects to its rights under contract 3, and to the rights of the issuing bank against its customer under contract 2. Were it otherwise, the confirming bank may, for example, be required to pay the beneficiary but unable to reclaim the money from the issuing bank. Alternatively, the issuing bank may be required under contract 3 to reimburse the confirming bank but be unable itself to claim reimbursement from its customer under contract 2. In reality, therefore, the obligations of the bank towards the beneficiary tie in with the obligations of the customer towards the bank (unless of course the bank exceeds its instructions in the issue of the credit). Hence contracts 2, 3 and 4 in Figure 2.2, although autonomous, are interconnected. The interconnection between these contracts is examined in more detail in Chapter 6.

1.6.2 Other contractual relationships

Wherever bankers' documentary credits are used, there will be one or more carriers involved. Sometimes only carriage by sea is involved, but frequently today the sea element forms part only of a wider transport operation. Containerised goods, for example, are often loaded on board a lorry or train at an inland terminal, for carriage to the port of shipment, and may either remain on board the same vehicle or be reloaded on board a lorry or train for

38. See section 2.1.
39. See section 8.3.1.4.

carriage from the port of discharge to a second inland terminal. In this case the transport operation includes land, sea and land elements, and there may well be more than one carrier involved.[40]

If the cargo is lost or damaged *en route*, whoever suffers loss may be able to sue the carrier for breach of the carriage contract. Under the sale contract, either the buyer or the seller will undertake to arrange for carriage of the goods, which will involve making a contract with one or more carriers. However, even if (for example) the contract of carriage is entered into by the seller, the buyer may still acquire rights under it, and have obligations imposed upon him in certain circumstances, as may any bank involved in financing the transaction.[41] For the purposes of bankers' documentary credits, the rights obtained by the bank (or banks) against the carrier (or carriers) form a major element in their security, since they will be thrown back upon them if the goods are lost or damaged at sea.

For each individual sale, therefore, it is necessary to consider in addition to the four autonomous contracts described above the relationships between seller and buyer and the carrier (or carriers), and (more particularly for present purposes) between any bank involved and the carrier (or carriers). This forms the subject matter of Chapter 7.

1.6.3 Whose law applies?

The assumption is made for the purposes of the book that all contracts are governed by the domestic laws of the United Kingdom, except where that is itself an issue.[42]

---

40. See further section 4.5.
41. See further, Chapter 7.
42. As in section 8.3.

CHAPTER 2

THE DOCUMENTARY CREDIT IN GENERAL: THE U.C.P., TYPES OF CREDIT AND THE BANK'S RIGHT TO REIMBURSEMENT

The purpose of this chapter is to describe the documentary credit in general terms, to outline the various forms of credit in use today and to describe the protection given to each of the parties. It should be borne in mind, however, that today nearly all credits are issued subject to the Uniform Customs and Practice for Documentary Credits (U.C.P.), and there is little point in embarking upon this exercise without reference to the U.C.P.

2.1 THE UNIFORM CUSTOMS AND PRACTICE FOR DOCUMENTARY CREDITS

2.1.1 An introduction to the Uniform Customs and Practice

Attempts at unification of law and practice across the world are rarely successful, but documentary credits constitute an outstanding exception to this observation. Nearly all credits, wherever issued in the world, are on the terms of the *Uniform Customs and Practice on Bankers' Commercial Credits*.

The U.C.P. was originally published by the International Chamber of Commerce (I.C.C.) in 1933, and was revised in 1951, 1962, 1974, and most recently in 1983, as a result of the deliberations of the I.C.C. Banking Commission. Revisions have therefore averaged about once a decade, and have usually been in response to changing trade and banking practices. It has already been explained, for example,[1] how the 1983 revisions responded to new forms of documentation, particularly for combined transport operations. In October 1989 the I.C.C. Banking Commission decided to embark on a further revision of the U.C.P., which will probably be completed in around 1993.

In addition to initiating periodic revisions, the I.C.C. Banking Commission also gives opinions on interpretation of the various Articles of the code. As the I.C.C. itself notes, "[a]lthough they do not have legal force, these Opinions are widely read and taken note of". Reference will be made in this

---

1. See above, section 1.2.

17

book to the most recent Opinions of the I.C.C. Banking Commission, covering 1975–1979,[2] 1980–1981[3] and 1984–1986.[4]

The U.C.P. has been adopted in 146 countries, and as has already been observed, nearly all credits issued today, except in China and Rumania, are on the terms of the *Uniform Customs and Practice*. However, this has not always been the case. Only since the 1962 revisions have banks in the United Kingdom adopted the U.C.P., for example, since before then the U.C.P. differed in a number of fundamental ways from "London Practice".

The 1983 revision will be referred to extensively in this book, and is fully set out in Appendix A.

In addition to the substantive changes made to the U.C.P. in 1983, the layout was also altered and made more logical. Part A, entitled "General Provisions and Definitions", deals with the application of the U.C.P., and sets out both a definition of the documentary credit, and the general principles applicable thereto. Part B, entitled "Form and Notification of Credits", describes the different varieties of credit. Part C deals with "Liabilities and Responsibilities". Part D, entitled "Documents", is further sub-divided into transport documents, insurance documents, the commercial invoice and other documents. Part E, entitled "Miscellaneous Provisions", mostly concerns formal requirements and in particular the correct use of words. Part F, entitled "Transfer", deals with transferable and divisible credits.

2.1.2 Application of U.C.P.

Although the U.C.P. is of almost universal application, it does not have the force of law in the United Kingdom, and has to be incorporated into the contracts which form the basis of the credit.[5] Article 1 of the U.C.P. provides:

"These Articles apply to all documentary credits, including, to the extent to which they may be applicable, standby letters of credit,[6] and are binding on all parties thereto unless otherwise agreed. They shall be incorporated into each documentary credit by wording in the credit indicating that such credit is issued subject to Uniform Customs and Practice for Documentary Credits, 1983 Revision, I.C.C. Publication, No. 400."

In the United Kingdom the U.C.P. has not been given the force of law, so that the first part of Article 1, providing that the Articles are binding on all parties thereto unless otherwise agreed, has no effect in the absence of express words of incorporation as provided at the end of the Article: English law does not recognise a principle whereby terms are compulsorily incorporated into a contract in the absence of provision to the contrary.

In fact, English banks have adopted the U.C.P. since the 1962 revisions, so

---

2. I.C.C. publication No. 371.
3. I.C.C. publication No. 399.
4. I.C.C. publication No. 434.
5. On which, see section 1.6.
6. On which, see section 8.2.

that their standard forms will invariably incorporate the U.C.P. provisions, but that does not affect the sale contract, which will be governed by the common law unless it expressly stipulates that any credit opened under it is governed by the U.C.P.[7] In most situations this will not matter, since the provisions of the U.C.P. do not in general operate in opposition to the common law, but rather elaborate upon it. Their purpose for the most part is to clarify, rather than alter the law. There are some differences, however, between common law and U.C.P. provisions, for example regarding the requirements for the commercial invoice,[8] in which case the provisions of the sale contract may conflict with those of the other contracts underlying the credit.

Another consequence of the fact that the U.C.P. is only given force in the United Kingdom by incorporation into the contracts which form the basis of the credit, is that its provisions cannot be used to determine whether those contracts have been made in the first place. Some of the consequences of this conclusion are elaborated upon in Chapter 8.[9]

The second part of the Article sets out the exact form of wording required for incorporation, in order to make clear that it is the 1983 revision which is incorporated, rather than earlier versions. It is not necessary for the wording to be incorporated into the text of the credit. In *Forestal Mimosa Ltd.* v. *Oriental Credit Ltd.*,[10] an insertion in similar words in the left-hand margin of the document was held by the Court of Appeal to be sufficient to incorporate the provisions of the U.C.P.

Inter-bank electronic messages sent by S.W.I.F.T. (the Society for Worldwide Interbank Financial Telecommunications), do not expressly state when the credit is subject to the U.C.P., but the phrase: "unless specifically stated, the Documentary Credit is issued subject to Uniform Customs and Practice for Documentary Credits, International Chamber of Commerce, Paris, France, which are in effect on the date of issue" is incorporated into the user handbook. On the effect of this procedure, see further Chapter 5.[11]

Banks are also required to notify the I.C.C. of their adherence to the 1983 revision.

2.2 PAYMENT UNDER DOCUMENTARY CREDITS

Because under an irrevocable credit the seller knows that he will eventually be paid by a reliable and solvent paymaster, the seller may not insist upon

---

7. Presumably the U.C.P. would also apply if the sale contract required the credit to be opened by a particular bank, which itself had adopted the U.C.P.
8. See sections 4.4.9 and 5.6.
9. Section 8.1.10.3.
10. [1986] 1 W.L.R. 631; [1986] 2 All E.R. 400.
11. Section 5.7.

payment of cash against documents. Credits sometimes provide for deferred cash payment. Alternatively (and more commonly), an acceptance credit may be used, in which case the bank undertakes to accept bills of exchange drawn on it by the beneficiary. Such bills can be in the form of sight drafts, but time drafts (maturing a fixed time, often 90 days, after sight) are more commonly used, and this provides an alternative method of deferring payment.

In reality, if the credit provides for cash payment or sight draft, the bank will usually provide the buyer with an advance for it against the security of the goods, but then of course the buyer will be liable for interest until the goods are sold and he is able to make reimbursement. Conversely, a seller who obtains a time draft can usually sell it to his own bank for immediate cash should he so wish, but of course the bank will then deduct interest until maturity (and presumably a commission). In effect, therefore, the difference between cash payment or sight draft on the one hand, and time draft on the other, comes down to a question of interest. As Devlin J. observed in *Midland Bank Ltd.* v. *Seymour*[12]:

"Well, of course, basically the confirmed credit is designed to give the seller the security he wants before he ships the goods. He can arrange to ship the goods in the confident knowledge that as soon as he tenders documents that are in order he is bound to be paid. If the letter of credit provides for a cash payment, or a sight bill, he will get paid at once. That will mean, of course, that the buyer, unless he sells the documents for cash, will be out of his money during the period of the voyage and until he disposes of the goods on arrival. But the buyer, of course, may not like that, and then the letter of credit he furnishes will not provide for a cash payment, but, as in this case,[13] for a bill after sight—a 90 days' bill. Then the seller, unless he sells the bill for cash, will be out of his money for 90 days. If the buyer does pay cash, he will probably do so by advance from his bank on the security of the goods. If the seller sells the bill to his bank it is only another way of getting an advance on the security of the bill. The only point of difference is, which of the two, buyer or seller, has to pay in the form of interest or discount for financing the goods during what one might call the barren period of transportation or delivery?"

Another possibility is the negotiation credit, where the issuing bank undertakes to negotiate (i.e., purchase) bills of exchange drawn by the beneficiary on a third party. The issuing bank can then itself, of course, present those bills to the third party (probably another bank). If the credit is irrevocable it is important that the issuing bank negotiates without recourse against the drawer (i.e., beneficiary under the credit), so that it is the issuing bank and not the drawer who takes the risk of default by the third party when the bills of exchange are presented.

All these possibilities are provided for by the U.C.P., Article 11(a) of which states: "All credits must clearly indicate whether they are available by sight payment, deferred payment, by acceptance or by negotiation." For an

---

12. [1955] 2 Lloyd's Rep. 147 at p. 165.
13. For more detailed consideration of this case, see section 6.3.2.

irrevocable credit Article 10(a) defines the undertaking of the issuing bank[14] as:

> "(i) if the credit provides for sight payment—to pay, or that payment will be made;
>
> (ii) if the credit provides for deferred payment—to pay, or that payment will be made on the date(s) determinable in accordance with the stipulations of the credit;
>
> (iii) if the credit provides for acceptance—to accept drafts drawn by the beneficiary if the credit stipulates that they are to be drawn on the issuing bank, or to be responsible for their acceptance and payment at maturity if the credit stipulates that they are to be drawn on the applicant for the credit or any other drawee stipulated in the credit;
>
> (iv) if the credit provides for negotiation—to pay without recourse to drawers and/or bona fide holders, draft(s) drawn by the beneficiary, at sight or at tenor, on the applicant for the credit or on any other drawee stipulated in the credit other than the issuing bank itself, or to provide for negotiation by another bank and to pay, as above, if such negotiation is not effected."

Article 10(a)(ii) was added for the first time in 1983. Deferred payment credits which were not acceptance credits were very uncommon at the time of the 1974 revision, but had come into increasing use by 1983.[15] It is arguable that the Article as it stands is too vague, and that the bank should give a written undertaking of deferred payment at the due date at the time of taking up documents.

2.3 TYPES OF CREDIT

The most important distinctions are between revocable and irrevocable, and confirmed and unconfirmed credits, and these distinctions (as explained in Chapter 1) are recognised by the U.C.P. The U.C.P. also defines transferable and divisible credits, but does not define any other type of credit.

The distinctions between revocable and irrevocable, and confirmed and unconfirmed credits, are sometimes confused. The first relates to the obligations of the issuing bank, the second to those of the correspondent bank.

Other classifications are commonly made, by both writers and practitioners. These classifications are largely descriptive, however, and have little or no legal significance. It should also be borne in mind that no single classification of credits is universally adopted, and that apart from those adopted by the U.C.P. itself, the definitions used are somewhat imprecise.

---

14. On the irrevocable nature of the undertaking, see below, section 2.3.1.1.
15. Bernard Wheble, *UCP 1974/1983 Revisions Compared and Explained*, I.C.C. publication No. 411, p. 23.

2.3.1 Revocable and irrevocable credits

2.3.1.1 Nature of issuing bank's undertaking under irrevocable credit

The essence of the issuing bank's undertaking under an irrevocable credit is set out in Article 10(a) of the U.C.P.: "An irrevocable credit constitutes a definite undertaking of the issuing bank, provided that the stipulated documents are presented[16] and that the terms and conditions of the credit are complied with . . . [17]" Article 10(d) provides: "Such undertakings can neither be amended nor cancelled without the agreement of the issuing bank, the confirming bank (if any), and the beneficiary . . . " The beneficiary is thus given the benefit of an irrevocable undertaking from the bank itself, under which payment is conditional only upon presentation of the stipulated shipping documents, and compliance with the terms and conditions of the credit.

2.3.1.2 Nature of issuing bank's undertaking under revocable credit

A revocable credit offers no security at all to the seller (though the buyer can gain from it). Not only can the issuing bank revoke at any time, but there is no obligation on the bank even to inform the seller that the credit has been revoked. In *Cape Asbestos Co. Ltd.* v. *Lloyds Bank Ltd.*,[18] Lloyds Bank advised the plaintiff sellers (of around 30 tons of asbestos sheets) that it had opened a credit in their favour, but added: "This is merely an advice of the opening of the above-mentioned credit and is not a confirmation of the same." A shipment of about 17 tons was made and the sellers were paid under the credit. About a fortnight later, Lloyds Bank were instructed by cable by the buyers' bankers (Banque de l'Est) that the credit was cancelled, but Lloyds did not inform the sellers of this. The evidence suggested that this was an oversight due to pressure of business, but that it was their usual practice to inform beneficiaries of the withdrawal of a revocable credit.

Being unaware of the cancellation of the credit the sellers made a second shipment of the remaining asbestos (about 12 tons), and about 7 weeks after Lloyds had been notified of the cancellation, tendered the shipping documents for payment. Lloyds Bank did not pay and the sellers sued, claiming that the bank was under a duty to give them reasonable notice of the cancellation of the credit. Bailhache J. (sitting in the King's Bench Division) held, however, that a bank may cancel a revocable credit at any time, and is under no duty to inform the seller that a revocable credit has been cancelled.

The *Weekly Notes* report (which is an extract from the judgment of Bailhache J., written in commentary form in the third party), states:

16. The requirement that stipulated documents be presented was added for the first time in 1983—it would seem to be superfluous, however, given the additional requirement that the terms and conditions of the credit be complied with.

17. Article 10 then goes on to describe methods of payment—this has already been set out above, section 2.2.

18. [1921] W.N. 274.

"It was to be observed that the letter of June 14, 1920, from the defendants to the plaintiffs announced the opening of a revocable and not of a confirmed credit. A letter in that form intimated to the person in whose favour the credit was opened that he might find that the credit was revoked at any time. That being the representation by the defendants to the plaintiffs, were the defendants under any legal duty to give notice to the plaintiffs when the credit was revoked. On consideration his Lordship had come to the conclusion that there was no legal obligation on the defendants to give notice in the circumstances. In a case of this kind the wise course for the seller to take before making a shipment of the goods would certainly be to inquire of the bank whether or not the credit had been withdrawn. The practice of the defendants to give notice in such cases was a most prudent, reasonable and business-like practice, and his Lordship hoped that nothing that he said in this case would lead banks to alter that practice, but at the same time it did not seem to be based upon any legal obligation or duty. It had been said that the defendants regarded the giving of notice as an act of courtesy which they always performed except when, as in this case, it was unfortunately forgotten. That was the true view of the proceeding. It was an act of courtesy which it was very desirable should be performed, but it was not founded upon any legal obligation. If that conclusion was right it disposed of the case."

There is in fact some confusion in the case between the terms "revocable" and "unconfirmed". It seems however (from a less than entirely clear report) that Lloyds, and not the Banque de l'Est, were acting as the issuing bank, so that the correct analysis is that this was a revocable, rather than unconfirmed credit.[19] The case is therefore authority that a revocable credit can be revoked without notice.

Nor was the bank taken to have waived its rights to revoke by its earlier conduct in paying against the first tender (for about 17 tons). The bank had waived its rights only in respect of that particular tender, and there was no reason to infer a general waiver. This aspect of the case is considered further in the next chapter.[20]

The U.C.P. adopts essentially the same position as that adopted by the common law in *Cape Asbestos*. Accordingly, Article (a) provides: "A revocable credit may be amended or cancelled by the issuing bank at any moment and without prior notice to the beneficiary." This was not altered by the 1983 revisions.[21] The provision allows the bank to amend or cancel the credit on its own initiative, whether or not on the instructions of the buyer.[22] However,

19. Uniform terminology does not appear to have been used until the first version of the U.C.P. was published some 13 years after this decision.

20. Section 3.1.5.

21. The first sentence of Article 2 of the 1974 revision is identical.

22. As in *Cape Asbestos*. The principle in *Cape Asbestos* is clearly intended to be of general application, however, and not limited to the case where the buyer instructs the bank to withdraw the credit.

Ventris argues that it cannot have been the intention of the draftsmen that the bank should be able to cancel on its own initiative: F.M. Ventris, *Bankers' Documentary Credits*, (first supplement to the second edition, Lloyd's of London Press Ltd. (1985)), p. 7. In fact it clearly was, however: Bernard Wheble notes that the applicant for the credit may get into difficulties, and that the bank should be able to protect itself from the possibility that he becomes unable to make reimbursement: *UCP 1974/1983 Revisions Compared and Explained*, I.C.C. publication No. 411, p. 20. Of course, however, a bank under an irrevocable credit does not have this protection.

Article 9(b) provides protection for any bank (other than the issuing bank itself) which has already accepted and paid against documents under a revocable credit[23]:

"However, the issuing bank is bound to:
  (i) reimburse a branch or bank with which a revocable credit has been made available for sight payment, acceptance or negotiation, for any payment, acceptance or negotiation made by such branch or bank prior to receipt by it of notice of amendment or cancellation, against documents which appear on their face to be in accordance with the terms and conditions of the credit.
  (ii) reimburse a branch or bank with which a revocable credit has been made available for deferred payment, if such branch or bank has, prior to receipt by it of notice of amendment or cancellation, taken up documents which appear on their face to be in accordance with the terms and conditions of the credit."

Perhaps because they provide the seller with such poor protection, it is usually assumed that where the sale contract does not indicate whether or not a credit is revocable, a requirement for an irrevocable credit is assumed.[24] The U.C.P. adopts the opposite position, however. Article 7 of the 1983 revision provides:

"(a) Credits may be either (i) revocable or (ii) irrevocable.
(b) All credits, therefore, should clearly indicate whether they are revocable or irrevocable.
(c) In the absence of such indication the credit shall be deemed to be revocable."

This is exactly the same as Article 1 of the 1974 revision, the I.C.C. Banking Commission rejecting (after serious consideration) a proposal that the principle of paragraph (c) should be reversed. The point was made that as the Article stands if the intention was to make the credit irrevocable it can later be so amended by the issuing bank, whereas if paragraph (c) were reversed, if the intention was to make the credit revocable it could not later be so amended.[25] This argument does not seem terribly convincing: surely it is not unreasonable to require the issuing bank to make up its mind from the outset whether the credit is to be revocable or not! No doubt, however, the matter will be considered again during the current revision process.

In practice, revocable credits are very rare in the United Kingdom, but are still used fairly extensively for transactions within the United States.

2.3.2 Confirmed credits

As explained in Chapter 1,[26] where an irrevocable credit is confirmed, the confirming bank effectively takes on towards the seller all the obligations

---

23. Article 9(b)(i) is substantively similar to the second sentence of Article 2 of the 1974 revisions. Article 9(b)(ii) was added for the first time in 1983.
24. See further section 3.1.1.
25. Bernard Wheble, *UCP 1974/1983 Revisions Compared and Explained*, I.C.C. publication No. 411, p. 18.
26. Section 1.5.3.

taken on by the issuing bank where the credit is unconfirmed. In other words, the seller need only deal with the confirming bank, and its undertakings may be regarded as irrevocable.

It is important to note that the confirming bank adds its own definite and irrevocable undertaking to pay to that of the issuing bank, and that if for any reason it is not reimbursed by the issuing bank (for example, where the issuing bank has gone into liquidation), it has no recourse against the beneficiary. In *Panoustos* v. *Raymond Hadley Corporation of New York*,[27] it was admitted by all parties that a credit was not confirmed where the "confirming" bank stated: "In advising you that this credit has been opened we are acting merely as agents for our foreign correspondents and cannot assume any responsibility for its continuance."

This was not confirmed because no irrevocable undertaking was entered into by the "confirming" bank.[28]

The definition of a confirmed credit under the U.C.P. conforms with the common law position. Article 10(b) states:

"When an issuing bank authorizes or requests another bank to confirm its irrevocable credit and the latter has added its confirmation such confirmation constitutes a definite undertaking of such bank (the confirming bank), in addition to that of the issuing bank, provided that the stipulated documents are presented and that the terms and conditions of the credit are complied with:

   (i) if the credit provides for sight payment—to pay or that payment will be made;

  (ii) if the credit provides for deferred payment—to pay, or that payment will be made on the date(s) determinable in accordance with the stipulations of the credit;

 (iii) if the credit provides for acceptance—to accept drafts drawn by the beneficiary if the credit stipulates that they are to be drawn on the confirming bank, or to be responsible for their acceptance and payment at maturity if the credit stipulates that they are to be drawn on the applicant for the credit;

 (iv) if the credit provides for negotiation—to negotiate without recourse to drawers and/or bona fide holders, draft(s) drawn by the beneficiary, at sight or tenor, on the issuing bank or on the applicant for the credit or on any other drawee stipulated in the credit other than on the confirming bank itself."

Article 10(b), describing the methods of payment, is in almost identical terms to Article 10(a),[29] except that references to the confirming bank are substituted for those of the issuing bank. However, whereas it would be rare for an issuing bank under an unconfirmed irrevocable credit to undertake to negotiate drafts drawn on a third party, it is quite common for a confirming bank to undertake to negotiate (i.e., purchase) drafts drawn by the beneficiary on the issuing bank. Again, such negotiation is without recourse to drawers—hence it is the confirming bank and not the beneficiary who takes the risk that the issuing bank will not honour the drafts drawn upon it when these are presented by the confirming bank.

27. [1917] 2 K.B. 473.
28. On this case see further below, section 3.1.5.
29. See section 2.2, above.

As noted above, Article 10(d) provides in respect of these undertakings to pay: "Such undertakings can neither be amended nor cancelled without the agreement of the issuing bank, the confirming bank (if any), and the beneficiary . . ."

This applies to the confirming bank under a confirmed credit just as it does to an issuing bank under an unconfirmed irrevocable credit. It follows that the effect of confirmation is to add the irrevocable undertaking of the confirming bank to that of the issuing bank.

In *Forestal Mimosa Ltd.* v. *Oriental Credit Ltd.*,[30] the Court of Appeal was concerned with an acceptance credit under Article 10(b)(iii), where the sellers drew 90 day drafts on the confirming bank. The issuing bank, on the instructions of the buyers, later refused to accept the shipping documents because of alleged discrepancies, and the defendants (confirming bank) refused to pay against the drafts at maturity. The Court of Appeal held that the alleged discrepancies were unarguable, and that once it was clear that the provisions of the U.C.P. applied, the defendants were responsible for the acceptance of the drafts and payment on their maturity, notwithstanding that the buyers had not accepted them. It is the confirming bank itself that makes the undertaking, and that undertaking is enforceable independently of the position taken by the issuing bank or the buyer.

2.3.3 The unconfirmed negotiation credit

Confirmed credits are always irrevocable, but irrevocable credits are often unconfirmed, even where a second bank (correspondent bank) is involved, situated in the seller's country of business. A common variety is the unconfirmed negotiation credit, where the bank undertakes merely to negotiate a bill of exchange drawn on the issuing bank, but does not itself undertake payment on its own behalf, nor does it add its own confirmation to the credit. Any payment made by the correspondent bank for such bills of exchange is subject to recourse against the drawer (i.e., seller or beneficiary) if the issuing bank does not reimburse the negotiating bank. By contrast, a correspondent bank which confirms a credit has no recourse if it is not itself reimbursed.[31]

A good illustration of the workings of an unconfirmed negotiation credit, including the right of recourse, can be found in *Maran Road Saw Mill* v. *Austin Taylor & Co. Ltd.*[32] The plaintiffs were Malaysian sellers of timber, and the defendants acted as their selling agents. In reality, however, under the agency agreement with the plaintiffs they were purchasers of the timber, who then arranged a sub-sale of the timber to sub-buyers, who paid cash against documents to the defendants. See figure 2.1.

Apparently it was not the normal practice of the defendants to agree to pay

30. [1986] 1 W.L.R. 631; [1986] 2 All E.R. 400.
31. See above, section 2.3.2.
32. [1975] 1 Lloyd's Rep. 156.

Figure 2.1 The contracts in Maran Road Saw Mill v. Austin Taylor & Co. Ltd.

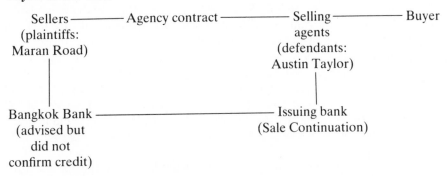

shippers in Malaya by letters of credit, because of the extra expense involved, but the plaintiffs insisted on payment under an irrevocable commercial credit, because according to Ackner J.[33]:

" . . . letters of credit were of advantage since *inter alia* these enabled them to borrow money from their banks against such documents. In fact, this was the very reason given by the plaintiffs to the defendants for insisting on the establishment of letters of credit in their favour. They relied upon overdrafts from their bankers and letters of credit were 'instrumental to our obtaining advances necessary for speeding up our production and shipments.' "

Accordingly, irrevocable letters of credit were opened in the plaintiffs' favour by Sale Continuation Ltd., trading as Sale & Co. Payment was to be made 90 days after sight, but the credits also provided that drafts were negotiable by the Bangkok Bank in Kuala Lumpur at sight rate. In other words the plaintiffs were assured of payment on sight by the Bangkok Bank, and there was a provision for interest to be claimed by the Bangkok Bank from Sale & Co. when they presented the documents for acceptance. The arrangement is described by Ackner J. as follows[34]:

" . . . when shipment time came under the contract for the sale of the timber, the plaintiffs drew bills of exchange on Sale & Co. made out to the order of the Bangkok Bank Ltd. for payment 90 days after sight. The sum involved would be the price of the goods less the defendants' commission.[35] The plaintiffs took the bills and shipping documents to the Bangkok Bank, [and] negotiated these bills with the bank at sight rate. The Bangkok Bank then took the shipping documents and the bills and obtained Sale & Co.'s acceptance in exchange for the shipping documents. The shipping documents would then be handed over to the defendants by Sale & Co. against payment or the provision of a trust letter."[36]

However, Bangkok Bank did not confirm the credit.

33. [1975] 1 Lloyd's Rep. 156, 157 (col. 2).
34. *Ibid*.
35. Which in the case was 4 per cent. of the f.o.b. value.
36. On which see below, section 2.4.1.

In accordance with the arrangement the plaintiffs shipped the timber, and obtained payment at sight rate from Bangkok Bank. Bangkok Bank tendered the shipping documents to Sale & Co., who released them to the defendants. The defendants later transferred them to the sub-buyers against payment of the purchase price by them. Unfortunately, however, before the bills of exchange, providing for payment 90 days after sight, had matured, Sale & Co. went into liquidation. Consequently the bills of exchange were dishonoured. Bangkok Bank accordingly called upon the plaintiffs to reimburse them, and the plaintiffs did so. The plaintiffs sued the defendants for recovery of the sum paid by them to the Bangkok Bank, and succeeded. Their claim in effect was that they had not received the purchase price for the goods, the credit having failed.[37]

One of the arguments advanced by the defendants was that the plaintiffs should not have reimbursed the Bangkok Bank, in other words that the credit had not failed and the plaintiffs had occasioned their own loss. Ackner J., in rejecting this contention, noted that a confirming bank would have had no right of recourse against the drawer, and that the beneficiary would have been under no obligation to reimburse it. He then referred to Article 3 of the U.C.P. (1962 revision), which is substantively similar to Article 10(b) of the 1983 revision set out above, and continued[38]:

"This Article makes it clear that a confirming bank may not have recourse. It is otherwise in the case of a non-confirming bank. The reason is that whereas the latter is the agent of the issuing bank for the purpose of advising the credit, it acts as principal vis-à-vis the beneficiary. He [negotiating bank] is under no duty to negotiate and if it does so, it may make whatever conditions it likes as to a pre-requisite to doing so. It follows that if the credit is available by 'time' draft, the negotiating bank may have recourse on the draft if this is ultimately unpaid."

Ackner J. also rejected a contention of the defendants that the Bangkok Bank could be taken to have confirmed because they had negotiated time drafts at sight rate. He saw no reason for any such implication.

2.3.3.1 Advantages of confirmation

Unlike the confirmed credit, therefore, the unconfirmed negotiation credit gives the beneficiary no protection against failure or refusal to pay by the issuing bank. It leaves the seller open to the possibility of having to litigate against the issuing bank, if for example the issuing bank rejects the documents, which litigation may of course take place abroad. Clearly it offers protection which is vastly inferior to that offered by the full confirmed credit.

On the other hand, so long as the issuing bank is reputable, sellers may not consider worthwhile the extra commission payable for confirmation. Indeed, confirmation may in practice add very little when the issuing bank is repu-

---

37. The precise nature of the action against the defendants is discussed in section 3.2.3.
38. [1975] 1 Lloyd's Rep. 156, 161 (col.1).

table. In *Enrico Furst & Co.* v. *W.E. Fischer Ltd.*,[39] a credit which was issued by a reputable bank in Italy should have been confirmed by a London bank, but the Westminster Bank in London was instructed[40]: "Please advise the beneficiaries of the opening of this letter of credit, without adding your confirmation." Hence the credit was not confirmed by a London bank, but the English sellers raised no objection to the lack of confirmation, and indeed were later held to have waived their right to rely on non-confirmation of the credit when an action was brought against them by the buyers for non-delivery of the goods. It did not surprise Diplock J. that they had not taken this point[41]:

"I have no doubt that the defendants [sellers], when they received the letter of credit, took no point on its not being 'an irrevocable credit opened in London'.[42] They took plenty of points, but they did not take that one. They treated it as valid in its nature and requested the plaintiffs [buyers] to extend it, which they did. No doubt the reason that they did not take any point about it is that, with a reputable [issuing] bank like Swiss-Israel Trade Bank, it made no real commercial difference whether the Westminster Bank, Ltd., added their own confirmation or not."

Clearly it is by no means necessary for sellers always to demand confirmation of credits, then. An unconfirmed irrevocable credit will frequently offer all the security that is required.

2.3.3.2 Confirmation and the U.C.P.

Where the U.C.P. applies, it is clear that the issuing bank cannot, merely by nominating a confirming bank, impose any obligations upon the nominated bank, but also requires the nominated bank to inform the issuing bank without delay should it not be prepared to add its confirmation. Article 11(b) and (c) provide:

"(b) All credits must nominate the bank (nominated bank) which is authorized to pay (paying bank), or to accept drafts (accepting bank), or to negotiate (negotiating bank), unless the credit allows negotiation by any bank (negotiating bank).

(c) Unless the nominated bank is the issuing bank or the confirming bank, its nomination by the issuing bank does not constitute any undertaking by the nominated bank to pay, to accept or to negotiate."

On the other hand, Article 10(c) provides:

"If a bank is authorized or requested by the issuing bank to add its confirmation to a credit but is not prepared to do so, it must so inform the issuing bank without delay. Unless the issuing bank specifies otherwise in its confirmation, authorization or request, the advising bank will advise the credit to the beneficiary without adding its confirmation."

The first sentence of Article 10(c), which was added in 1983, is clearly a

---

39. [1960] 2 Lloyd's Rep. 340. See further section 3.1.5.
40. [1960] 2 Lloyd's Rep. 340, 344 (col. 2).
41. [1960] 2 Lloyd's Rep. 340, 348 (col. 2).
42. This terminology is a little confusing. This statement appears to mean "confirmed in London", since an irrevocable credit had in fact been opened, and a London bank had advised but not confirmed the credit.

sensible provision, but it can be argued that the procedure in the second sentence is not ideal. If the nominated bank is unwilling to confirm the credit, the issuing bank may well prefer to re-route the credit through another bank which is. Additionally, of course, the beneficiary may be unprepared to accept an unconfirmed credit. Arguably it would be better, therefore, to relieve the nominated bank from its duty to advise the credit at all, rather than require it to advise the credit without adding its confirmation.

2.3.4 Transfer of credits

Early forms of credit were sometimes addressed to anybody negotiating bills of exchange drawn upon it.[43] Today credits will normally be opened in favour of a named beneficiary—usually the seller under the sale contract. If so, only the beneficiary can tender shipping documents required by the credit, and in the absence of an assignment of the benefit of the credit, only the original beneficiary can require the issuing bank to pay, or accept or negotiate bills drawn on it.[44]

At common law a beneficiary may assign the benefit of any credit (or indeed any other contract) to his supplier, or any other third party. Under the Law of Property Act 1925, section 136, express notice in writing must be given to the bank as debtor, but an oral notice is sufficient for an equitable assignment.[45] Assignment is also provided for by Article 55 of the U.C.P.: "The fact that a credit is not stated to be transferable shall not affect the beneficiary's right to assign any proceeds to which he may be, or may become, entitled under such credit, in accordance with the provisions of the applicable law." Although this provision, which adds little to the general law, allows the assignee to require the bank to accept bills drawn upon it by the original beneficiary, the obligation to present correct shipping documents remains with the original beneficiary, only the proceeds being assigned. Additionally, the rights of the assignee are no better than those of the original beneficiary, and so depend upon the terms and validity of contract 4 in figure 1.2.

If the seller is a middleman, obtaining the goods from a supplier, or selling goods which are supplied by a number of different suppliers, he may use a transferable credit, defined under Article 54 of the U.C.P. It must be designated "transferable", but if it is so designated the original (or first) beneficiary can request the issuing, confirming or negotiating bank to make the credit available to one or more other parties (second beneficiaries), who are likely to be his suppliers. The credit can thus be used as part or full payment for one or more suppliers.

43. See, for example, the discussion of the credit in *Re Agra and Masterman's Bank* (1867) L.R. 2 Q.B. 391: section 8.1.3.
44. In the analysis of section 8.1, the offer to open the credit is made by the bank to the beneficiary and nobody else.
45. *Ex parte Agra Bank* (1868) L.R. 3 Ch. App. 555. Note that this case has nothing to do with *Re Agra and Masterman's Bank* (1867) L.R. 2 Q.B. 391, discussed in section 8.1.3.

Transfer operates not by way of assignment by novation (of contract 4 in figure 1.2), which is to say that once the credit has been transferred to the second beneficiaries only they, and not the first beneficiary, can enforce it. The first beneficiary of course remains party to the sale contract between himself and his buyer (contract 1).

The general requirements are set out in Article 54. Article 54(a) provides:

"(a) A transferable credit is a credit under which the beneficiary has the right to request the bank called upon to effect payment or acceptance or any bank entitled to effect negotiation to make the credit available in whole or in part to one or more other parties (second beneficiaries)."

Article 46 of the 1974 revision was in similar terms except that the beneficiary could give instructions to the bank, rather than merely request it to transfer. The new Article makes it clear that the bank can refuse. Article 54 continues:

"(b) A credit can be transferred only if it is expressly designated as 'transferable' by the issuing bank. Terms such as 'divisible', 'fractionable','assignable', and 'transmissible' add nothing to the meaning of the term 'transferable' and shall not be used.

(c) The bank requested to effect the transfer (transferring bank) shall be under no obligation to effect such transfer except to the extent and in the manner expressly consented to by such bank.

(d) Bank charges in respect of transfers are payable by the first beneficiary unless otherwise specified. The transferring bank shall be under no obligation to effect the transfer until such charges are paid."

A transferable credit can only be transferred once,[46] but it can be split up. Thus the original credit can be divided to pay various suppliers, if more than one. Article 54 continues:

"(e) A transferable credit can be transferred once only. Fractions of a transferable credit (not exceeding in the aggregate the amount of the credit) can be transferred separately, provided partial shipments are not prohibited, and the aggregate of such transfers will be considered as constituting only one transfer of the credit. The credit can be transferred only on the terms and conditions specified in the original credit, with the exception of the amount of the credit, of any unit prices stated therein, of the period of validity, of the last date for presentation of documents in accordance with Article 47[47] and the period for shipment, any or all of which may be reduced or curtailed, or the percentage for which insurance cover must be effected, which may be increased in such a way as to provide the amount of cover stipulated in the original credit, or these articles. Additionally, the name of the first beneficiary can be substituted for that of the applicant for the credit, but if the name of the applicant for the credit is specifically required by the original credit to appear in any document other than the invoice, such requirement must be fulfilled."

The last part of this provision allows the first beneficiary to keep the name of the applicant of the credit (i.e., his buyer) secret from the second beneficiary (i.e., his supplier), and *vice versa*. The following provision allows the

---

46. U.C.P., Article 53(e).
47. See further section 8.4.6.

first beneficiary to keep his profit secret from his supplier by substituting his own invoices. Article 54 continues:

"(f) The first beneficiary has the right to substitute his own invoices (and drafts if the credit stipulates that drafts are to be drawn on the applicant for the credit[48]) in exchange for those of the second beneficiary, for amounts not in excess of the original amount stipulated in the credit and for the original unit prices if stipulated in the credit, and upon such substitution of invoices (and drafts) the first beneficiary can draw under the credit for the difference, if any, between his invoices and the second beneficiary's invoices.

When a credit has been transferred and the first beneficiary is to supply his own invoices (and drafts) in exchange for the second beneficiary's invoices (and drafts) but fails to do so on demand, the paying, accepting or negotiating bank has the right to deliver to the issuing bank the documents received under the credit, including the second beneficiary's invoices (and drafts) without further responsibility to the first beneficiary."

Further general provisions are contained in paragraph (g):

"(g) Unless otherwise stipulated in the credit, the first beneficiary of a transferable credit may request that the credit be transferred to a second beneficiary in the same country, or in another country. Further, unless otherwise stipulated in the credit, the first beneficiary shall have the right to request that payment or negotiation be effected to the second beneficiary at the place to which the credit has been transferred, up to and including the expiry date of the original credit, and without prejudice to the first beneficiary's right subsequently to substitute his own invoices and drafts (if any) for those of the second beneficiary and to claim any difference due to him."

As in paragraph (a) the word "request" has been substituted for earlier wording to make it clear that the bank has the right to refuse.

2.3.5 Back-to-back credits

Since a transferable credit can only be transferred once, it is suitable only where there is a single middleman obtaining the goods from one or more suppliers for a single re-sale. It is not suitable for chain sales, where the same goods are sold over and over again through many intermediaries. The back-to-back credit, however, may be used for any number of transactions.

In a back-to-back credit, a seller's bank, on the security of the credit opened in the seller's favour, opens a similar credit for his supplier (for a smaller sum). The original credit, and the second opened in favour of the supplier, will be in identical terms apart from the price. This is not really a transfer of the original credit, and indeed there is no reason for the original credit to be made transferable for a second to be opened on its back, because there are in reality two separate credits involved here, and eight autonomous contracts. To call the two credits back-to-back is simply to describe the situation in which the second is opened, and the term has practical but no legal

---

48. This would be rather unusual, but see, e.g., *Borthwick* v. *Bank of New Zealand* (1900) 6 Com. Cas. 2, considered in detail in section 4.4.10.1.

significance. The supplier can use his credit as security for a further credit in favour of his own supplier, and theoretically there is no reason why this should not continue indefinitely.

It is clear, therefore, that where an irrevocable credit is opened, not only is the seller relying on receiving the price whatever happens, subject only to presenting the correct documents, but many others, including for example his suppliers, may well be making similar assumptions. The law to a great extent recognises this.[49]

2.3.6 Revolving credits

Revolving credits are mentioned in all the textbooks on documentary credits, but if it is possible to form any judgments on the basis of reported cases, appear to be extremely rare. They are also not recognised as a separate category by the U.C.P.

Where the sale contract covers a number of shipments, say for a regular supply over a period, the seller will want from the start a documentary credit covering all the shipments. It is no good setting up fresh credits for each shipment, since the seller needs to know from the outset that he is guaranteed payment for the entire period. One possibility is to provide the type of credit that was provided in *Urquhart Lindsay & Co.* v. *Eastern Bank Ltd.*,[50] where the credit required the bank to pay the amounts of the sellers' invoices for each shipment up to a top limit of £70,000, which sum was sufficient to cover all the shipments.

Under the *Urquhart Lindsay* type of credit, the bank's undertaking extends to the value of the entire contract, and it may be unwilling to take this risk. Under a revolving credit, on the other hand, the seller is guaranteed a maximum credit whose amount will be less than the total value of all the shipments, but the credit will continually be topped up to that amount as the buyer reimburses the bank. Hence the bank can limit its liability to a stated maximum amount, while still providing a credit covering all the shipments.

The sellers, who were paper exporters, argued that a confirmed revolving credit for £50,000[51] had been established in their favour in *Nordskog & Co.* v. *National Bank*.[52] In the event Bailhache J. rejected this contention on the facts, but there was considerable discussion as to what a revolving credit would have been, had the sellers' contention been correct. Bailhache J. refused finally to decide, since even at the end of the case he was still unclear,[53] but he appeared to accept the following expert witness testimony[54]:

"It is a little difficult to define, but a revolving credit technically means a credit for a

49. See, e.g., section 6.2.2.1.
50. [1922] 1 K.B. 318; (1921) 9 Lloyd's Rep. 572; see section 8.1.10.1.
51. This being about one-sixth of the total value of the shipments.
52. (1922) 10 Ll.L. Rep. 652.
53. (1922) 10 Ll.L. Rep. 652, 663 (col.2).
54. (1922) 10 Ll.L. Rep. 652, 656 (col.1).

certain sum at any one time outstanding, which is automatically renewed by putting on at the bottom what has been taken off at the top. If you have a revolving credit for £50,000 open for three months, to be operated on by drafts at 30 days' sight as drafts are drawn, they temporarily reduce the amount of the credit below £50,000. As these drafts run off and are presented and paid they are added again to the top of the credit, and restore it again to £50,000. That is what is known technically as a revolving credit, and it is automatic in its operation and does not need any renewal."

In other words, a revolving credit of £50,000 does not mean that that is the maximum sum that can be advanced. Rather, £50,000 is available at any one time. It is reduced by the amount that the seller claims as payment on each shipment, or for which he accepts time drafts, but is topped up again as the buyer reimburses the bank. So long as the buyer continues to reimburse the bank, therefore, up to £50,000 is available under the credit for each shipment. The seller's protection is not as good as in *Urquhart Lindsay*, however, since the credit is only available for the entire series of shipments as long as the buyer continues to reimburse the bank.

2.3.7 Standby credits

Standby credits are not true documentary credits at all, but are essentially a form of bank guarantee. Sometimes they are used to guarantee payment where a true documentary credit cannot be used, and sometimes they are used, by way of performance bond, to guarantee performance by a seller or contractor. Nevertheless, much of the law relating to documentary credits also applies to guarantees and performance bonds, and indeed since 1983, so do the provisions of the U.C.P., so far as they can be made applicable. Both forms of stand-by credit are commonly used in international sales of goods and services. They require their own detailed treatment, therefore, and are further considered in Chapter 8.[55]

2.4 REIMBURSEMENT OF THE ISSUING BANK

2.4.1 Trust receipts

On the assumption that the purchaser has not put the issuing bank in funds in advance, the issuing bank will need to recoup its costs, and its own commission, from him. Usually, however, the purchaser cannot reimburse the issuing bank before he has himself re-sold the goods, but he cannot re-sell the goods without obtaining the bill of lading. The bank, however, will be reluctant to release the bill of lading to the buyer, without some form of security being provided against the bankruptcy of the buyer.

---

55. See section 8.2.

2.4.1.1 Security against bankruptcy of buyer

The problems of security will normally only arise once the goods are sold. If the bank has, through its possession of the bill of lading, obtained special property in the goods,[56] this gives it a legal title to the goods as pledgee. Special property (also referred to as possessory title) remains with the bank until the buyer makes reimbursement to it, whether or not it gives up the bill of lading to the buyer. Thus, if the buyer goes bankrupt before selling the goods the bank can still assert its special property as against the other creditors, and can sell the goods as if it were owner. There is no need for the provision of any alternative form of security.

In the old case, on appeal from Scotland, of *North Western Bank Ltd.* v. *John Poynter, Son, & MacDonalds*,[57] Charles Page & Co. pledged bills of lading for a cargo of phosphate rock which was at sea, with the appellants, a Liverpool bank, as security for an advance of £5,000. Under the terms of the pledge the bank obtained special property as pledgee, and also the power to sell the goods[58]:

"It is distinctly agreed that we [the bank] are to have immediate and absolute power of sale, and that under that power we authorise and empower you [the pledgors] to enter into contracts of sale of the merchandise on our behalf in the ordinary course of business, and we expressly direct you to pay to us from time to time the proceeds of all such sales immediately and specifically as received by you to be applied towards payment of the said advance, interest, commission, and all charges.

You are at any time at our request to give us full authority to receive all sums due or to become due from any person or persons in respect of any sales of the merchandise so made by you on our behalf."

In other words, the bank was in exactly the same position as an issuing bank with which documents of title had been placed under a documentary credit, and which had thereby obtained the special property in the goods.

Later, the bank released the bills of lading to the pledgors, in order to enable them to resell the goods, under a contract of sale which had already been made. It was made clear that the pledgors obtained the documents in order to take delivery of the goods and sell them as agent for the bank. The House of Lords held that by so releasing the documents the bank had not thereby prejudiced its rights as pledgee, nor its special property as pledgee. Lord Herschell L.C. observed[59]:

"There can be no doubt the pledgee might hand back to the pledgor as his agent for the purpose of sale, as was done in this case, the goods he had pledged, without in the slightest degree diminishing the full force and effect of his security."

Page & Co. sold the goods to A. Cross & Co. of Glasgow, but Cross & Co.

---

56. See section 3.3.
57. [1895] A.C. 56.
58. [1895] A.C. 56, 57.
59. [1895] A.C. 56, 68. The position was said to be different under Scottish law, but English law was held to apply, although the disputed fund was situated in Scotland, because both the bank and the pledgor were situated in England.

had not yet paid either Page & Co. or the bank. Nor had Page & Co. reimbursed the bank. John Poynter, Son, & MacDonalds, a creditor of Page & Co., took arrestment proceedings against the debt, the money still being held by Cross & Co., situated in Scotland. The details of arrestment, an action peculiar to Scotland, are beyond the scope of this discussion, except to observe that if the debt was owed by Cross & Co. to Page & Co. the arrest would be valid, whereas if the goods were still the property of North Western Bank, the fund could not be attached by a creditor of Page & Co. The decision of the House was that Page & Co. were merely acting as agents in selling the bank's goods, so that the debt was owed to the bank directly, and could not be attached. It is clear that the decision rests on the bank's special property in the goods as pledgee having been retained, in spite of its release of the bills of lading to the pledgor to sell the goods as its agent.

However, special property in the goods will not avail the bank, at any rate in a dispute between the bank and the buyer's creditors,[60] once they have been sold, except in the special circumstances of *North Western Bank Ltd.* v. *John Poynter, Son, & MacDonalds*, where the proceeds of sale were still held in an indentifiable fund, and had not simply become mixed with the buyer's general funds. Once the proceeds of sale are paid into the buyer's general account, the entire property in them will pass to the buyer,[61] and the bank will lose the protection of its special property. The bank needs to be certain, therefore, before releasing the documents, that it obtains security in the proceeds of sale should the buyer go bankrupt after selling the goods. Of course, if the bank has *not* obtained special property as pledgee, by releasing the bill of lading to the buyer it is giving up its entire security. Obviously an alternative form of security needs to be provided in this case, covering the bank both before and after the goods are sold.

The solution is for the bank to release the bill of lading in exchange for a trust receipt. Normally, a trust receipt constitutes the buyer trustee for the bank of the documents of title and the goods until sold, and of the proceeds of sale once the goods are sold.[62] Thus the bank as beneficiary under the trust retains equitable title in the goods and (if sold) the proceeds of sale. Since the buyer obtains the property only as trustee, if he goes bankrupt, whether before or after the goods are sold, the bank will be able to claim in preference to the general creditors.

It is also worthy of note that the bank's equitable title depends only on the

---

60. On the assertion of legal title against the buyer of the goods, see the discussion of *Lloyds Bank* v. *Bank of America National Trust and Savings Association*, below, section 2.4.1.2.

61. There can be no tracing in this situation at common law.

62. For an example of a modern trust receipt, see the discussion of *Sale Continuation* v. *Austin Taylor*, below, section 2.4.2. However, terms of trust receipts can vary. The documents were, for example, released in exchange for a trust receipt in *North Western Bank* v. *Poynter*, but the decision in no way depended upon this. In any case, it constituted the pledgor trustee only of the bills of lading, and not of the proceeds of sale once the goods were sold: the terms of the trust receipt are set out at [1895] A.C. 56, 65 (bottom of page).

buyer having constituted himself trustee of the goods until sold, and the proceeds of sale thereafter. Whether or not the bank also has special legal property as pledgee is immaterial; so long as the buyer has the general property in the goods, the bank will obtain equitable property as beneficiary under a trust. In this situation at least, the possessory title of a pledgee is irrelevant.

2.4.1.2 Protection against buyer's fraud

Trust receipts give no protection, however, against the buyer's fraud. A trust receipt may give the bank equitable title in the goods and proceeds of sale, but release of the bill of lading will certainly deprive the bank of its constructive possession in the goods. The trust receipt is of no avail, for example, if the buyer uses the bill of lading to obtain the goods from the vessel and simply absconds with them.

Nor will it be of any avail if the buyer re-sells or re-pledges the goods and dishonestly misappropriates the proceeds. There would now be no point in the bank proceeding against its customer, and in order to succeed it would need to sue whoever had come into possession of the documents. In *Lloyds Bank* v. *Bank of America National Trust and Savings Association*,[63] Lloyds Bank released shipping documents to their customer, Strauss & Co. Ltd., in exchange for a trust receipt. The purpose was to enable Strauss & Co. Ltd. to re-sell the goods, but instead Strauss & Co. Ltd. fraudulently pledged the shipping documents with another bank, the Bank of America National Trust and Savings Association, thereby raising further money on the goods. On the liquidation of Strauss & Co. Ltd., Lloyds Bank sued the Bank of America for the return of the shipping documents. However the Court of Appeal held that ownership had passed to the Bank of America.

It is clear that under the terms of the trust receipt, Lloyds Bank released the bills of lading to Strauss & Co. "in order to enable the company to sell the merchandise as trustees for the plaintiffs . . . ",[64] so that Lloyds Bank retained equitable title to the goods. It was of no avail to them, however, because the Bank of America had taken up the documents in good faith, in ignorance of Lloyds Bank's interest. If the Bank of America had thereby obtained legal title to the goods it would be a *bona fide* purchaser for value without notice, and thus, on general equitable principles, defeat any prior equitable title on the part of Lloyds Bank. The issue, therefore, was whether the Bank of America obtained the legal title which Lloyds Bank had by virtue of being pledgee. If so, Lloyds Bank lost not only its security as pledgee, but also any equitable title it may have had in the goods under the trust receipts. It is interesting to note, therefore, that whether or not the bank had equitable title under the trust receipt was irrelevant: if it lost its legal title as pledgee,

---

63. [1938] 2 K.B. 147.
64. [1938] 2 K.B. 147, 159 (bottom).

then any equitable title it may have had would be lost along with it. The existence and terms of the trust receipt were therefore irrelevant to the decision.

The Court of Appeal held that Strauss & Co. Ltd. was able to pass good title to the Bank of America, because of the application of the Factors Act 1889, section 2(1). This provision allows mercantile agents in possession of goods (or documents representing the goods) with the consent of the owner, to pass good title to a third party. Lloyds Bank was regarded as owner for these purposes, by virtue of its special property as pledgee, and Strauss & Co. Ltd. was treated as a mercantile agent within the meaning of the section (even though he also, as pledgor, had the general property in the goods).

The trust receipt did not therefore protect Lloyds Bank against Strauss & Co. Ltd.'s fraud. The position is similar if a buyer under a commercial credit re-sells the goods and fraudulently dissipates the proceeds. If the bank has possessory legal title to the goods it passes to the sub-buyer under the Factors Act provision. Its equitable title to the goods is defeated by the transfer of legal title to the sub-buyer, and the proceeds of sale (in which the bank still has equitable title under the trust receipt) no longer exist. There is therefore nothing left in which the bank can claim any property. Of course, if the bank had not obtained special property as pledgee, its equitable title in the goods under the trust receipt would be defeated simply by the transfer on sale of the (entire) legal title of the buyer to the sub-buyer, at least on the assumption that the sub-buyer was a *bona fide* purchaser for value without notice. There would be no need to invoke the Factors Act provision.

The only protection against this type of fraud is either for the issuing bank to make certain of the honesty of the buyer before agreeing to open the credit, or to refuse to release the shipping documents except against full reimbursement of the sums advanced, interest and commission.

The bank's property at the various stages of the transaction is diagrammatically represented in Figure 2.2 on page 39.

2.4.2 Right to reimbursement where bank does not itself pay: Sale Continuation Ltd. v. Austin Taylor & Co. Ltd

It may seem self-evident that the right of the issuing bank to reimbursement, and to its commission, depends upon it making payment under the letter of credit, but the bank argued the contrary in *Sale Continuation Ltd.* v. *Austin Taylor & Co. Ltd.*[65]

2.4.2.1 The facts of the case

The facts were almost identical to those in the *Maran Road* case,[66] and indeed arose from the liquidation of the same issuing bank. The contractual relationships are illustrated by Figure 2.3 on page 39.

65. [1968] 2 Q.B. 849; [1967] 2 Lloyd's Rep. 403.
66. Above, section 2.3.3.

Figure 2.2 Bank's property in goods and proceeds

Tender of documents.	Bank obtains either no property, or special property as pledgee—see section 3.3.
Release of documents to buyer.	If trust receipt used, bank obtains equitable property, whether or not previously obtained special property as pledgee.
Re-sale of goods.	Bank loses both legal and equitable property in goods—obtains equitable property in proceeds of sale under trust receipt.

Figure 2.3 The contracts in Sale Continuation Ltd. v. Austin Taylor & Co. Ltd.

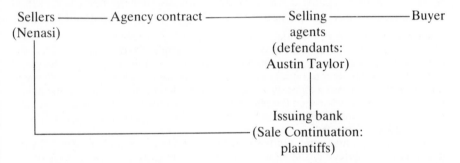

The defendants were again selling agents for a firm of timber exporters in Kuala Lumpur, Malaysia, and as in *Maran Road* were effectively in the position of buyers under an irrevocable credit, opened by Sale Continuation Ltd. As in *Maran Road*, the sellers drew 90 day drafts on the bank in exchange for the shipping documents. The documents were released to the defendant agents against trust receipts which provided[67]:

"We hereby acknowledge the receipt of the under-mentioned documents of title relating to the under-mentioned goods (now in pledge to you as security for advances) to be held by us on the following terms and conditions:

67. [1968] 2 Q.B. 849, 856G–857A; [1967] 2 Lloyd's Rep. 403, 407 (col.1).

We undertake to hold the documents of title and the said goods when received (and the proceeds thereof when sold) as trustees for you . . . further to pay you the proceeds of sale without deduction of any expenses immediately on receipt thereof . . . "

The effect of the trust receipt was to constitute the defendant trustees for Sale Continuation Ltd. of the documents and the goods until sold, and the proceeds of sale thereafter. The goods were in fact sold and the issue in the case concerned the proceeds.

As in *Maran Road*, however, Sale Continuation went into liquidation before the 90 day drafts matured. The main difference between this case and *Maran Road* is that in this case the defendants had not already reimbursed the bank before winding-up proceedings were commenced. Instead, when the drafts were dishonoured, the defendants forwarded the proceeds of sale directly to the sellers, thereby bypassing the bank altogether.

The liquidators for the bank claimed also to be entitled to the proceeds of sale, their commission, charges and interest from the defendants. Their argument was that the consideration for the commission, charges and interest was merely opening the credit, and that they were entitled to the proceeds of sale under the terms of the trust receipt. Paull J. rejected both these arguments.

2.4.2.2 The consideration argument

So far as the first argument was concerned, on whether the bank had earned its commission, and was entitled to claim charges and interest, Paull J. said[68]:

"In my judgment it is an essential element in the contract between the plaintiffs [issuing bank] and the defendants that there was an implied term that, provided the defendants put the plaintiffs in funds to meet any accepted draft, the plaintiffs would in fact honour the accepted draft. That term is necessary to give business efficacy to the contract . . . It may well be, however, that if the defendants did not put the plaintiffs in funds, then, as between the plaintiffs and the defendants, there is no obligation to meet the accepted drafts although there would be as between the drawer [beneficiary] and the plaintiffs.

I therefore hold that under the terms of the contract there was an obligation by the plaintiffs to the defendants to honour drafts properly presented under the letter of credit provided that the defendants put the plaintiffs in funds to do so."

It is not enough, in other words, merely for the issuing bank to open the credit. The contract contained an additional implied term. Of course, in the actual case the defendants had not put the plaintiffs in funds, but the obligations were mutual: they were under no obligation to provide funds to meet the drafts if it were known in advance that the drafts were not going to be met. Here the bank had (by appointing a receiver and commencing winding-up proceedings) evinced their intention not to fulfil their obligation to honour the draft. This constituted a wrongful repudiation of their contract with the defendants, so that the defendants' obligation to reimburse them did not arise.

68. [1968] 2 Q.B. 849, 859 C-E; [1967] 2 Lloyd's Rep. 403, 408 (col. 2).

2.4.2.3 The trust receipt argument

The bank also claimed reimbursement of the proceeds of sale on the basis of the trust receipt, arguing that the defendants had acted in breach of the trust thereby created in paying over the proceeds of sale to the sellers (Nenasi). Paull J. rejected this argument also, but the reasoning is, I would suggest, limited to the case where the documents are released to agents of the sellers, and would not apply where they are released to buyers under the more usual form of credit. He said[69]:

"In this case by the terms of the contract with the buyers, entered into by their agents (the defendants), Nenasi [sellers] parted with their property for all purposes when the goods were shipped except for their vendor's lien for the unpaid purchase price[70] and when Nenasi sent the documents to the plaintiffs Nenasi retained that lien as against the buyers. Having that lien they pledged the documents to the plaintiffs who took them as security against not receiving the purchase price before they had to honour the draft, subject to the buyers' right to demand them as soon as they paid for the goods. The application states that the drafts are to be secured by the delivery of the documents of title as collateral security.

Now the essence of a pledge is that it is security against either an immediate advance or against a present liability to make a future payment. The trust receipt contemplated that the defendants would part with the documents to the Belgian buyer and recover the purchase price. It was no breach of trust to do so. In my judgment the same principle applies to the money [proceeds of sale] as applies to the obligation to put the plaintiffs in funds before the maturity date of the draft. Once the draft is dishonoured (or notice of intention to dishonour given) Nenasi are entitled to cancel the contract of pledge by returning the draft for cancellation and claiming the purchase money from their agents, the defendants. It is as though a pawnbroker having received the pledge and given his pawn ticket to the pledgor refused to hand over the sum agreed to be lent. The pledgor can say: 'Very well, here is your pawn ticket. Hand me back my goods.' In this case 'the goods' (being the documents of title, or rather the money received for them) were already in the hands of the pledgor [Nenasi]."

The result of the case was that the defendants, having paid the proceeds of sale to the seller, did not need also to pay them to the bank. By contrast in *Maran Road*, where the sellers' agents had reimbursed the bank first, they had to pay twice over. At first sight, therefore, it seems that when a bank goes into liquidation in circumstances such as these, having released the documents to agents of the seller, the seller's agents should pay the seller in preference to reimbursing the bank.

2.4.2.3.1 WHAT IF DEFENDANTS HAD NOT BEEN AGENTS OF THE SELLERS?

I would suggest, however, that the same reasoning would not apply where (as is the usual case) the documents are released to a buyer who is not acting as

---

69. [1968] 2 Q.B. 849, 861E–862B; [1967] 2 Lloyd's Rep. 403, 410 (col. 1).
70. This is (probably) not the usual position: see further, section 3.3.4. However, nothing turns on this here.

seller's agent. It is necessary to examine Paull J.'s reasoning in some detail. From the above passage it is clear that:

1. Nenasi having pledged the documents against the 90 day draft, were entitled to cancel the pledge when the bank gave notice that it intended to dishonour the draft. Since Nenasi could not demand return of the documents themselves, the bank no longer being in possession of them, as pledgor he was entitled instead to the purchase price, into which they had been converted.
2. Parting with the documents to the Belgian buyer did not constitute a breach of trust by the defendants.

It is noteworthy that the first of these points deals only with the relationship between Nenasi and the bank, and not that between the bank and the defendants. It is indeed arguable that nothing remained to be done as between Nenasi and the bank, since Nenasi were entitled to cancel the pledge and demand the purchase price, and they had of course been paid this by the defendants.[71] On this basis, the bank could not have sued Nenasi. The problem is that they sued not Nenasi, but the defendants. I would suggest that the decision depended on defendants being agents of the seller: because they were acting on Nenasi's behalf, rather than as principals in their own right, it was Nenasi rather than the defendants who could be regarded as having undertaken obligations under the trust receipt. Consequently, it was necessary to consider only the relationship between the bank and Nenasi, and of course Nenasi were entitled to cancel the pledge.

Suppose, however, the normal case where the documents, having originally been pledged by the seller, are released to the buyers directly, for re-sale to a sub-buyer. It is not enough now to consider only whether the sellers are entitled to cancel the pledge, since it is the buyers who are being sued, and they have now undertaken obligations as principals under the trust receipt. The issue would instead be whether the buyers themselves had acted in breach of trust. Of course, it would no more be a breach of trust for them to part with the documents to the sub-buyer than it was for the defendants in *Sale Continuation* to part with them to the Belgian buyer, but that would not be the issue either. The question would instead be: "would the buyers be acting in breach of trust in paying the proceeds of sale over to the sellers"? If the trust receipt was in the same terms as that in *Sale Continuation*, under which the defendants undertook to hold the proceeds on trust for the bank, then the answer would surely be a resounding "Yes". That question did not arise in *Sale Continuation* itself, and is not discussed anywhere in the case, because the defendants were regarded not as undertaking any trust obligations in their

---

71. But there is a contrary argument, that by parting with the documents and transferring the property in the goods to the buyer, Nenasi must have been content to be treated as an unsecured creditor of the bank: Benjamin, *Sale of Goods* (3rd ed., 1987), para. 1510. See also Gutteridge & Megrah, *The Law of Bankers' Commercial Credits* (7th ed., 1984), pp. 43–45.

own right as principals, but merely undertaking obligations on Nenasi's behalf.

What then is the position if documents are released to a buyer directly? I suggest that the buyers would be required, on the assumption that the terms of the trust receipt are similar to those in *Sale Continuation*, to pay the proceeds of sale to the bank. It would be a breach of trust to pay them to the seller directly. Of course, if the seller had not been paid by the bank, then he would undoubtedly be entitled, just as Nenasi was, to cancel the pledge, and sue the bank. In that event, however, he would recover from the liquidator only a proportion of the proceeds. The seller would then be able to sue the buyers under the sale contract for the balance.[72]

If that analysis is correct, then the buyer would gain nothing by paying the seller first, rather than the bank. This may be thought unfair on the buyer, who would thereby have been forced to pay twice over (or almost twice over). On the other hand:

1. If the buyer chooses to reimburse the bank first, his position is exactly the same as that of the defendants in the *Maran Road* case. He is still liable to the seller under the sale contract, so has to pay twice over. It is very difficult, as a matter of logic or principle, to justify putting him into a better position merely because he had decided to pay the seller rather than the bank.

2. If a buyer chooses to undertake trusteeship of the proceeds of sale for the bank, in the knowledge that the seller has not yet been paid, he is clearly taking the risk that he will come under obligations to both seller and bank. That undertaking of risk being entirely voluntary, it would be difficult to justify the buyers in such a case taking priority over the other creditors.

---

72. The issues are identical to those discussed in section 3.2.3.

CHAPTER 3

THE CONTRACT OF SALE

3.1 GENERAL REQUIREMENTS OF PROVISION OF CREDIT

Documentary credits, as seen in Chapter 2, are of various types, and the type of credit which the buyer must provide will be determined by the sale contract. Because the credit is provided in pursuance of the contract of sale, the sale contract is sometimes referred to as the underlying transaction.

It is important to appreciate, however, that because the contract of sale is autonomous,[1] it has no direct effect on the obligations of the banks under the credit. The contracts constituting the credit (contracts 2 and 3 in figure 1.2) are independent of the underlying contract (contract 1). If the required form of credit is not provided by the buyer the seller may thereby have an action against the buyer under the sale contract (contract 1), but his relationship with issuing or confirming bank will be determined by the terms of the credit actually provided (contract 4). Therefore, if the credit does not conform to the sale contract requirements the seller may sue the buyer on the contract of sale, but can take no steps to remedy the situation against either bank directly.

3.1.1 Implied requirement for irrevocable credit

As was observed in Chapter 2, where the sale contract provides for sale by documentary credit, the courts presume a requirement for an irrevocable credit unless the contrary is expressly stated.[2] The usual authority given for this proposition is *Giddens* v. *Anglo-African Produce Ltd.*,[3] an action by c.i.f. purchasers (under two contracts) of South African yellow maize against the sellers for damages for non-fulfilment of the contracts. The defendant sellers contended that the credit required by the sale contract had not been opened, so that the condition precedent for their performance had not arisen, and Bailhache J. accepted this proposition. In giving judgment for the defendants he said:

1. See section 1.6.1.2.
2. The U.C.P. requirement is opposite: see section 2.3.1.
3. (1923) 14 Ll.L. Rep. 230.

"I think this case is quite hopeless. Here is a contract which calls for an established credit and in purported satisfaction of what this contract calls for what they get is this: 'Negotiations of drafts under these credits are subject to the bank's convenience. All drafts hereunder are negotiated with recourse against yourselves.' How that can be called an established credit in any sense of the word absolutely passes my comprehension."

This was not, of course, an irrevocable credit because under an irrevocable negotiation credit the drafts must be negotiated without recourse against the drawer.[4] It appears from the (very short and not very clear) report of the case that the sale contract did not call expressly for an irrevocable credit, but it is usually assumed that a requirement for an irrevocable credit was implied.

There is no presumption, by contrast, that a credit is required to be confirmed, unless the sale contract expressly so states.

3.1.2 Credit more than simply means of paying the price

A fundamental principle, which has been recognised over and over again by the courts, is that the credit is more than simply a means of paying the price, and that the seller may be relying on it to finance the transaction. Two consequences follow from this fundamental principle, that the seller is under no obligation to perform at all until the credit is opened, and that it must be opened within a reasonable time.[5]

3.1.2.1 Opening of credit condition precedent of seller's performance under sale contract

In *Trans Trust S.P.R.L.* v. *Danubian Trading Co. Ltd.,*[6] the buyers failed to procure the opening of a credit in accordance with the requirements of sale contract, and Denning L.J. categorically stated that the sellers were under no obligation to perform at all in the absence of a credit[7]:

"What is the legal position of such a stipulation [that a credit should be provided]? Sometimes it is a condition precedent to the formation of a contract, that is, it is a condition which must be fulfilled before any contract is concluded at all. In those cases the stipulation 'subject to the opening of a credit' is rather like a stipulation 'subject to contract'. If no credit is provided, there is no contract between the parties. In other cases a contract is concluded and the stipulation for a credit is a condition which is an essential term of the contract. In these cases the provision of the credit is a condition precedent, not to the formation of the contract, but to the obligation of the seller to deliver the goods. If the buyer fails to provide the credit, the seller can treat himself as discharged from any further performance of the contract and can sue the buyer for damages for not providing the credit."

4. See section 2.3.1. Although the report is rather inadequate, the credit appears to be an old-fashioned negotiation credit, where drafts are drawn on the buyer, not the issuing bank, the bank undertaking merely to negotiate the drafts. This form of credit is obsolete except in the Middle East.
5. A further consequence, affecting measure of damages, is considered below, at section 3.1.5.
6. [1952] 2 Q.B. 297; [1952] 1 All E.R. 970; [1952] 1 Lloyd's Rep. 348; [1952] W.N. 184.
7. [1952] 2 Q.B. 297, 304.

The difference between the two types of case is that in the first type both sellers and buyers are relieved of any obligation to perform in the absence of a credit being provided, whereas in the second variety only the sellers are relieved of this obligation to perform, the buyers remaining liable in damages for breach of contract. Denning L.J. went on to hold that in the particular case, the credit was of the second type, and this is the normal situation. The buyers were accordingly liable for damages for breach, on principles discussed below.[8]

3.1.2.2 Time of opening of credit

Ideally, the sale contract should stipulate the period within which the credit should be opened, and if it does then no problems arise. If it does not, or if the term is too vague to be treated as an express stipulation as to time,[9] then the courts have again had regard to the fact that the seller may be relying on the provision of the credit in order to finance the transaction, and require the credit to be opened as soon as the buyer reasonably can.

The starting point is the judgment of Porter J. in *Garcia* v. *Page & Co Ltd.*[10]:

"In my view, under the original contract there was a contract by which a confirmed credit in the terms specified was a condition precedent, and it had to be opened immediately. That means that the buyer must have such time as is needed by a person of reasonable diligence to get the credit established."

There was no express stipulation in the contract itself, and Porter J. took the view that three months was an unreasonably long time to establish the credit.

What is a reasonable time will depend on all the circumstances, and it is not therefore possible to state a general rule. The courts have adopted Lord Watson's test from *Hick* v. *Raymond & Reid*[11]:

"When the language of a contract does not expressly, or by implication, fix any time for the performance of a contractual obligation, the law implies that it shall be performed within a reasonable time. The rule is of general application, and is not confined to contracts for the carriage of goods by sea. In the case of other contracts the condition of reasonable time has been frequently interpreted; and has invariably been held to mean that the party upon whom it is incumbent duly fulfils his obligation, so long as such delay is attributable to causes beyond his control, and he has neither acted negligently nor unreasonably."

In *Etablissements Chainbaux S.A.R.L.* v. *Harbormaster Ltd.*,[12] the

---

8. Section 3.1.5.
9. E.g., "within a few weeks", as in *Etablissements Chainbaux S.A.R.L.* v. *Harbormaster Ltd.* [1955] 1 Lloyd's Rep. 303, below, f.n. 13.
10. (1936) 55 Ll.L. Rep. 391, 392 (col.1).
11. [1893] A.C. 22, 32–33. This is not a banking case, but concerns the obligations of a consignee under a carriage contract. However, the test is of general application.
12. See f.n. 9.

contract of sale required the credit to be "opened in London within a few weeks". Devlin J. treated this as too vague a term to be treated as an express provision as to time,[13] and therefore thought that a reasonable time should be allowed. Applying the above passage from *Hick* v. *Raymond & Reid*, he thought that one month was about the outside limit. This is far longer than in the normal case, because all the circumstances are taken into account. Here, French buyers had to provide a sterling letter of credit, and there was an inevitable delay in obtaining exchange control permission from the French Government. In *Baltimex Ltd.* v. *Metallo Chemical Refining Ltd.*,[14] Sellers J. took into account the fact the sellers' knowledge at the time of the contract that delay was likely, since they were to be paid out of the proceeds of a sub-sale by their buyers to Russian sub-buyers, and they knew that there was likely to be a delay in the establishment of the credit by the Russian sub-buyers.

Because the seller may be relying on the credit to finance the transaction, the requirement to provide a credit within a reasonable time prevails even where under the contract, delivery is postponed until a considerable time into the future. As Devlin J. observed in *Etablissements Chainbaux S.A.R.L.* v. *Harbormaster Ltd.*, where delivery was not to take place for eight months[15]:

"It is to be observed that the provision as to the letter of credit is to be contrasted with the provision as to delivery. Delivery is not to start until the lapse of eight months; the letter of credit, on the other hand, is to be 'opened in London within a few weeks'. It is plain, therefore, that although the letter of credit is to provide for payment against shipping documents, and therefore payment could not in any event be due until some eight months, when deliveries started, the buyers offered to establish the letter of credit before that. One can well understand the business reason for that. Sometimes a letter of credit is wanted merely because the seller is unwilling to make arrangements for shipment, which may involve him in expense, unless he knows he is going to be paid. That might be the normal case where the seller has got the goods and the only expense he has to incur in relation to them is to put them on board ship or otherwise arrange for their transport, but in this case it plainly is not so: the seller had to manufacture the goods, and what he desires is to have the letter of credit for it is plainly so that he will have the assurance, within a few weeks and before he begins manufacture, that he is certain to be paid and that the labour of manufacture will not therefore be done in vain."

In addition to the reasonable time requirement, the courts have consistently held that if the contract provides for shipment by the seller at any time over a stated period, then in the absence of an express stipulation, the buyer must open the credit and make it available by the beginning of the shipment period. The authority for a c.i.f. contract is the Court of Appeal decision in *Pavia & Co. S.p.A.* v. *Thurmann-Nielsen*.[16] The buyers claimed that since the credit was simply a means of paying the price, there was no reason why the

---

13. [1955] 1 Lloyd's Rep. 303, 306 (col.1).
14. [1955] 2 Lloyd's Rep. 438.
15. [1955] 1 Lloyd's Rep. 303, 305 (col. 2).
16. [1952] 2 Q.B. 84; [1952] 1 Lloyd's Rep. 153.

credit should be provided before the price became payable (i.e., in a c.i.f. sale, on tender of shipping documents). The Court of Appeal took the view that this was the wrong approach. The credit was not simply a means of paying the price, but was also intended to provide the seller with security. Denning L.J., echoing the fundamental principles already set out, said[17]:

"The question in this case is this: In a contract which provides for payment by confirmed credit, when must the buyer open the credit? In the absence of an express stipulation, I think the credit must be made available to the seller at the beginning of the shipment period. The reason is because the seller is entitled, before he ships the goods, to be assured that, on shipment, he will get paid. The seller is not bound to tell the buyer the precise date when he is going to ship; and whenever he does ship the goods, he must be able to draw on the credit. He may ship on the very first day of the shipment period. If, therefore, the buyer is to fulfil his obligations he must make the credit available at the very first date when the goods may be lawfully shipped in compliance with the contract."

The argument that the provision of the credit is merely another way of paying the price was also rejected in a different context, considered below.[18]

Similar reasoning was applied to an f.o.b. contract by Diplock J. in *Ian Stach Ltd.* v. *Baker Bosley Ltd.*[19] The buyers argued that unlike *Pavia*, it was they rather than the sellers who were entitled to choose the time of shipment, within the stipulated period. Diplock J.'s view was that this made no difference to the principle in *Pavia*, relying again on the fundamental principle that the seller needs the assurance given by the credit from as early as possible. The view was stated yet again that a commercial credit is not simply a means of paying the price.[20]

The requirement that the credit must be available by the beginning of the shipment period is additional to the reasonable time requirement, and does not allow the buyer to delay where the shipment period does not begin until after more than a reasonable time has elapsed.

3.1.3 Terms of credit

Apart from the requirements in the previous sections, the courts are reluctant to imply others into the sale contract. In particular, the buyer has considerable freedom over the terms of the credit, in the absence of express stipulation to the contrary.

In *Soproma S.p.A.* v. *Marine & Animal By-Products Corporation.*,[21] the buyer agreed to buy 1,000 tons of Chilean fish fullmeal from the seller c. & f., the sale contract also requiring a 70 per cent. protein content. Under the sale

17. [1952] 2 Q.B. 84, 88.
18. Section 3.1.5.
19. [1958] 2 Q.B. 130; [1958] 2 W.L.R. 419; [1958] 1 All E.R. 542; [1958] 1 Lloyd's Rep. 127.
20. [1958] 2 Q.B. 130, 139. He also cited the remarks of Jenkins L.J. in *Hamseh Malas & Sons* v. *British Imex Industries Ltd.* [1958] 2 Q.B. 127; [1958] 2 W.L.R. 100; [1957] 2 Lloyd's Rep. 549, set out in their context in section 6.2.1.
21. [1966] 1 Lloyd's Rep. 367.

contract, payment was to be by irrevocable documentary credit, but apart from stipulating the identity of the advising bank (Marine and Midland Trust Co., New York), the sale contract was otherwise silent as to the details of the credit. It was unclear whether the credit was also required to be confirmed by Marine and Midland Trust Co.

The sale contract was later varied twice, first to allow two shipments of 500 tons, one in September 1962 and one in October 1962, in place of the single shipment of 1,000. The second variation was to vary the respective shipments to 600 tons in September and 400 tons in October. Before the second variation, however, an irrevocable credit, to which the U.C.P. applied,[22] had already been opened by the buyers' bank in respect of the 500 ton September shipment, and advised (but not confirmed) by Marine and Midland Trust Co. The credit stipulated that the shipping documents must include (among others) a certificate of analysis stating that it had a minimum protein content of 70 per cent., and full set of on board ocean bills of lading, issued to order and blank indorsed, and marked "freight prepaid". Shortly after the sale contract had been varied for the second time, a second credit was opened in respect of the additional 100 tons to be shipped in September, and the two letters of credit later consolidated by one set of documents.

No letter of credit was ever opened for the remaining 400 tons, and the buyers were clearly liable for that failure. For present purposes, only the two credits (later consolidated) regarding the first shipment of 600 tons are relevant.

The sellers tendered a bill of lading marked "freight collect", and naming the confirming bank as consignee, but not issued to order. A quality certificate was also tendered certifying a minimum protein content of only 67 per cent. The bank rejected the documents,[23] and the sellers attempted to make a second tender, directly to the buyers. This was also rejected.[24] The sellers went to arbitration, claiming that the buyers were in breach of the contract of sale, and the Umpire found in their favour. The buyers appealed to the Board of Appeal of the London Cattle Food Trade Association (L.C.F.T.A.), which stated a special case for decision by the High Court. One of the issues was whether the buyers, by procuring credits which stipulated additional documents to those required by the sale contract itself, were thereby acting in breach of the contract of sale. McNair J. held that they were not[25]:

"It may be that [the credits opened by the buyers] were . . . defective in that they called for documents in addition to those specified in the contract itself. This was the view expressed by the Board of Appeal in par. 39 (c) of their findings of fact set out above. But as at present advised, I should not feel disposed to accept this conclusion. It seems to me to be a necessary implication from the use of the words 'payment

22. 1951 revision. The U.C.P. is irrelevant to the present discussion, but is relevant to the further discussion of this case in section 6.3.
23. On this aspect of the decision, see further section 6.3.
24. On this aspect of the decision, see further below, section 3.2.2.
25. [1966] 1 Lloyd's Rep. 367, 386 (col.1).

against letters of credit' that the credit itself should set out in detail the specific conditions under which it can be operated including the period of its availability and that so long as these conditions are fair and reasonable and not inconsistent with the terms of the contract itself no objection can be taken to them by the sellers."

McNair J.'s view, in other words, was that the terms of the credit are contained in the credit itself, and cannot generally be implied from the sale contract. The only implication in the sale contract is that the credit terms must be fair and reasonable, and must not conflict with the express terms of the sale contract. Otherwise, subject of course to express terms in the sale contract, buyers may open credits on any terms they wish.

Two qualifications ought to be made to this statement. The first is that *Soproma* is not a strong authority on this issue. Apart from being only a decision at first instance, McNair J.'s above comments were only *obiter dicta*, since it was not, in the event, necessary to decide the point. The seller also claimed that the credits were defective in other, far more serious respects, namely that they were not confirmed (as required, he claimed, by the sale contract), and that they were not opened in time to cover the whole shipment period.[26] Had these inconsistencies been made out, the seller would clearly have won, whatever view had been taken on the documentary requirements. However, the arbitrators had found that the letters of credit were not in fact inconsistent with the terms of the sale contract.[27] Even if they had been, however, the seller was estopped by his conduct (applying for the two letters of credit to be consolidated, and operating the letters of credit by the tender of a consolidated set of documents) from relying on the inconsistencies.[28]

In spite of their weaknesses as authority, however, I would suggest that the remarks of McNair J., set out above, are correct.

The second qualification is that the documents must not be inconsistent with the terms of the contract itself. The documents required here were obviously consistent with the sale contract, in that the 70 per cent. protein requirement was the same, and freight prepaid bills would be usual under c. & f. contracts (although buyers do not normally object to freight collect bills so long as freight is deducted from the invoice price, or a freight receipt tendered by the sellers.[29]) A requirement for a certificate of analysis showing 80% protein would clearly be inconsistent with the sale contract, however.

Some documents would in any case be inconsistent with any c.i.f. (or c. & f.) contract, and could not be stipulated. It is a fundamental principle, for example, that a c.i.f. seller is required only to ship conforming goods, but is not responsible if they do not arrive at the port of discharge, or arrive damaged. A requirement for a quality certificate issued on discharge, therefore, or at any other time after shipment, could not be stipulated under a c.i.f.

---

26. And hence came within the *Pavia* principles, above, section 3.1.2.2.
27. [1966] 1 Lloyd's Rep. 367, 386 (col. 2).
28. [1966] 1 Lloyd's Rep. 367, 386 (col. 1). See also below, section 3.1.4.
29. [1966] 1 Lloyd's Rep. 367, 387 (col. 1).

contract. Further, if such a document was stipulated in the credit, the terms of the credit would be inconsistent with the sale contract, and the buyer would be in breach.

3.1.4 Waiver and estoppel

3.1.4.1 General principles

Even where a sale contract calls for a particular type of credit, it may be open to the seller to accept a different type, providing him with less security. So long as the benefit is wholly for the seller, he may waive that benefit.

Furthermore, by accepting a credit which provides inferior security to that provided for under the contract, he may by his conduct be taken as having waived his right to demand the greater security, at any rate without giving reasonable notice. In *Panoustos* v. *Raymond Hadley Corporation*,[30] the sale contract (for a number of shipments of flour) provided that payment should be by confirmed bankers' credit. The seller accepted payments for a number of shipments by means of a credit which was not confirmed, and the Court of Appeal held that he was unable to repudiate the contract when the buyer provided an unconfirmed credit for a later shipment. Because the seller had waived for a time the buyer's breach of condition in failing to provide a confirmed credit, he was unable to repudiate the contract on that ground without giving reasonable notice. As Viscount Reading C.J. observed[31]:

"In *Bentsen* v. *Taylor, Sons & Co.*[32] Bowen L.J. stated the law as to waiver thus: 'Did the defendants by their acts or conduct lead the plaintiff reasonably to suppose that they did not intend to treat the contract for the future as at an end, on account of the failure to perform the condition precedent?' Reading sellers for defendants and buyer for plaintiff in that passage, it applies exactly to the present case. The sellers did lead the buyer to think so, and when they intended to change that position it was incumbent on them to give reasonable notice of that intention to the buyer so as to enable him to comply with the condition which up to that time had been waived."

Another similar case is *Enrico Furst & Co.* v. *W.E. Fischer Ltd.*[33] As in *Panoustos* the buyers were in breach by providing a credit which was not confirmed by a London bank, but instead of relying on this as a ground to throw up the contract the sellers made no objection to the lack of confirmation, and indeed requested extension of the credit.[34] In an action by the buyers for non-delivery of the goods (cast-iron piping), the sellers were held to have waived their right to rely on non-confirmation of the credit as a breach of condition by the buyers.[35]

---

30. [1917] 2 K.B. 473.
31. [1917] 2 K.B. 473, at p. 478.
32. [1893] 2 Q.B. 283, a case on a sale contract.
33. [1960] 2 Lloyd's Rep. 340.
34. Diplock J. commented that since the issuing bank was clearly reputable it made no commercial difference whether or not the credit was confirmed: [1960] 2 Lloyd's Rep. 340, 348 (col. 2).
35. [1960] 2 Lloyd's Rep. 340, 349 (col. 2).

Estoppel operates in much the same way as waiver. The seller will be estopped from asserting his strict legal rights if he has made a representation to that effect, upon which the buyer has relied to his detriment. Whether the seller has waived his right or is regarded as being estopped from asserting it seems to matter little for practical purposes, since the test for a waiver in the above passage is virtually identical to that for an estoppel. As with waiver, the representation may be inferred from words or conduct, and the effect of the estoppel will be to prevent the seller from going back on the representation without giving reasonable notice.[36]

Another example where sellers were taken to have waived the inconsistencies (if any) in a credit, or to be estopped from relying on them, was the *Soproma* case. It is clear from McNair J.'s judgment that he regards it as a matter of indifference whether the matter is put as waiver, variation or estoppel[37]:

"It is to be observed that the Board of Appeal . . . found that the letters of credit were not inconsistent with the terms of the contract. But, assuming for the purposes of the point at present being considered that the letters of credit were defective both in respect of the matters mentioned above, namely, not being confirmed and not covering the whole shipment period, and also in respect of the additional requirements, the material question is as to the effect of the sellers' acceptance of the letters of credit. On the assumption stated, the sellers could, I think, plainly have treated the buyers' failure to open proper letters of credit as a breach of condition entitling them to rescind and claim damages. In fact (i) the sellers applied for the two letters of credit to be varied by the authorization of the tender of one consolidated set of documents under the two letters of credit and (ii) in fact after this authorization had been given they operated the letters of credit by the tender of a consolidated set of documents. In my judgment, by so acting, the sellers must be taken to have accepted the position that their letters of credit were in order and, not having at any time given notice to the buyers that they required letters of credit in strict conformity with the contract, they are precluded (whether the matter is put as waiver, variation or estoppel) from now saying that the letters of credit were not in order and did not accurately define the contractual mode of obtaining payment including the period of availability.[38]

The request by the sellers in [*Enrico*] for an extension of the defective letters of credit is indistinguishable in principle from the request in the present case for a variation of the two letters of credit by the authorisation of presentation of a single consolidated set of shipping documents. This result, as it seems to me, both accords with well-settled principles of law and is also consistent with good business sense. Unless the concession asked for by the sellers had been granted, the sellers would have been in plain default since by shipping the whole 600 tons under one bill of lading they had

---

36. A detailed discussion of the difference between waiver and estoppel is beyond the scope of this book, but see, for example, Treitel, *The Law of Contract* (7th ed., 1987), pp. 83–96, and in particular 92–96. Both estoppel and waiver should be distinguished from variation of a contract. Variation requires consideration to move from both parties, and therefore cannot arise from the unilateral act of one party, and variation permanently affects the rights of the parties. Waiver and estoppel probably operate only to suspend rights, however: the seller in *Panoustos* could have reasserted his original rights under the contract upon reasonable notice.

37. [1966] 1 Lloyd's Rep. 367, 386 (col. 2).

38. McNair J. referred to *Panoustos* v. *Raymond Hadley Corporation of New York* [1917] 2 K.B. 473, and *Enrico Furst & Co.* v. *W.E. Fischer, Ltd.* [1960] 2 Lloyd's Rep. 340.

put it out of their power to tender two bills of lading, namely, a separate bill of lading under each letter of credit. Accordingly, they can only succeed in the present case if they can establish that in law they made a valid tender of documents under the letters of credit as so modified and within the period of availability of these letters . . . "

3.1.4.2 Waiver and periodic actions

In *Panoustos* the sellers made the first of a number of shipments without insisting on the confirmed credit to which they were entitled. The Court of Appeal held that they had waived their right to a confirmed credit not only in respect of that particular shipment, but also in respect of future shipments, since they would be required to give the buyers reasonable notice before again availing themselves of their right to confirmation. It does not necessarily follow, however, that where there are a number of shipments waiver of a right in respect of the first shipment will necessarily preclude the seller from reasserting his right in respect of a subsequent shipment: an act by one party may be held only to operate in respect of each individual shipment, and it may not always be possible to infer a waiver for the future in addition.

In *Cape Asbestos Co. Ltd.* v. *Lloyds Bank Ltd.*,[39] it has already been explained that the bank was able to revoke without notice a revocable credit. The bank raised a further defence that the bill of lading tendered did not conform to the terms of the credit, since the bill of lading instead of being to the order of the defendant bank, was made out to the order of the buyers. The sellers claimed, relying on *Panoustos*, that the bank having accepted a bill of lading in similar terms on a previous shipment had waived its right to reject on those grounds for the subsequent shipment. In the event the point did not arise for decision since the credit had been validly revoked,[40] but Bailhache J. said that in any event *Panoustos* was not authority for the proposition claimed[41]:

"That case [*Panoustos*] was an authority for the proposition that where an act had to be done by the buyer of goods, such, for instance, as the opening of a confirmed banker's credit, and he did not perform that act, and the seller nevertheless went on delivering the goods with knowledge that the act had not been performed, the seller could not suddenly cancel the contract and refuse to make further deliveries without giving the buyer reasonable notice of his intention so as to give the buyer an opportunity of putting himself right. That case was no authority for the proposition, that where an act had to be done periodically, as, for instance, the delivery of a bill of lading in such a case as the present, the fact that it had been done irregularly in the past justified the assumption that the irregularity would be waived in the future. The *Panoustos* case had only reference to an act which had to be done once and for all, and not to an act which had to be done periodically."

The distinction, then, appears to be between an act which has to be done

39. See above, section 3.1.4.2.
40. See above, section 2.3.1.2.
41. [1921] W.N. 274, 275 (col. 2).

once and for all, as in the confirmation of the credit in *Panoustos*,[42] and one which has to be done periodically, as in tendering bills of lading for each shipment in *Cape Asbestos*.

Panoustos is authority only for the former type, not for the latter. Although there were several separate shipments in *Panoustos*, confirmation of the credit should have occurred when the credit was opened. The credit opened in the seller's favour covered all the separate shipments, so that the act of confirmation was a once and for all act. It follows that waiver of the right to insist on confirmation of the credit ought to have operated (and did) not only in respect of the first shipment, but also in respect of future shipments, or at any rate until reasonable notice was given to the contrary. In *Cape Asbestos*, on the other hand, bills of lading were issued separately in respect of each shipment, so that there was no reason to infer from waiver in respect of the first shipment waiver in respect of any subsequent shipments.

3.1.4.3 Only unilateral benefits may be waived

It is very important to note that both waiver and estoppel only operate where the stipulation is inserted only for the benefit of the party waiving the right, or being estopped from relying on it, and it is clear, for example, that the *Panoustos* case refers only to this situation.[43] By contrast, the stipulation that payment is to be made by commercial credit benefits both seller and buyer, and it is not generally open to the seller unilaterally to waive it by insisting on making payment directly to the buyer.[44]

3.1.5 Consequences of failure to open credit, or failure to provide reliable and solvent paymaster

3.1.5.1 Seller can claim loss of profit on transaction

It has already been explained that the provision of a credit is more than simply a way of paying the price, because the seller may use it as security to raise finance for the transaction, for example for purchasing or manufacturing the goods.[45] In other words, the provision of the credit may be essential to the seller's performance.

If the buyer fails to open a credit, he is in breach of contract, and the damages will be anything that is recoverable under ordinary principles applicable to contractual damages. In *Trans Trust S.P.R.L.* v. *Danubian Trading Co. Ltd.*,[46] the buyers of a quantity of steel failed to procure the opening of a

---

42. Although there were several separate shipments in *Panoustos*, confirmation of the credit should have occurred when the credit was opened. The credit opened in the seller's favour covered all the separate shipments, so that the act of confirmation was a once and for all act.
43. [1917] 2 K.B. 473, at p. 477 (bottom).
44. See below, 3.2.2.
45. Above, section 3.1.2.
46. See section 3.1.2.1.

credit in accordance with the sale contract, and the sellers claimed as damages the loss of profit which they would have made on the sale. It has already been explained that the buyers were liable for breach of contract,[47] but they claimed that the credit was no more than a way of paying the price. Since the steel market was rising, they claimed that the sellers could have resold at a profit. Therefore they had suffered no loss, so the damages ought to be nominal only.

In fact, the sellers had not resold the steel at a profit, because in the absence of a credit they were unable to purchase it from the manufacturers in the first place. In other words, they were relying on the provision of the credit to finance the transaction. This is, of course, quite normal, and Denning L.J. thought that it was wrong to treat the provision of the credit as simply an alternative way of paying the price[48]:

"This argument reminds me of the argument we heard in *Pavia & Co.* v. *Thurmann-Nielsen*.[49] It treats the obligation to provide a credit as the same thing as the obligation to pay the price. That is, I think, a mistake. A banker's confirmed credit is a different thing from payment. It is an assurance in advance that the seller will be paid. It is even more than that. It is a chose in action which is of immediate benefit to the seller. It is irrevocable by the banker, and it is often expressly made transferable by the seller. The seller may be relying on it to obtain the goods himself. If it is not provided, the seller may be prevented from obtaining the goods at all. The damages he will then suffer will not in fact be nominal. Even if the market price of the goods has risen, he will not be able to take advantage of the rise because he will not have any goods to resell. His loss will be the profit which he would have made if the credit had been provided. Is he entitled to recover that loss? I think he is [subject to the normal rules of remoteness of damage in contract] . . . "

This reasoning can of course equally apply on a falling market. Diplock J. applied *Trans Trust S.P.R.L.* v. *Danubian Trading Co. Ltd.*, on a falling market, in *Ian Stach Ltd.* v. *Baker Bosley Ltd.*[50] The facts of this case have already been set out[51]: the sellers repudiated the sale contract because the credit had not been opened in time. Diplock J. had held that the measure of damages was the difference between the contract price and market price at the time of repudiation. The market price having fallen between the time of entering the contract and the time of its repudiation, the damages included compensation for the market loss suffered by the sellers through having to sell on a falling market.[52] This seems reasonable, since had the buyers properly

---

47. Section 3.1.2.1.
48. [1952] 2 Q.B. 297, 305 (bottom).
49. Above, f.n. 16.
50. [1958] 2 Q.B. 130; [1958] 2 W.L.R. 419; [1958] 1 All E.R. 542; [1958] 1 Lloyd's Rep. 127.
51. See section 3.1.2.2.
52. [1958] 2 Q.B. 130, 145. The contract price was 205 dollars per tonne, and the market price was found to be 194 dollars at the time of repudiation. It will not always be easy in practice to ascertain market price, but here evidence was accepted that a Swiss company was prepared to pay 194 dollars for the goods on the relevant date.

performed by opening the credit in time, they would have obtained the contract price under the credit and would not have suffered any market loss.

3.1.5.2 Position where there are a number of shipments

The buyer will also be in breach of contract if, having opened a credit in the required form, the bank later refuses to pay against conforming documents. Even if the credit were regarded as no more than a means of paying the price, it would not follow that damages would necessarily be limited to that amount. In *Urquhart Lindsay & Co.* v. *Eastern Bank Ltd.*,[53] the sale contract was for a number of shipments of machinery by instalments, payment for each instalment to be by irrevocable letter of credit. After two instalments had been shipped and paid for, the buyers disputed the amount of the price payable on the third, and the bank, on the buyers instructions, refused to pay. The sellers sued the bank, but the main issue was as to the measure of damages,[54] and in deciding this Rowlatt J. considered what would have been the consequences of the buyers refusing to pay on the instalment. He took the view that in a sale by instalments this would entitle the sellers to cancel the entire transaction. If they did this, their loss would be their loss of profit on the entire transaction, and in principle they would be entitled to recover this, and not merely non-payment for one shipment[55]:

"Now if a buyer under a contract of this sort declines to pay for an instalment of the goods, the seller can cancel and claim damages upon the footing of an anticipatory breach of the contract of sale as a whole. These damages are not for non-payment of money. It is true that non-payment of money was what the buyer was guilty of; but such non-payment is evidence of a repudiation of the contract to accept and pay for the remainder of the goods; and the damages are in respect of such repudiation."

It may be said in conclusion that if the buyer fails to open a credit, or if the credit fails to operate, he is in breach of the sale contract. The breach is not regarded as being simply non-payment of money, because as far as the seller is concerned the credit means much more to him than that. Accordingly, the damages are not limited to the payment of the price, but will be anything that is recoverable under ordinary principles applicable to contractual damages. Further, if the bank fails to pay that puts the buyer into repudiatory breach of contract, and if in a sale by instalments the seller elects to bring the contract to an end, he is relieved of any obligations to perform in respect of future instalments, and can claim as damages loss of profits not only in respect of the present instalment, but also in respect of all remaining instalments due under the sale contract.

53. [1922] 1 K.B. 318; (1921) 9 Lloyd's Rep. 572.
54. See further section 8.1.10.1.1.
55. [1922] 1 K.B. 318, 323 (bottom) – 324 (top).

3.2 PROVISION OF RELIABLE AND SOLVENT PAYMASTER

3.2.1 Mutual advantage of credit to both seller and buyer

As was explained in Chapter 2,[56] both parties to the contract of sale enjoy mutual advantages under an irrevocable documentary credit. The seller can arrange shipment in the sure knowledge that he will be paid by a "reliable paymaster", in his own country in the case of the confirmed credit. The buyer, on the other hand, can use a credit to raise funds. The credit is not, in other words, to be regarded as being solely for the benefit of the seller, which privilege he can therefore waive.

It ought therefore to follow that, so long as the seller continues to enjoy the benefits he obtains under the credit, he should not be able unilaterally to withdraw from it. If he were able to short-circuit the credit, and demand payment directly from the buyer, he would be able to retain his benefits under the credit, while denying the buyer his.

3.2.2 No short-circuiting of credit

It has already been explained how payment by commercial credit is to the mutual advantage of both parties. Therefore, once it has been agreed that payment is to be by documentary credit, it is not open to the seller to short-circuit the credit, to tender the documents directly to the buyer, and demand payment directly from him.

The facts of *Soproma S.p.A.* v. *Marine and Animal By-Products Corp.* have already been outlined[57]: a contract for the sale of fishmeal c. & f. included a stipulation for payment to be by irrevocable letter of credit. Two tenders were made. The buyers having validly instructed their bank to reject the first tender of documents,[58] the sellers made a second tender. This was made directly to the buyers. The buyers rejected this tender also, and McNair J. held that they were entitled to do so. One reason was that the second tender was too late, being outside the time stipulated in the credit. The second reason was of more general application. Even if it had been tendered within the time stipulated in the credit, the tender was invalid because it was made directly to the buyer.

McNair J. emphasised that payment by documentary credit is to the advantage of both parties. It is not merely a privilege to the seller, which he can therefore unilaterally waive. It is[59]:

" . . . of advantage to the seller in that by the terms of the contract [of sale] he is given . . . 'a reliable paymaster' generally in his own country whom he can sue, and of advantage to the buyer in that he can make arrangements with his bankers for the

56. E.g., section 2.3.5.
57. Section 3.1.3.
58. See further section 6.3.
59. [1966] 1 Lloyd's Rep. 367, 385 (col. 2).

provision of the necessary funds, his banker retaining the drafts and the documents as his security for making payment to the seller and the buyer being freed from the necessity of having to keep the funds available to make payment against presentation of documents to him at an uncertain time which is no further defined in the authorities [on c.i.f. contracts] than being at a reasonable time after shipment by the seller of documents covering goods which he has shipped or are already afloat."

Obviously, to allow the seller to short-circuit the credit would be to deny the buyer his advantages of the credit while allowing the seller to retain his. McNair J. continued:

"Under this form of contract, as it seems to me, the buyer performs his obligation as to payment if he provides for the sellers a reliable and solvent paymaster from whom he can obtain payment—if necessary by suit—although it may well be that if the banker fails to pay by reason of his insolvency the buyer would be liable; but in such a case, as at present advised, I think that the basis of the liability must in principle be his failure to provide a proper letter of credit which involves (*inter alia*) that the obligee under the letter of credit is financially solvent. (This point as to the buyers' liability for the insolvency of the bank was not fully argued before me and I prefer to express no concluded opinion upon it as I understand that it may arise for decision in other cases pending in this Court.) It seems to me to be quite inconsistent with the express terms of a contract such as this to hold that the sellers have an alternative right to obtain payment from the buyers by presenting the documents direct to the buyers. Assuming that a letter of credit has been opened by the buyers for the opening of which the buyer would normally be required to provide the bank either with cash or some form of authority, could the seller at his option disregard the contractual letter of credit and present the documents direct to the buyer? As it seems to me, the answer must plainly be in the negative."

3.2.3 Conditional nature of payment: position if bank does not pay

The position is different, of course, if the seller does not obtain the advantages due to him under the credit, for example if the buyer does not provide a "reliable and solvent paymaster". In the above passage, for example, McNair J. was prepared to accept that the position may be different where the bank failed to pay by reason of insolvency. The principle may be of more general application than this, however, and not limited to insolvency. There is authority suggesting that as a general presumption, payment under a letter of credit is conditional and not absolute payment. If the bank does not pay when the seller has complied with the requirements of the credit and tendered conforming documents, then the buyer is obliged to pay, whatever the reason for the bank's non-payment. The buyer's liability does not arise only on the insolvency of the bank. Alternatively, in this situation the buyer is in breach of the term of the sale contract requiring him to provide a reliable and solvent paymaster.[60]

In *W. J. Alan & Co. Ltd.* v. *El Nasr Export and Import Co.*,[61] letters of

60. In which case he can be sued for damages: see, for example, the discussion of the *Urquhart Lindsay* case, above, section 3.1.5.
61. [1972] 2 Q.B. 189; [1972] 2 W.L.R. 800; [1972] 2 All E.R. 127; [1972] 1 Lloyd's Rep. 313.

credit were opened which did not conform in a number of respects to the provisions of the sale contract, and in particular provided for payment in U.K. sterling rather than Kenyan currency. Sterling was devalued before payment was made, and the Court of Appeal held that in general, where the bank fails to meet its obligations the seller can claim payment from the buyer directly, unless express provision to the contrary is made in the contract of sale. The letter of credit was said to be a conditional, rather than an absolute payment of the price, so that if the bank failed to meet its obligations the seller could look to the buyer directly.[62] Lord Denning M.R. said[63]:

"In my opinion a letter of credit is not to be regarded as absolute payment, unless the seller stipulates, expressly or impliedly, that it should be so. He may do it impliedly if he stipulates for the credit to be issued by a particular bank in such circumstances that it is to be inferred that the seller looks to that particular banker to the exclusion of the buyer . . .

If the letter of credit is conditional payment of the price, the consequences are these: the seller looks in the first instance to the banker for payment: but if the banker does not meet his obligations when the time comes for him to do so, the seller can have recourse to the buyer. The seller must present the documents to the banker. One of two things may then happen: (1) the banker may fail or refuse to pay or accept drafts in exchange for the documents. The seller then, of course, does not hand over the documents. He retains dominion over the goods. He can resell them and claim damages from the buyer. He can also sue the banker for not honouring the credit: see *Urquhart Lindsay & Co. Ltd.* v. *Eastern Bank Ltd.*[64] But he cannot, of course, get damages twice over. (2) The bank may accept time drafts in exchange for the documents, but may fail to honour the drafts when the time comes. In that case the banker will have the documents and will usually have passed them on to the buyer, who will have paid the bank for them. The seller can then sue the banker on the drafts: or if the banker fails or is insolvent, the seller can sue the buyer. The banker's drafts are like any ordinary payment for goods by a bill of exchange. They are conditional payment, but not absolute payment. It may mean that the buyer (if he has already paid the bank) will have to pay twice over. So be it. He ought to have made sure that he employed a 'reliable and solvent paymaster'."

The *dicta* from *W. J. Alan & Co. Ltd.* v. *El Nasr Export and Import Co.* were applied by Ackner J., as part of the *ratio*, in *Maran Road Saw Mill* v. *Austin Taylor Ltd.*[65] The facts of this case were set out in Chapter 2.[66] It will be remembered that the issuing bank failed, and that the seller repaid the purchase money to the Bangkok Bank, which had purchased time drafts drawn on the issuing bank but had not confirmed the credit. The seller then brought an action against its agent, who was in the position of buyer under the commercial credit, and succeeded. The case was a direct application of the principles of *W. J. Alan & Co. Ltd.* v. *El Nasr Export and Import Co.*,

---

62. Technically this is *obiter*, since in the event the seller was held to have waived this right by accepting payment under the sterling letters of credit.
63. [1972] 2 Q.B. 189, at p. 220.
64. See above, section 3.1.5.
65. [1975] 1 Lloyd's Rep. 156.
66. Section 2.3.3.

Ackner J. taking the view that they were equally applicable to an agency agreement as to an ordinary sale by way of commercial credit. He said[67]:

"Can it then be said that [the defendants] have discharged their contractual obligation, when, although they have established a letter of credit, payment has not been made under it? To my mind, the answer is a simple one and is in the negative. I respectfully adopt and slightly adapt the language used by Stephenson L.J. in *W. J. Alan & Co. Ltd.* v. *El Nasr Export and Import Co.*[68] The agents promised to *pay* by letter of credit not to provide by a letter of credit a source of payment which *did not* pay."

The principles of *W. J. Alan & Co. Ltd.* v. *El Nasr Export and Import Co.* create only a presumption, which is rebuttable, so it is open for the courts in appropriate circumstances to treat payment under a credit as absolute rather than conditional payment. One possibility, mentioned in the case itself, is where the seller "stipulates for the credit to be issued by a particular bank in such circumstances that it is to be inferred that the seller looks to that particular banker to the exclusion of the buyer". Normally, of course, the choice of issuing bank is left to the buyer, and therefore the seller should not be required to take the consequences of its failure. In the *Soproma* case, by contrast, the banker (the Marine and Midland Trust Co. of New York) was selected by the seller, which may account for McNair J.'s limited view that only in the event of its insolvency might the seller be able to tender documents to the buyer directly.

This was not however the situation in *Maran Road Saw Mill* v. *Austin Taylor Ltd.*, where the presumption in *W. J. Alan & Co. Ltd.* v. *El Nasr Export and Import Co.* was not rebutted. Ackner J. observed[69]:

"The principal has not, for example, stipulated for the credit to be issued by a particular banker, in such circumstances that it is to be inferred that he is looking to that particular banker to the exclusion of the agent . . .

The plaintiffs did not expressly or impliedly agree that the liability of the issuing bank should be accepted by them in place of that of the defendants. Thus, the defendants were obliged to employ a reliable and solvent paymaster and if they failed to do so, despite having put him in funds, they like the buyer in the case of the contract for the sale of goods, have to pay twice over."

Nor is it enough to rebut the *Alan* v. *El Nasr* presumption for the identity of the bank to be merely agreed between the parties. In *E.D. & F. Man Ltd.* v. *Nigerian Sweets & Confectionery Co. Ltd.*,[70] the respondent buyers (under three contracts for the sale of white crystal sugar) argued that the opening of the credit should be treated as absolute payment because the sellers had agreed on the identity of the issuing bank. The facts were similar to those in the *Maran Road* case: the issuing bank, Merchant Swiss Ltd., was wound up after the buyers had reimbursed it, but before payment had been made to the sellers under 90 day drafts drawn on it. The sellers sued the buyers directly.

67. [1975] 1 Lloyd's Rep. 156, 159 (col.1).
68. [1972] 2 Q.B. 189, at 220.
69. [1975] 1 Lloyd's Rep. 156, 159 (col. 2) – 160 (col.1).
70. [1977] 2 Lloyd's Rep. 50.

In an appeal from arbitrators on a point of law, Ackner J. held that, on the facts found, the buyers were liable. Applying *Alan* v. *El Nasr* directly, he thought that the seller's agreement as to choice of bank was merely one factor, and not in any way conclusive[71]:

"Mr Evans [for the buyers] sought to submit as a proposition of law, that where the identity of the bank is agreed between the parties, and not left to the choice of the buyers, it must follow that the sellers impliedly agree that the liability of the issuing bank has been accepted by them in place of that of the buyers. I do not think that this is correct. The fact that the sellers have agreed on the identity of the issuing bank is but one of the factors to be taken into account when considering whether there are circumstances from which it can be properly inferred that the sellers look to that particular bank to the exclusion of the buyer. It is in no way conclusive. In this case . . . , there were other circumstances which clearly supported the presumption that the letters of credit were not given as absolute payment but as conditional payment . . .

The sellers' remedy in such circumstances is to claim from the buyers either the price agreed in the contract of sale or damages for breach of their contractual promise to pay by letter of credit.[72]"

In fact the case was not particularly strong, because principal shareholders of the respondent buyers were also principal shareholders of Merchant Swiss Ltd. It seems likely, then, that the buyers chose the identity of the issuing bank and the sellers merely acquiesced. Would the position be different if the sellers had insisted on the identity of the issuing bank? No doubt the presumption of absolute payment would then be stronger, but it would still presumably not be conclusive. There appears to be a strong presumption in favour of construing letters of credit as conditional payment only, in the absence of an express stipulation to the contrary.[73]

A similar position obtains, at least under the U.C.P., as between issuing bank and advising or confirming bank. Payment by a confirming bank is conditional only, and if the confirming bank does not pay, the issuing bank must. Article 21(b) and (c) of the U.C.P. provides:

"(b) An issuing bank will not be relieved from any of its obligations to provide reimbursement itself if and when reimbursement is not effected by the reimbursing bank.

(c) The issuing bank will be responsible to the paying, accepting or negotiating

71. [1977] 2 Lloyd's Rep. 50, 56.
72. Not only does the buyer remain liable for the price but he is also liable in damages for failure to provide a reliable and solvent paymaster. In other words, the failure to pay by the bank also puts the buyer in breach of the contract of sale: see above, section 3.1.5., where the consequences of the contract action can be clearly seen where the contract called for shipment by instalments. In other cases the damages claim is usually academic because an action for the price will almost certainly be a better option for the seller, but the tort action discussed in section 8.1.11.2 depends on the bank's failure to pay putting the buyer in breach of contract.
73. However, the cases considered in this section were distinguished by Millett J., in a different context, in *Re Charge Card Services Ltd.* [1986] 3 All E.R. 289, 302–303. Payment for consumer goods under a charge card may be regarded as absolute payment where the charge card company goes into liquidation. Millett J. emphasised, however, that the situation was very different from payment under a commercial credit, and no doubt was cast on the correctness of the decisions considered here.

bank for any loss of interest if reimbursement is not provided on first demand made to the reimbursing bank, or as otherwise specified in the credit or mutually agreed, as the case may be."

3.3 EFFECT OF PASSING OF PROPERTY UNDER CONTRACT OF SALE ON BANKERS' COMMERCIAL CREDIT, AND VICE VERSA

3.3.1 Importance of passing of property

3.3.1.1 As between parties to the sale contract

The question when property passes from seller to buyer under the contract of sale has taken on a greater importance within the last year or so, for the parties to the sale contract.

Apart from the security which property confers should the other party go bankrupt, the operation of the Bills of Lading Act 1855, section 1, which transfers contractual rights under the carriage contract from the shipper to the holder of the bill of lading, depends on when property passes. In other words, the timing of the passing of property can affect the question whether anybody but the original shipper of the goods can sue the carrier in contract, should the goods be lost or damaged on the voyage.

As will become apparent in Chapter 7,[74] as a result of recent case law development the exact timing of the passing of property is far more critical than was once thought to be the case. In general it can be said that for the section to be triggered, if the bill of lading is made out to order then property must pass on indorsement, or at any rate indorsement must be an essential process in the passing of property. If the bill of lading names a consignee, property must pass on consignment.

3.3.1.2 Effect of passing of property on bank's security

The passing of property under the sale contract can also affect the security of the bank. The bank is, in general, unconcerned with the problems of section 1, since it cannot rely upon that section.[75] However, a major part of the security provided by the bill of lading is that the bank can obtain the special property, or possessory title of a pledgee. The issuing bank must obtain special property in order adequately to be protected against the bankruptcy of the buyer before reimbursement is made to it, and a confirming bank may need equally to guard against the bankruptcy of the issuing bank. However, if the property in the goods has already passed from seller to buyer before the documents are pledged by the seller to the bank, then clearly the seller can pass no

74. See section 7.1.1.
75. See section 7.1.1.

property to the bank as pledgee. Only if property passes under the sale contract on or after tender of documents is the bank likely to be adequately protected against the bankruptcy of the buyer (or in the case of a confirming
bank, the bankruptcy of the issuing bank).

Clearly, then, the passing of property under the sale contract can have
major implications for the bank's security. However, it may also be the case
that the connection works both ways: the existence of a commercial credit
may affect the passing of property under the sale contract.[76]

Different considerations apply to specific and unascertained goods.

3.3.2 Unascertained goods

Goods may be either specific or unascertained. Specific goods can be identified from the time of contract as being destined for the buyer, and him alone.
A common example of the sale of specific goods might be the sale of a particular manufactured item.

Goods are unascertained when the buyer cannot point to the particular
goods which are destined for him. Any goods to be manufactured or grown in
the future must be unascertained. So will be purely generic goods, where the
contract states simply quantity, quality and description, without defining the
goods further. An example of a contract for the sale of generic goods might be
a contract for 150 tons of copra, c.i.f. London, October shipment. No vessel is
specified, and the seller can supply goods satisfying the description from anywhere in the world. Clearly the buyer cannot point to the particular consignment destined for him in such a case.

Another possibility is part of an undivided but specified bulk (whether
liquid or dry cargo). An example might be 200 tons of copra from an undivided bulk of 20,000 tons on a specified vessel. The buyer cannot say which
200 tons are his until the bulk is divided.

Section 16 of the Sale of Goods Act 1979[77] provides that property in unascertained goods cannot pass unless and until the goods are ascertained:
"Where there is a contract for the sale of unascertained cargo no property in
the goods is transferred to the buyer unless and until the goods are ascertained." Unascertained goods become ascertained by appropriation. Appropriation must be an unconditional and irrevocable act by the seller, and once
the goods have been appropriated to the buyer's contract the buyer knows
that the contract will be fulfilled by the provision of those goods, and no
others. The act of appropriation is final and irrevocable, and is usually the last
act performed by the seller. In the case of manufactured goods appropriation
normally takes place on or immediately before shipment, but if a number of
identical consignments are shipped by the same seller for different buyers,

---

76. See section 3.3.4.1.
77. The sections of the Sale of Goods Act considered in this section re-enact without alteration
those of the Sale of Goods Act 1893.

appropriation will not take place until the seller has decided which consignment is destined for which buyer, and this may not occur until tender of the bill of lading.

Once the goods are appropriated to the buyer's contract, property does not necessarily pass immediately, but on the principles discussed below.[78]

3.3.3 Undivided bulk cargo

Sales of undivided bulk cargo, whether in liquid or dry cargo form, are sales of unascertained goods if parts of the bulk are sold to a number of different buyers: no individual buyer can state which part of the bulk will be his until it is appropriated to him (by being divided out). This will usually occur on the splitting of the bulk on discharge, and only then does the cargo become ascertained.

Because of the absolute rule stated in section 16, therefore, property in part of an undivided bulk cargo cannot usually pass until delivery, and clearly whether or not payment is by irrevocable documentary credit can have no effect on this. This conclusion has major implications for buyers of undivided bulk cargoes, since the Bills of Lading Act 1855, section 1 can never apply in their favour, and therefore they cannot sue the carrier in contract if the goods are lost or damaged on the voyage. The Law Commission has recently considered proposals to amend both section 16 and section 1, in order to deal with this problem, but has not made any conclusive recommendations.[79]

It also follows that where an undivided bulk cargo is sold to a number of different buyers, the original seller has property to pledge to the bank on tender of documents, but if one of the buyers re-sells, he will have no property to pledge to any bank financing the sub-sale.

If an entire bulk cargo is sold to a single buyer (as often happens with oil cargoes), the cargo is ascertained and the principles discussed in the next section apply. Similarly if the cargo is divided, for example by being carried in a number of holds, if the whole of the cargo in the same hold is destined for the same buyer, the cargo is ascertained.

3.3.4 Specific or ascertained goods

Where the sale is of specific goods, or once goods are ascertained, section 17 of the Sale of Goods Act provides that property passes when the parties intend it to pass:

"(1) Where there is a contract for the sale of specific or ascertained goods the property in them is transferred to the buyer at such time as the parties to the contract intend it to be transferred.

(2) For the purpose of ascertaining the intention of the parties regard shall be had

78. Section 3.3.4.
79. Law Commission Working Paper No. 112 (Rights to Goods in Bulk), 1989. See further section 7.3.

to the terms of the contract, the conduct of the parties and the circumstances of the case."

There are various guidelines laid down in sections 18–20 of the Sale of Goods Act 1979. For sales that are not c.i.f. or f.o.b. (or variations thereon), the contract itself will normally stipulate when property is to pass. Usually it will be at the point of delivery, for example on discharge in an ex ship contract. For c.i.f. and f.o.b. contracts (or variations thereon), the position is rather more complicated, and will often depend on the form of the bill of lading. Sections 19(1) and (2) of the Sale of Goods Act 1979 provide:

"(1) Where there is a contract for the sale of specific goods or where goods are subsequently appropriated to the contract, the seller may, by the terms of the contract or appropriation, reserve the right of disposal of the goods until certain conditions are fulfilled; and in such a case, notwithstanding the delivery of the goods to the buyer, or to a carrier or other bailee or custodier for the purpose of transmission to the buyer, the property in the goods does not pass to the buyer until the conditions fulfilled by the seller are fulfilled.

(2) Where goods are shipped, and by the bill of lading the goods are deliverable to the order of the seller or his agent, the seller is prima facie to be taken to reserve the right of disposal."

A detailed review of the passing of property under the sale contract is beyond the scope of this book, but in general it can be said that with the exception of sales of undivided bulk cargoes, under c.i.f. and f.o.b. contracts, property passes on payment (which will usually occur on indorsement) when the seller intends to retain the bill of lading as security against payment, and on consignment when he does not. Where the bill of lading is made out to seller's order, section 19(2) (set out above) creates a statutory presumption that the bill of lading is retained as security against payment; where it is made out to a named consignee, or to the order of a consignee, any presumption that the bill of lading is retained as security against payment is weakened.

As a general rule, therefore, property passes on indorsement when the bill of lading is made out to the order of the seller, and on consignment where a consignee is named. In either case, the Bills of Lading Act, section 1, operates in the buyer's favour. If the sale is financed by documentary credit, the bank obtains the special property as pledgee if the bill of lading is made out to the order of the seller, but not where a consignee is named, since in the latter case property will already have passed to the buyer before the documents are tendered.

It must be emphasised, however, that the general rule does not invariably apply. At the end of the day, the passing of property depends on the intention of the parties, and the form of the bill of lading is just one element (albeit an important element) of evidence of intention. Property may, for example, pass under an express term in the sale contract, whatever the form of the bill of lading[80]—contracts for the sale of oil cargoes, for example, frequently pro-

80. As, for example, in *Sale Continuation Ltd.* v. *Austin Taylor & Co. Ltd.*, f.n. 84 below.

vide for property to pass on shipment, and this may be conclusive, even where the bill of lading is taken out to seller's order. It should also be borne in mind that where the bill of lading is made out to seller's order, the statutory presumption under section 19(2) is that he reserves a right of disposal against payment, not against indorsement, in which case property may pass after indorsement if payment is made later. This will not affect the position of a bank, but can have consequences for the buyer, since he may no longer be able to rely on section 1, or sue the carrier in tort.[81]

It should perhaps be added that even once property has passed, an unpaid seller retains a lien on the goods.

3.3.4.1 Effect of payment being by documentary credit

Since the passing of property depends on the intention of the parties to the sale contract, and since all relevant circumstances can be taken into account in ascertaining that intention, the question arises whether it is affected by payment being by banker's documentary credit.

One view is that where payment is by documentary credit the presumption of property passing on tender of documents is strengthened, because the bank needs to obtain from the seller a special property in the goods as pledgee. This will only happen if the seller has not before tender to the bank (for example, on shipment) passed all property to the buyer. As Lord Wright observed in *Ross T. Smyth & Co. Ltd.* v. *T.D. Bailey Son & Co.*[82]:

"In general . . . the importance of the retention of the property is not only to secure payment from the buyer but for purposes of finance. The general course of international commerce involves the practice of raising money on the documents so as to bridge the period between shipment and the time of obtaining payment against documents. These credit facilities, which are of the first importance, would be completely unsettled if the incidence of the property were made a matter of doubt. By mercantile law, the bills of lading are the symbols of the goods. The general property in the goods must be in the seller if he is to be able to pledge them. The whole system of commercial credits depends on the seller's ability to give a charge on the goods and the policies of insurance. A mere unpaid seller's lien would, for obvious reasons, be inadequate and unsatisfactory."

A similar view is taken by the editors of Benjamin's *Sale of Goods*[83]:

"The suggestion that such a seller has adequate security for the payment of the price by reason of his rights of lien or stoppage in transit has not been accepted by the courts; and their refusal to accept it is based on a realistic appreciation of modern methods of financing overseas sales. A bank willing to advance money on the security of property in goods would be much less ready to accept the somewhat perilous security of the rights of lien or stoppage. These rights may be useful, in the last resort, when other methods of securing payment have failed; but it is unlikely that a bank (or conse-

---

81. An example of this is *The Ciudad de Pasto*, below, f.n. 92. See also section 7.2.
82. [1940] 3 All E.R. 60.
83. Benjamin's *Sale of Goods*, 3rd ed., para 1484. The extensive footnotes in Benjamin are not reproduced here.

quently a seller wanting to raise money on the security of shipping documents) would intend to rely solely on them. In overseas sales, there is, therefore, a fairly strong presumption that the seller does not intend to part with property until he has either been paid or been given an adequate assurance of payment."

The bank only requires the protection of possessory title, or the special property of a pledgee, to protect it against the bankruptcy of the buyer not only before it has been reimbursed, but also before the documents have been released to the buyer under a trust receipt. The reason for this is that even if the bank does not obtain legal title on tender of documents, it will usually only release the documents on the terms that the buyer constitutes himself trustee of the goods for the bank. Thereafter, the bank will be adequately protected by its equitable property as beneficiary under the trust. In *Sale Continuation Ltd.* v. *Austin Taylor & Co. Ltd.*,[84] for example, property passed from seller to buyer before the documents were pledged, so that the bank could not have obtained a possessory title as pledgee.[85] However, the documents were later released to an agent of the seller against a trust receipt the effect of which was expressly to constitute the agent trustee of the goods for the bank. The second transaction, creating a trust of property that had already passed, was not in any way dependent on the original pledge, so the bank could obtain equitable title under the trust even though it had obtained no legal title under the pledge. Consequently, the bank's possessory title will often only be of importance for a relatively short time.

One difficulty with the view propounded by Lord Wright in *Ross T. Smyth & Co. Ltd.* v. *T.D. Bailey Son & Co.* is that the question when property passes under the sale contract depends only on the intention of the parties to that contract (i.e., seller and buyer), and not on the intention of the bank. It is necessary therefore to infer that the parties to the sale contract intend to protect the bank against the buyer's insolvency. Such an inference can of course theoretically be drawn from the mere fact that the parties have agreed that sale is to be by documentary credit, but it is arguably a somewhat artificial inference.

In any case an alternative view is sometimes taken, which tends towards the opposite conclusion. Since where payment is by documentary credit the seller ships goods in the sure knowledge that he is going to be paid, there is no need for him to retain the bill of lading as security against payment. Therefore there is no reason for property not to pass on shipment. An early expression

---

84. [1968] 2 Q.B. 849; [1967] 2 Lloyd's Rep. 403. See further section 2.4.2. See also on the passing of legal and equitable title, figure 2.3.

85. Property passed on shipment by virtue of an express clause in the sale contract: [1968] 2 Q.B. 849, 855E; [1967] 2 Lloyd's Rep. 403, 406 (col. 2). The bank went into liquidation, and the editors of Benjamin's *Sale of Goods* observe (presumably tongue in cheek): " . . . the bank appears to have accepted a pledge of documents from the seller after the property had passed to the buyer. Perhaps the fate of the bank suggests that this was not good business practice": *ibid.*, f.n. 96.

of such a view can be found in *The Kronprincessan Margareta*.[86] Lord Sumner observed[87]: "It is said that, as a matter of business, the confirmed credit relieved the consignors of all further concern in the goods, for they could have no doubt that they would be paid by the bank in any event and that the failure to insure is proof positive of this."

In the event, however, property passed on indorsement, Lord Sumner taking the view that the bank had not in fact given the benefit of any enforceable undertaking to the consignor, so that in other words there was no irrevocable or confirmed credit in existence.[88] In any case, he said, payment by documentary credit is no more than indirect evidence of the intention of the parties under section 17:

"The special circumstance of the existence of a confirmed banker's credit . . . is only indirectly relevant. It no doubt enhances the likelihood that the bills of lading will eventually be taken up and the goods be paid for, and so diminishes the importance to the seller of being still able to say that the goods are his, but it is not direct evidence of intention; it is only a reason why a particular intention is more likely to have been formed in such a case than in others. The intention has still to be inferred . . . "[89]

On the other hand, given that the only relevant intention is that of the parties under the sale contract, there is a certain logic in the view that if the seller knows that he is going to be paid by a reputable bank, there is less need for him to reserve a right of disposal. If property passes before tender of documents that may well prejudice the security of the bank, but that is arguably not the concern of the parties to the sale contract.

In general, however, the courts have been reluctant to infer that the existence of a documentary credit is a reason for passing property on shipment. In *The Glenroy*,[90] a cargo shipped from Japan to Germany was seized as enemy property in October 1939 (which was, of course, before Japan entered the war), and in order to justify the seizure the British Crown had to argue that property had already passed to the German buyers at the time of the seizure. One of their arguments was that because the sellers had obtained an undertaking from a bank under a letter of credit, they were no longer interested in the goods, because they had been assured of payment in full. Lord Porter, rejecting this argument, observed that the bank might fail.[91]

In *The Ciudad de Pasto*,[92] sellers agreed to sell a quantity of prawns f.o.b. 80 per cent. of the price had been paid before shipment, the balance to be paid (or so the Court of Appeal assumed) by letter of credit. The bill of lading made the goods deliverable to the order of the seller, but the Court of Appeal

---

86. [1921] 1 A.C. 486.
87. [1921] 1 A.C. 486, 515.
88. [1921] 1 A.C. 486, 513–514.
89. [1921] 1 A.C. 486, 517.
90. *Part Cargo ex Glenroy* [1945] A.C. 124.
91. [1945] A.C. 124, 135 (bottom).
92. *Mitsui & Co. Ltd.* v. *Flota Mercante Grancolombiana S.A., The Ciudad de Pasto* [1989] 1 All E.R. 951; [1988] 2 Lloyd's Rep. 208.

applied the section 19(2) presumption, and inferred that the seller retained the bill as security against payment of the remaining 20 per cent. There was no evidence either as to when or if the remaining 20 per cent. was paid, or that the bill of lading was indorsed in favour of the purchasers, although the cargo was eventually discharged (in a damaged condition) to them. The evidence was indeed described as woefully inadequate,[93] but on the limited facts available the Court of Appeal refused to infer that property had ever passed to the f.o.b. purchaser.

On the effect on passing of property of the letter of credit, Staughton L.J. said[94]:

"Nor can I attach much weight to the fact that the balance of the price was (as I assume) payable by letter of credit. Even the most copper-bottomed letter of credit sometimes fails to produce payment for one reason or another; and the seller who has a letter of credit for 100 per cent. of the price will nevertheless often retain the property in his goods until he has presented the documents and obtained payment."

On the other hand, the existence of a standby letter of credit guaranteeing payment was treated by Leggatt J. as a reason for holding that property in an oil cargo had passed on shipment, the bill of lading was to sellers' order, in *The Filiatra Legacy*.[95] I would suggest, however, that it is very difficult to reconcile this view with the views expressed in the cases set out above. No doubt, since intention is ultimately a question of fact and not of law, no hard and fast rules can be laid down. Also, in *The Filiatra Legacy* the bank had no interest in when property passed, since unlike a bank under a conventional documentary credit, it obtained no security under the standby letter of credit whatever happened.[96] Nevertheless, I would suggest that Leggatt J.'s view in this case is wrong.

What conclusions can be drawn from this discussion? I would start by re-iterating that since the passing of property depends on intention, no hard and fast rules can be laid down. With the exception of *The Filiatra Legacy*, there appear to be no cases where the existence of a letter of credit, or bank guarantee, has clearly had any effect either way on when property passed. Although the existence of a letter of credit may therefore be relevant in ascertaining the intention of the parties, it is very unlikely to tip the balance, and displace the usual presumptions for the passing of property under c.i.f. and f.o.b. contracts.

93. [1989] 1 All E.R. 951, 953c.
94. [1989] 1 All E.R. 951, 957j.
95. *Anonima Petroli Italiana S.p.A. and another* v. *Marlucidez Armadora S.A., The Filiatra Legacy* [1990] 1 Lloyd's Rep. 354. On the nature of standby letters of credit, see section 8.2.
96. See further section 8.2.

CHAPTER 4

DOCUMENTARY REQUIREMENTS: GENERAL PRINCIPLES

4.1 INTRODUCTION

The detailed documentary requirements under the U.C.P. are covered in the next chapter, where it will become clear that the banking community has been forced, by changing transport practices, to move away from the traditional requirement of the shipped bill of lading, policy of insurance and invoice. It is not easy to understand the U.C.P. provisions without first appreciating some general principles of documentation, however. Accordingly, this chapter examines the main features of the various types of documentation, and why they are used, and considers their advantages and disadvantages from the point of view of a bank advancing money under a documentary credit. It will probably become clear in this chapter that the move away from the traditional documentation is by no means necessarily in the best interests of the banking community.

It may seem at first sight that it would have been more sensible to consider each variety of document along with the relevant U.C.P. provision, and so indeed it would, except that the layout of the U.C.P. itself unfortunately makes this approach impossible. When the U.C.P. was last revised in 1983, Article 25 was inserted for the first time, to set out the broad characteristics of acceptable documentation in any case where a traditional bill of lading is not called for. Article 25 does not, however, further distinguish between types of documentation, and so covers, for example, both a negotiable combined transport document and a non-negotiable waybill. Yet, apart from the undoubted fact that neither is a traditional bill of lading, these documents have virtually nothing in common, and the security afforded by each is very different.

The structure of the book is therefore determined by that of the U.C.P. itself. Because the U.C.P. makes no distinctions except between the traditional bill of lading and other documents, it is convenient to deal with the different varieties of documentation in principle in this chapter, and then to consider the overall policy of the U.C.P. in relation to the different types of documentation in Chapter 5.

4.2 THE TRADITIONAL BILL OF LADING

4.2.1 Advantages of using shipped bill of lading

As has been explained in Chapter 1,[1] the traditional banker's documentary credit calls for documents that are similar to those used in c.i.f. and f.o.b. international sale contracts,[2] namely the clean shipped (or on board) bill of lading, policy of insurance and invoice. From the point of view of the buyer and bank, the clean shipped bill of lading has the following advantages:

1. It provides best evidence that the seller has performed his contractual obligations. Under a c.i.f. or f.o.b. contract the seller is required to ship the goods, and not merely to deliver them into the charge of the carrier. Hence the usual requirement for a shipped, as opposed to received for shipment bill of lading. The reason for the requirement that the bill of lading be clean is to provide evidence that the goods have been shipped in apparent good order and condition. Ideally, no doubt, buyers (and banks) would prefer a statement as to the actual, as opposed to the apparent condition of the goods on shipment, but this is assumed to be outside the competence of the master. The clean shipped bill of lading is thus the best evidence that the seller has performed his contractual obligations.

2. It triggers section 1 of the Bills of Lading Act 1855, so as to transfer contractual rights under the contract of carriage to the holder for the time being of the bill of lading. The Act also imposes liabilities under the carriage contract. There is authority that only the shipped bill of lading can perform this function,[3] and that the received for shipment bill of lading does not trigger the operation of section 1. For reasons that will become apparent in Chapter 7, the 1855 Act is a material consideration only for a buyer, not for a bank.

3. It is a document of title, which transfers constructive possession of (i.e., right to possess) the goods to the holder. Only the holder of an original bill of lading may claim those goods from the vessel when they are discharged.

4.2.2 Disadvantages of using shipped bill of lading

There are nevertheless serious problems with the shipped bill of lading. Because it is a document of title, a carrier is taking an enormous risk in

1. Section 1.4.
2. Where the underlying sale contract is c.i.f. or f.o.b., or a variation thereon, it is sensible for the documents required under the credit to match as closely those required by the sale contract. The documentary requirements under c.i.f. and f.o.b. contract are therefore set out below, section 4.4.
3. *Diamond Alkali Export Corp.* v. *Fl. Bourgeois* [1921] 3 K.B. 443. But see section 4.4.3., below.

delivering without production of an original bill of lading: if he delivers to someone who is not entitled to the cargo, he is liable to the true owner for the full value of the cargo wrongly delivered.[4] Obviously this protects the holder of an original bill of lading, and is indeed one of the reasons why it provides such valuable security to a seller or bank should the buyer fail to pay.

4.2.2.1 Ship arrives before documents

The requirement that delivery be made only against production of an original bill of lading is not generally a problem so long as it reaches the receiver before the goods arrive at their destination. Over the last quarter century or so, however, whereas the speed of ships has increased, in particular for example on North Atlantic container routes, the documentation still has to be processed and posted, and the speed of the documents has not kept pace. This is particularly a problem if a shipped bill of lading is insisted upon, since obviously that cannot be negotiated until after the vessel has been loaded.

Problems which are similar in nature also arise with oil cargoes, although for different reasons: the documents rarely arrive before the vessel, since frequently there are multiple re-sales of the cargo at sea, with banks involved in the financing of each sale, and it is simply impossible to process the documentation sufficiently quickly.

Naturally the shipowner does not wish to wait until the documents catch up. Not only will the vessel not be earning freight, but especially in the case of oil there may well be pressures from port authorities for a quick turn-round. It is sometimes possible to discharge the cargo into a warehouse, and only to deliver from there on production of an original bill of lading, but it is usually impossible for the shipowners to arrange storage of bulk liquid cargo otherwise than on the vessel itself, or of course, in the receiver's cargo tanks.

Nor does the shipowner wish to take the enormous risk of delivering without production of a bill of lading, although today this is quite a common practice, particularly where the receiver furnishes the carrier with a bank indemnity.[5] From the point of view of the carrier it is far better for a bill of lading not to be issued at all, so that the risks of delivering to the wrong person are lessened. Unless a negotiable document is clearly required (for

---

4. *Sze Hai Tong Bank Ltd.* v. *Rambler Cycle Co. Ltd.* [1959] A.C. 576. Where bills of lading are issued in sets of three originals, the carrier is protected so long as he delivers against production of any original; he need not require tender of all three, nor need he take steps to enquire whether the holder of the original presented is in fact entitled to take delivery of the cargo: *Glyn Mills Currie & Co.* v. *East and West India Dock Co.* (1882) 7 App. Cas. 591.

5. In *Hansen-Tangens (A/S) Rederi III* v. *Total Transport Corporation, The Sagona* [1984] 1 Lloyd's Rep. 194, the bill of lading was delayed where payment was by banker's commercial credit, and the bank had refused to pay against the documents because of alleged discrepancies. The shipowners delivered without production of a bill of lading, and clearly this is a common practice with oil cargoes. In his evidence the master of the vessel (who had been in command of tankers for some 14 years), asked how often an original bill of lading had been presented to him prior to discharge, answered: "I have never seen it!" In fact, it is not uncommon for it to take months or even years for the documentation to catch up.

example, where multiple re-sales are envisaged), carriers prefer if possible to use non-negotiable waybills.[6] Manufactured goods are not often resold in transit, and unless negotiability is of the essence, a non-negotiable waybill can be used instead. If electronic mail can be used, then so much the better, since postal delays can then be obviated.

Where a negotiable document *is* required, one possible solution is for it to be issued earlier: obviously, a received for shipment bill of lading, or perhaps even a mate's receipt, can be negotiated far sooner than can a shipped bill of lading.[7] A rather more dubious (but apparently common) practice is for the carrier to carry one original of the set on board, so that he is in effect acting as a postal service, and can indeed ensure that delivery is made only against production of an original bill. If the other two bills in the set are separately negotiated, perhaps via a bank, then the security afforded by the negotiated bills is seriously diminished. Perhaps this is a reason for banks generally to require tender of all three originals in a set.

4.2.2.2 Where carriage by multimodal transport

The traditional bill of lading assumes carriage from port to port, and is not well suited to combined transport operations, where the shipment is part of a larger transaction (e.g., container transport from an inland terminal in one country to an inland terminal in another). There will usually be at least three different carriers involved in the total operation, which will involve at least one sea and two land legs, but there is no reason why one document (combined or multimodal transport document) should not cover all three legs.[8]

The development of containerisation has significantly increased the

---

6. A liner (or sea or ocean) waybill is also sometimes called a data freight receipt or cargo key receipt. Sir Anthony Lloyd, Lord Justice of Appeal, has recently observed that: "I have been told that on the North Atlantic route, for example, perhaps 70 per cent. of all liner goods are carried on sea waybills": *The bill of lading: do we really need it?* [1989] L.M.C.L.Q. 47, 49. But banks should be very wary about accepting non-negotiable waybills as security: see further below, section 4.6.

7. One problem is that Article III of the Hague-Visby Rules allows a shipper to demand a shipped bill of lading:

"3. After receiving the goods into his charge the carrier or the master or agent of the carrier shall, on demand of the shipper, issue to the shipper a bill of lading . . .

7. After the goods are loaded the bill of lading to be issued by the carrier, master, or agent of the carrier, to the shipper shall, if the shipper so demands, be a 'shipped' bill of lading, provided that if the shipper shall previously have taken up any document of title to such goods, he shall surrender the same as against the issue of the 'shipped' bill of lading, but at the option of the carrier such document of title may be noted at the port of shipment by the carrier, master, or agent with the name or names of the ship or ships upon which the goods have been shipped and the date or dates of shipment, and when so noted, if it shows the particulars mentioned in paragraph 3 of Article III, shall for the purpose of this article be deemed to constitute a 'shipped' bill of lading."

There is no reason, however, why the shipowner should not charge for its issue. This could discourage its use where inappropriate, and also compensate the shipowner for the additional costs and risks which the bill of lading carries with it.

8. See below, sections 4.5. and 5.3.

importance of combined transport operations. Indeed, one of the main advantages of containers lies in their ability to be transferred easily from rail or road to ship and vice-versa.

4.3 EXTENT OF SECURITY REQUIRED BY BANK

While it is clear from the previous section that alternative documentation can clearly benefit carriers, and the parties to the sale contract in appropriate circumstances, they were by no means devised in the interests of the banking community. It is necessary to consider, therefore, what a bank loses by accepting any document other than a traditional shipped bill of lading.

4.3.1 Bills of Lading Act 1855, section 1

A shipped bill of lading triggers the provisions of the Bills of Lading Act 1855, section 1, but it is probable that no other document does. Even a "received for shipment" bill of lading probably does not.[9] Only holders of a shipped bill of lading, therefore, have an automatic action in contract against the carrier should the goods be lost or damaged while at sea. It might therefore be thought that a bank's security is seriously jeopardised if it accepts any other document. In reality, however, this is not a material consideration since banks can rarely rely on section 1 in any event.[10]

4.3.2 Evidence of shipment required?

Where the seller's obligation is to ship the goods, a loaded or on board document is the best evidence that the contractual obligation has been performed. On the other hand, these advantages may be outweighed by the practical disadvantages imposed by requiring a shipped bill of lading. With multimodal transport operations in particular, it would be very inconvenient if an on board document were required, since the document-handling process would be seriously delayed. Also, the obligations of the seller normally end on delivery to the forwarding agent, rather than on shipment, and there is therefore no advantage in requiring an on board document.

4.3.3 Common law document of title required

4.3.3.1 Definition of document of title at common law

The one feature of the traditional shipped bill of lading which the banking community ought to be most reluctant to give up is that it is a document of title at common law[11]:

9. *Diamond Alkali Export Corp.* v. *Fl. Bourgeois* [1921] 3 K.B. 443. See further section 4.4.3, below.
10. See section 7.1.1.
11. Benjamin, *Sale of Goods* (3rd ed., 1987) para. 1433.

"There is no authoritative definition of 'document of title to goods' at common law, but it is submitted that it means a document relating to goods the transfer of which operates as a transfer of the constructive possession of the goods, and may operate to transfer the property in them."

Because a document of title at common law[12] transfers constructive possession of the goods, the holder of an original document of title, and only the holder of such a document, can demand delivery of the goods to him when they arrive at their destination. Thus, a bank which requires this security should the buyer default must take a document of title to the goods. Transfer of a document of title may also operate to transfer the property in the goods. Again therefore, if a bank under a commercial credit requires the security afforded by the special property of a pledgee,[13] a document of title must be used.

The dangers of accepting a document which is not a common law document of title are illustrated by *Nippon Yusen Kaisha* v. *Ramjiban Serowgee*.[14] Shipowners issued bills of lading, against a letter of indemnity, without the mate's receipts being given up in exchange. The mate's receipts and bills of lading were negotiated separately and ended up in the hands of different persons. The shipowner delivered the goods against tender of the bills of lading, and the holders of the mate's receipts sued them for damages. The Privy Council held that the mate's receipts were not documents of title, and that the holders of the mate's receipts had neither the property in nor possession of the goods. Furthermore, in the circumstances of the case, the shipowner was entitled to issue bills of lading other than to the holders of the mate's receipts. A bank would be very unwise, therefore, to advance money on the security of a mate's receipt, except in the unusual circumstance that it constitutes a document of title on the principles discussed below.

A document becomes a document of title at common law by custom of merchants, and for two centuries the common has recognised that the shipped bill of lading is a document of title. In *Lickbarrow* v. *Mason*,[15] the special verdict of the jury in the second trial was that[16]:

"by the custom of merchants, bills of lading, expressing goods or merchandizes to have been shipped by any person or persons to be delivered to order or assigns, have been, and are, at any time after such goods have been shipped, and before the voyage performed, for which they have been shipped, negotiable and transferable by the shipper or shippers of such goods to any other person or persons, by such shipper or shippers indorsing such bills of lading with his, her or their name or names, and delivering or transmitting the same so indorsed, or causing the same to be so delivered or

---

12. To be distinguished from the meaning of "document of title to goods" under section 1(4) of the Factors Act 1889, the transfer of which by a non-owner may confer good title on the transferee. Documents of title under the Factors Act do not necessarily transfer constructive possession of the goods, however.
13. Section 3.3.1.
14. [1938] A.C. 429.
15. (1794) 5 Term Rep. 683; 101 E.R. 380.
16. (1794) 101 E.R. 380, 382.

transmitted to any such other person or persons; and that by such indorsement and delivery, or transmission, the property in such goods hath been, and is transferred and passed to such other person or persons . . . "

No doubt, had it been an issue, bills of lading would also have been taken to transfer constructive possession in the goods to the transferee.

It should be noted that jury's remarks in the above passage applied only to the shipped bill of lading, and not to any other document. It is also clear, however, that whether a document is a document of title is a question of fact, depending on the custom of merchants, and is not laid down as a matter of law. It follows that a document which is not a shipped bill of lading may also be held, as a matter of fact, to be a document of title.

4.3.3.2 Effect of local custom

It is also clear that the custom of merchants need not be a worldwide custom, so that what is a document of title can vary as between different trades and different parts of the world. In *Kum* v. *Wah Tat Bank Ltd.*,[17] the Privy Council, on appeal from the Malaysian Court of Appeal,[18] could "see no reason in principle why a document of title should not be created by local custom",[19] and were prepared to accept that even a mate's receipt could in principle be a document of title. Thus the existence of a local custom is sufficient, and it is not necessary to show a worldwide custom. The test was stated by Lord Devlin as follows[20]:

"Universality, as a requirement of custom, raises not a question of law but a question of fact. There must be proof in the first place that the custom is generally accepted by those who habitually do business in the trade or market concerned. Moreover, the custom must be so generally known that an outsider who makes reasonable enquiries could not fail to be made aware of it. The size of the market or the extent of the trade affected is neither here nor there. It does not matter that the custom alleged in this case applies only to part of the shipping trade within the State of Singapore, so long as the part can be ascertained with certainty, as it can here, as the carriage of goods by sea between Sarawak and Singapore."

In the end, however, their Lordships, differing from Wee Chong Jin C.J. in the Malaysian Court of Appeal, were not prepared to hold that the mate's receipt was a document of title in the particular case, because it was marked "Not Negotiable"[21]:

"The factor that in the end compels them to differ from his conclusion is the presence on the mate's receipt of the words 'NOT NEGOTIABLE'.

These words are part of the printed form. Their presence on a mate's receipt which is to be used simply as such may be superfluous, but it is not incongruous. The only

17. [1971] 1 Lloyd's Rep. 439.
18. [1967] 2 Lloyd's Rep. 437.
19. [1971] 1 Lloyd's Rep. 439, 443 (col. 2).
20. [1971] 1 Lloyd's Rep. 439, 444 (col.1).
21. [1971] 1 Lloyd's Rep. 439, 445 (col.1).

meaning, whether it be a popular or a legal meaning, that can be given to this marking is that the document is not to pass title by endorsement and delivery."

It follows from this decision that any document which is negotiable can become a document of title by local custom, but that a non-negotiable document can never be a document of title.

4.3.3.3 Documents of title without proof of custom

The courts recognise that shipped bills of lading are always, by custom of merchants, documents of title, and there is no need to prove a local (or more widespread) custom. It is not clear, however, that any other document is always treated as a document of title, even without proof of custom. In Benjamin's *Sale of Goods*, it is argued that even received for shipment bills of lading are not documents of title without proof of custom, and a justification for distinguishing between shipped and received for shipment bills is made[22]:

"There is, moreover, a practical reason for distinguishing for this purpose, between shipped and received bills. Once goods have been shipped, it is impossible or extremely difficult for the shipper or consignee to deal with them physically and it is that impossibility or extreme difficulty which led to the recognition of shipped bills of lading as documents of title. There is no such impossibility or extreme difficulty in dealing with goods before they have been shipped, and correspondingly less need to regard documents relating to them as documents of title."

It is not disputed, of course, that a received for shipment bill of lading can, like any other negotiable document, become a document of title through trade usage.

There is some authority, however, that received for shipment bills of lading are to be generally regarded as documents of title. In *The Marlborough Hill*,[23] the judicial committee of the Privy Council held that a received for shipment bill was a bill of lading for the purposes of the Admiralty Court Act 1861, section 6. The issue was whether a writ *in rem* could be issued against the *Marlborough Hill*[24] by some 20 consignees and indorsees of bills of lading in an action for non-delivery of goods under the bills of lading. Admiralty jurisdiction in New South Wales was the same as Admiralty jurisdiction in England, and section 6 gave the High Court of Admiralty:

" . . . jurisdiction over any claim by the owner or consignee or assignee of any bill of lading of any goods carried into any port . . . in any ship, for damage done to the goods or any part thereof by the negligence or misconduct of or for any breach of duty or breach of contract on the part of the owner, master, or crew of the ship . . . "

The question at issue was whether bills of lading which merely stated that goods had been "received for shipment by the sailing vessel *Marlborough Hill*, or by some other vessel owned or operated by the Commonwealth and

---

22. *Op. cit.*, f.n. 11, at para. 1448.
23. [1921] 1 A.C. 444; (1920) 5 Ll.L. Rep. 362.
24. I.e., whether the vessel could be arrested.

Dominion Line, Ltd., Cunard Line, Australasian service",[25] but which did not state that the goods had actually been "shipped on board", were bills of lading within the Act. Lord Phillimore was not disposed to distinguish in any regard between shipped and received for shipment bills of lading, even where the carrier had power to substitute another vessel, and it must therefore be inferred that received for shipment bills were now to be regarded as documents of title[26]:

"It is a matter of commercial notoriety, and their Lordships have been furnished with several instances of it, that shipping instruments which are called bills of lading, and known in the commercial world as such, are sometimes framed in the alternative form 'received for shipment' instead of 'shipped on board,' and further with the alternative contract to carry or procure some other vessel . . . to carry, instead of the original ship.

There can be no difference in principle between the owner, master or agent acknowledging that he has received the goods on his wharf, or allotted portion or quay, or his storehouse awaiting shipment, and his acknowledging that the goods have actually been put over the ship's rail. The two forms of bill of lading may well stand, as their Lordships understand that they stand, together. The older is still in the more appropriate language for whole cargoes delivered and taken on board in bulk; whereas 'received for shipment' is the proper phrase for the practical business-like way of treating parcels of cargo to be placed on a general ship which will be lying alongside the wharf taking in cargo for several days, and whose proper stowage will require that certain bulkier or heavier parcels shall be placed on board first, while others, though they have arrived earlier, wait for the convenient place and time of stowage."

Obviously the question whether received for shipment bills of lading were documents of title was *obiter dicta* in *The Marlborough Hill*, since the actual decision was limited to an interpretation of the Admiralty Court Act 1861, section 6. However, the issue arose directly for decision in *Ishag* v. *Allied Bank International*,[27] where a shipper of a cargo of various containers of insecticide and rolls of electric cable (Fuhs) deposited a received for shipment bill of lading, issued in January 1980, with the plaintiff (Ishag) as security for an advance of $1,450,000. In fact, it was arguably not even a received for shipment bill, since it stated merely that the goods were "at the disposal of" the carrier's agents "intended to be shipped . . . with M.S. 'LYCAON' from Bremen to Douala", and in fact the goods were in warehouses many miles from the vessel at the time. Unlike the bills of lading in *The Marlborough Hill*, however, it was clear that the intended vessel was *Lycaon*, and the carrier had no option to substitute another.

The purpose of the advance was to finance an entirely independent transaction involving uncut diamonds. The shipper had already agreed to sell the cargo of insecticide and electric cable c.i.f. to a Mr. Kotalimbora, who was apparently acting for General Kolingba of the Central African Republic, but

25. [1921] 1 A.C. 444, 450.
26. Although this was not clearly stated. The quote is taken from [1921] 1 A.C. 444, 451.
27. [1981] 1 Lloyd's Rep. 92.

it was assumed that the bill of lading would be released by the plaintiff in time for it to be used to effect this sale.

In February 1980, the cargo of insecticide and electric cable was shipped on the *Lycaon*, and a second, shipped bill of lading issued covering the same goods.[28] This (February) bill of lading was indorsed in favour of Mr. Kotalimbora, who had not however yet paid for the goods. Ishag sought to enforce his security, and the question arose directly whether he had a document of title. Fuhs argued that he had not. Lloyd J. applying *The Marlborough Hill*, held that he had.[29] He clearly assumed that a received for shipment bill was a document of title, even without proof of custom, and that the only issue here was whether this bill of lading was indeed equivalent to a received for shipment bill[30]:

"I now come to the third main argument put forward on behalf of Mr. Fuhs. It is said that the January bill of lading is not a document of title. The word 'Shipped/' has been deleted; instead there is a typed clause as follows:

'We herewith confirm that the a.m. consignment is at the disposal of Messrs. Karl Geuther & Co., Bremen, as Agents of the Joint Service (NEPH) and that same is intended to be shipped in 1 Lot with MS 'LYCAON' from Bremen to Douala.'

So far from being a 'shipped' bill it is said that this is not even a 'received for shipment' bill as ordinarily understood. All it does is to acknowledge that the goods are at the disposal of the vessel's agents. It is submitted that I ought not to regard such a document as a document to title without proof of custom, such as was found to be proved in *The Marlborough Hill* and *Kum* v. *Wah Tat Bank Ltd*. There has admittedly been no attempt to prove any such custom here.

I would not take so narrow a view of the January bill of lading. It is true that it does not use the traditional language 'received for shipment'. But the language which it does use comes to the same thing. Nobody suggests that the goods have to be received by the shipowners themselves. It is enough that they are received by their agents. For myself, I can see no practical or commercial difference between goods being received by agents on behalf of the shipowners and held in their own warehouse and goods being held at the disposal of the agents in the warehouse of another. Nor is there any difference, as was suggested, between 'for shipment' in a received for shipment bill and 'intended to be shipped with' in the present document. The document acknowledges that the goods are at the carriers' disposal. It provides for the terms on which the goods are to be carried to their destination, namely Douala, and there delivered to the consignee or his assigns. It states the name of the ship by which it is intended that the carriage should be performed. In my judgment the legal effect of the bill of lading is precisely the same as in any other received for shipment bill of lading. I would hold that it is covered by the custom as found proved in *The Marlborough Hill*. It follows that Mr. Fuhs has failed to satisfy me that the January bill of lading is not a document to title. On the contrary I am satisfied that it is."

28. Obviously this should not have happened. The circumstances were examined in more detail in later proceedings arising out of the same facts: *Elder Dempster Lines* v. *Zaki Ishag, The Lycaon* [1983] 2 Lloyd's Rep. 548, 551–552.

29. In the later proceedings, above, f.n. 28, no issue was taken on this point, but it was reserved if necessary for the Court of Appeal: *Elder Dempster Lines* v. *Zaki Ishag* [1983] 2 Lloyd's Rep. 548, 500 (col. 2). There were also a number of other issues in both *Ishag* cases, which are not relevant to the present discussion.

30. [1981] 1 Lloyd's Rep. 92, 97 (col. 2)–98 (col.1).

This appears at first sight to be a very strong authority, but arguably the above passage does not form part of the *ratio* of the case, since Lloyd J. also thought that the deposit of the documents with Ishag constituted an equitable pledge even if the January bill of lading was not a document of title. Ishag's equitable title would of course be defeated by a subsequent disposition of the legal title for valuable consideration without notice, and Fuhs argued that there was such a disposition when the February bill of lading was transferred to Mr. Kotalimbora. Lloyd J. held that the property in the goods had never passed to Mr. Kotalimbora, however, since he had not paid for the goods, and Fuhs had (in his view) retained a right of disposal until payment. Consequently Ishag could rely on his equitable title, whether or not the received for shipment bill was a document of title.

In *Diamond Alkali Export Corp.* v. *Fl. Bourgeois*,[31] a case surprisingly not mentioned in *Ishag*, McCardie J. took the opposite view, that only a shipped bill of lading is a document of title. He also criticised adversely the views taken by Lord Phillimore in *The Marlborough Hill*.[32] However, the actual decision was merely that a received for shipment bill of lading was not good tender under a c.i.f. contract, and this is clearly correct in principle. A c.i.f. buyer needs to know that the goods have actually been shipped,[33] and therefore needs a shipped bill of lading whether or not a received for shipment bill might also be a document of title. In fact, McCardie J.'s reasoning in part was that a c.i.f. buyer required a document which came within section 1 of the Bills of Lading Act 1855, that a received for shipment bill of lading was not by custom of merchants a document of title at the time when the 1855 Act was passed, and that since that Act covered only mercantile practice at the time,[34] it followed that section 1 could not apply to the received for shipment bill. It does not, of course, necessarily follow that the received for shipment bill could not be a document of title today.

4.3.3.4 Conclusion on documents of title

The conclusion that I would draw is as follows. Shipped bills of lading are documents without proof of custom. The position is unclear with received for shipment bills, but they can of course be documents of title on proof of custom. There is no reason in principle why mate's receipts and combined transport documents should not also be documents of title if a trade custom is established.

Banks should nevertheless be wary about moving away from traditional documentation for two reasons. First, since the existence of a trade custom is one of fact not law, it will not be easy to establish in advance of actual litiga-

31. [1921] 3 K.B. 443.
32. [1921] 3 K.B. 443, 452–453.
33. See below, section 4.4.2.
34. This was also one of the main reasons for the narrow view adopted by the Court of Appeal of that section in *The Delfini*, section 7.1.1.2.

tion to determine whether the document tendered is a document of title. Secondly, it is clear from *Kum* v. *Wah Tat Bank Ltd.* that a non-negotiable document cannot be a document of title in any circumstances, so that a non-negotiable waybill will provide very poor security indeed.

It is also clear that only an *original* bill of lading can be a document of title, and a copy will not do. It follows that as the law presently stands, a facsimile or computer print-out cannot be a document of title, since a computer print-out is merely a copy of whatever information is stored electronically within the computer at the time at which it is made. It cannot possibly (at least under existing law) be regarded as equivalent to an original bill of lading.[35]

4.4 DOCUMENTARY REQUIREMENTS UNDER C.I.F. AND F.O.B. SALE CONTRACTS

Although for reasons explained above,[36] the shipped bill of lading is no longer the most appropriate document for certain types of transaction, the fact nevertheless remains that a large proportion of the world's tonnage is still carried under c.i.f. and f.o.b. sale contracts, or variations thereon. In that event, the traditional documentation will still be used, and U.C.P., Article 26 sets out the requirements where a traditional bill of lading is still called for.[37] It is obviously inconvenient if the requirements under the credit differ markedly from those under the sale contract. If the U.C.P. applies, however, the credit (contract 4 in Figure 1.2) is governed by the Code, whereas the sale contract (contract 1) will be governed by the common law.

The requirements under both sale contract and credit can of course be altered by express term, although certain documentary requirements will be regarded as repugnant to a contract on c.i.f. terms. However, it is clearly preferable if the requirements under both contracts are similar even in the absence of extensive re-writing of one or other of them.

This section sets out the documentary requirements under c.i.f. and f.o.b. sale contracts. When, as explained above, the requirements under the U.C.P. are dealt with in the next chapter, it will be seen that they are similar but not identical to those set out in this section.

4.4.1 Negotiable bill of lading required

Unlike bills of exchange, bills of lading, and other shipping documents, are not negotiable unless they are expressly made so by the shipper. A negotiable bill of lading may be made out to the bearer, in which case it is transferred by delivery, but more commonly it will be made out to the order of one of the

---

35. See further section 4.4.5.
36. Section 4.2.2.
37. Section 5.2.

parties to the sale contract (usually the seller), and transferred by delivery and indorsement. Usually bills of lading are indorsed personally, but they can be indorsed in blank, in which case further transfer is by delivery alone, as with bearer bills. This practice seems to be rare.[38]

It is important that a c.i.f. of f.o.b. purchaser can use the bill of lading to claim the goods from the vessel, so that it must be made negotiable, unless the purchaser is named as consignee.

4.4.2 Shipped bill of lading required

Another function of the bill of lading is to provide evidence that the seller has performed his contractual obligations. In a c.i.f. contract, and an f.o.b. contract where the obligation to ship falls upon the seller, the purchaser needs to know that the goods were shipped (and not merely received for shipment), and that they conformed (or at any rate apparently conformed) to the contractual description when they were shipped. Hence the requirement for a clean shipped bill of lading in all c.i.f. contacts (and variations thereon) and most f.o.b. contracts. Also, particularly for sales of commodity futures, the shipment date is material, and this will not be shown on a received for shipment bill of lading.

In *Diamond Alkali Export Corp.* v. *Fl. Bourgeois*,[39] McCardie J. held that the seller was required to tender a shipped bill of lading under a c.i.f. contract, and that a received for shipment bill would not do. The main basis of the reasoning seems to be that only a shipped bill of lading would satisfy the requirements of the Bills of Lading Act 1855, section 1. Even f.o.b., since the seller is under a duty to load the goods on board, a shipped bill of lading is required, and a received for shipment bill will not usually suffice. In *Yelo* v. *S.M. Machado & Co. Ltd.*,[40] f.o.b. sellers of mandarin oranges from a Spanish port claimed that they were entitled to tender received for shipment bills by virtue of a trade custom in the Spanish ports concerned. Sellers J. held that they were not, and thought that an f.o.b. seller would need very strong evidence of a trade custom in order successfully to argue the contrary.

It is doubtful whether the *Diamond Alkali* decision is affected at all by trade customs, and therefore, shipped bills of lading are always required to constitute a valid tender c.i.f. Indeed, a contract calling for a received for shipment bill may not be regarded as being a contract on c.i.f. terms at all.

4.4.3 Clean and claused bills of lading

The seller is also required, under both c.i.f. and f.o.b. contracts, to tender bills of lading which are clean. A clean shipped bill of lading states that the

---

38. But see the discussion of *Sewell* v. *Burdick*, section 7.1.1.1.
39. [1921] 3 K.B. 443.
40. [1952] 1 Lloyd's Rep. 183.

goods were loaded on board in apparent good order and condition. If the bill of lading is claused, and those clauses cast doubt on the apparent order and condition of the goods on loading, then it will not be good tender. Because the seller's obligations in regard to the goods end on shipment, however, the bill of lading will still be valid tender f.o.b. or c.i.f. if it is claused by notations indicating that the goods have deteriorated, or been damaged or destroyed *after* shipment.

The Galatia[41] concerned a c. & f. contract of sale for shipment of a quantity of sugar. The sellers shipped the sugar in Kandla according to contract, but after loading 200 tonnes of it was destroyed by fire, or the water used to extinguish the fire and discharged. The separate bill of lading issued in relation to that part of the cargo that had been discharged acknowledged that it had been shipped in apparent good order and condition, but bore a typewritten notation: "Cargo covered by this Bill of Lading has been discharged Kandla view damaged by fire and/or water used to extinguish fire for which general average declared." The Court of Appeal held that the bill of lading was clean, and that the buyers were therefore bound to accept it. The clausing, relating as it did to damage after shipment, cast no doubt on the apparent condition of the cargo on loading, and thus did not invalidate the bill.

4.4.4 Other requirements

In addition to the above requirements, to be valid for c.i.f. tender a bill of lading must be procured on shipment or not long afterwards, must cover the contract goods and none other, and must show that shipment has occurred within the time stipulated in the sale contract.

4.4.5 One original of set required

An original bill of lading must also be tendered, but bills of lading are usually issued in sets of three originals "one of which being accomplished, the others stand void". In early days of international trade this probably provided protection against loss, but it can also increase the risk of fraud, where for example each of the three originals is separately negotiated.

In *Glyn Mills & Co.* v. *East and West India Dock Co.*,[42] the House of Lords held that a shipowner's duties extend no further than to deliver the goods to the first person to present an original bill of lading. He need not require all originals to be tendered, nor need he take further steps to ensure that the presenter of the document is in fact the consignee. A justification for this rule advanced by Earl Cairns was that the practice of issuing bills in sets of three

---

41. *Golodetz (M.) & Co. Inc.* v. *Czarnikow-Rionda Co. Inc.* [1980] 1 W.L.R. 495; [1980] 1 All E.R. 501.
42. (1882) 7 App. Cas. 591.

was for the benefit of either the shipper or consignee, if indeed it was a benefit at all, and was certainly not for the benefit of the shipowner.

There is no reason why the sale contract should not expressly require tender of all three originals.[43] In an ordinary sale contract, however, in the absence of an express stipulation, tender of one is sufficient. In *Sanders Brothers* v. *MacLean & Co.*,[44] the contract was for the sale of a quantity of old railway iron, and two tenders of documents were made. The buyers refused the first tender on the ground that only two of the three bills were tendered, and the second on the ground that the bills of lading could not have been forwarded in time to arrive before the goods.

The sellers sued for breach of contract, and the Court of Appeal held that they were entitled to damages for non-acceptance. The first tender was valid because in an ordinary sale contract, where payment is to be made against bills of lading, the buyer must accept and pay on one bill and cannot demand all three originals. The second tender was also valid, Brett M.R. refusing to imply as a term of the sale contract that the documents would arrive before the ship, so long as the seller made every reasonable exertion to send them forward as soon as possible.

4.4.6 Charterparty bills

Another function of the bill of lading is that its terms are evidence of those of the contract of carriage.[45] Indeed, when (and if[46]) the rights and obligations under the contract of carriage are transferred to a consignee or indorsee, the terms of the relationship between carrier and consignee or indorsee are those of the bill of lading itself.[47] The bill of lading will determine whether the receiver is to become liable for freight or demurrage, for example, and if so at what rate. The obligation on the seller is to enter into a contract of carriage which is reasonable, and the bill of lading should reflect this. Under a c.i.f. contract, the seller is also responsible for payment of the freight, so that if under the bill of lading the receiver becomes liable, either a freight receipt should be provided by the seller, or the invoice and the price should be adjusted accordingly.

This creates no particular difficulties where all the terms of the contract of carriage are evident from the bill of lading itself, but it is common for a bill of lading to import terms from a charterparty.[48] For example, the bill may state that freight and demurrage is payable as per charterparty. If the charterparty

43. Where payment is by bankers' documentary credit, banks usually demand all three sets as security for their advance. See section 5.2.1.4, below.

44. (1883) 11 Q.B.D 327.

45. *Ardennes (cargo owners)* v. *Ardennes (owners), The Ardennes* [1951] 1 K.B. 55; [1950] 2 All E.R. 517, (1950) 84 Ll.L. Rep. 340, [1950] W.N. 374.

46. See further Chapter 7, and in particular section 7.1.

47. *Leduc & Co.* v. *Ward* (1888) 20 Q.B.D. 475.

48. Banks will not accept charterparty bills unless expressly instructed to do so. See further section 5.2.1.3.

is not tendered along with the bill of lading the terms of the contract of carriage will not be known, but unless the seller is himself charterer of the vessel, the charterparty is unlikely to be available.

Even where the charterparty is not available, however, charterparty bills are generally acceptable tender in an ordinary f.o.b. or c.i.f. sale, at any rate where the charterparty is on a well-known standard form, commonly used in the trade. In *Finska Cellulosaforeningen* v. *Westfield Paper Co. Ltd.*,[49] one of the issues was whether a seller of woodpulp c.i.f. could validly tender a bill of lading containing the clause "All conditions and exceptions as per charterparty dated (blank)" when no charterparty was produced.[50] The sellers tendered the documents and successfully sued for the price. Viscount Caldecote, L.C.J. observed[51]:

"The bill of lading contained a clause as follows:
  'All conditions and exceptions as per charterparty dated (blank).'
  . . . I do not think that the fact that the clause in this case was left with the words 'charterparty dated' standing really affects the interpretation of the clause. I think that the defendants and their agents well understood what was intended by the clause, and were aware that shipments would take place, as in the past, in vessels chartered on the terms of the Baltpulp charter . . . Counsel for the defendants put his case as high as to say that, in all cases of c.i.f. contracts, the charterparty must be tendered where it is a relevant document. As authority for that proposition, he referred to a passage from the judgment of Blackburn J., in *Ireland* v. *Livingston*[52]:
    ' . . . for the balance a draft is drawn on the consignee which he is bound to accept (if the shipment be in conformity with his contract) on having handed to him the charterparty, bill of lading and policy of insurance.'
  It is to be observed that neither in the judgment of Hamilton J. in *Horst (E. Clemens) Co.* v. *Biddell Brothers*[53] nor in the judgment of Kennedy L.J. in that case in the Court of Appeal is there any mention of the charterparty as one of the necessary documents to complete delivery in accordance with the agreement . . .
  In the circumstances of this case, at any rate, the tender of the bill of lading duly indorsed was, in my opinion, a sufficient compliance with the contract of sale to entitle the sellers to payment of the price of the goods . . . "

The view expressed in this passage depends on the circumstances of the particular case, and is not of general application. Here the charterparty concerned was on the Baltpulp form, as both parties knew from previous dealings, and which was also the standard form used for the particular trade. It does not necessarily follow that a charterparty need never be tendered in a

---

49. [1940] 4 All E.R. 473; (1940) 68 Ll.L.Rep. 75.
50. There was also an insurance issue, which is not relevant to this book.
51. [1940] 4 All E.R. 473, 475H–477A.
52. (1872) L.R. 5 (H.L.) 395, 406. The statement of Blackburn J., from which this quote forms a part, is a classic early statement of the duties of the parties under a c.i.f. contract. See further section 4.4.9.
53. *Biddell Bros.* v. *E. Clemens Horst Co.* [1912] A.C. 18 (H.L.). The House of Lords approved the dissenting judgment of Kennedy L.J. in the Court of Appeal: [1911] 1 K.B. 934, 955, and the judgment of Hamilton J. at first instance: [1911] 1 K.B. 214, 220. These too have widely been adopted as classic statements of the duties of the parties under a c.i.f. contract.

c.i.f. contract, along with a charterparty bill. In *S.I.A.T. Di Del Ferro* v. *Tradax Overseas S.A.*,[54] Donaldson J. observed[55]:

"Nor need the charter-party be produced if the bill of lading refers to a known standard form and it is only the printed clauses of that form which are relevant, e.g., 'Centrocon Arbitration clause'. If the decision in *Finska Cellulosaforeningen v. Westfield Paper Company Ltd.* is correct, it is justified upon this ground."

It follows that if the charterparty is not on a known standard form, or has been heavily amended, or differs from that used in past dealings between the parties, the seller is probably under an obligation to tender it in addition to the bill of lading. The problem is, though: how is the buyer to know that, if the charterparty is not tendered?

4.4.7 Through bills of lading

The bill of lading must also cover the goods for the entire voyage, from shipment to port of destination. If the goods are to be transhipped during the voyage, for example where a large bulk cargo is shipped from outside Europe to a European port, and then placed aboard smaller vessels for distribution throughout Europe, then a through bill of lading is required.

The essence of the through bill of lading is that one carrier (probably the ocean carrier in the above example) takes on obligations for the whole voyage, but with a liberty to sub-contract on-carriage from the port of transhipment. There must also be an express liberty to tranship in the carriage contract, for in the absence of an express stipulation transhipment will put the carrier in breach.

Whether a through bill of lading constitutes a valid tender probably depends on what is usual and customary in the particular trade, but in any event it must provide coverage for the cargo for the entire voyage. The leading case is *Hansson* v. *Hamel & Horley Ltd.*[56] in the House of Lords. Cod guano was to be shipped c.i.f. from Braatvag, Norway to Yokohama, Japan, and it was initially put on board a local vessel, for transhipment at Hamburg on to a Japanese steamer, bound for Japan along with other cargoes from elsewhere. A document called a through bill of lading was issued, but only at Hamburg by the second carrier. The House of Lords held that this was a bad tender, because whatever the document purported to be, it was not in reality a through bill of lading at all.[57] Because it was not issued until Hamburg, it did not cover the local voyage. Had the goods been damaged at the local stage, the consignee would have had no action against the first carrier. In principle, however, a tender c.i.f. of a genuine through bill can be valid, so long as each stage is effectively covered, and so long as either they are usual

---

54. [1978] 2 Lloyd's Rep. 470.
55. [1978] 2 Lloyd's Rep. 470, 492 (col. 2).
56. [1922] 2 A.C. 36; (1922) 10 Ll.L. Rep. 507.
57. [1922] 2 A.C. 36, (*per* Lord Sumner) at p. 48.

and customary in the trade, or if the contract expressly provides for their tender.

4.4.8 Delivery orders

A bill of lading is not acceptable if it mentions other cargo, so only a single set of bills of lading can be issued for a particular consignment. Bills of lading are not therefore always suitable where a single undivided bulk consignment is sold to a number of buyers.

If the shipper knows on shipment how the total bulk is to be split between the various buyers, he can obtain a number of sets of bills of lading from the carrier, each for a part of the total bulk, and these can be sent to various buyers. Since bills of lading are issued on shipment, however, or shortly thereafter, this is only possible if the number of buyers is known then. More importantly, perhaps, an intermediate purchaser of bulk cargo afloat, who has become holder of a single bill of lading (or single set of bills), cannot use that bill of lading (or set) to resell the bulk to a number of different sub-buyers. Nor can he at this stage obtain fresh bills for smaller amounts.

Although he cannot use the single set of bills for the sub-sales, however, he can use delivery orders. These are directions to the carrier to deliver to the holder the amount of cargo mentioned, so a sub-sale can be effected by sending to each sub-buyer a delivery order in respect of that part of the cargo sold to him. Delivery orders fall into two categories: merchant's delivery orders, which in this example would be issued by the intermediate purchaser, and ship's delivery orders, which are either issued by the carrier or his agent, or attorned to by the carrier to the receiver.

Only ship's delivery orders, which can also provide rights against the carrier,[58] are acceptable tender under a c.i.f. contract, and even then only if the contract expressly so stipulates. In *Colin & Shields* v. *W. Weddel & Co. Ltd.*,[59] Singleton L.J. said of a ship's delivery order[60]: "As counsel for the sellers said, a ship's delivery order has never been defined with precision. I will not attempt any general definition, but for the purposes of this contract I take it to mean an order on the ship given by a person who had a right to give it." *Colin & Shields* v. *W. Weddel & Co. Ltd.* is authority for the proposition that not only must a ship's delivery order be addressed to and accepted by the ship, but also that this must happen while the goods are still in the ship's possession. The case concerned a c.i.f. contract which allowed the sellers to tender a ship's delivery order in place of a bill of lading. The goods (1,000 ox-hides) were supposed to be shipped to Liverpool, but instead were put on a vessel bound for Manchester, and then transhipped on to a dumb barge to carry them onwards to Liverpool. The sellers tendered a document signed by

58. See section 7.1.2.
59. [1952] 2 All E.R. 337; [1952] 2 Lloyd's Rep. 9; [1952] W.N. 420.
60. [1952] 2 All E.R. 337, 342.

the shipowners directing the master of the hide berth in Liverpool to deliver the goods to the buyers. The buyers rejected this document or to make payment. The Court of Appeal held that it was not a ship's delivery order, because it was addressed to someone who was no longer in physical possession of the goods. Had the goods been lost after their transfer at Manchester to the dumb barge the delivery order tendered would have conferred no rights on the buyers. Denning L.J. began his judgment by commenting generally on the commercial use of ship's delivery orders[61]:

"The contract of sale was a c.i.f. contract—modified, no doubt, in some respects, but, nevertheless, a c.i.f. contract . . . The most important modification . . . enables the sellers to supply a ship's delivery order instead of a bill of lading. This modification is made so as to enable a seller to split up a bulk consignment into smaller parcels and to sell them to different buyers while the goods are still at sea. A seller often only has one bill of lading for the whole consignment, and he cannot deliver that one bill of lading to each of the buyers because it contains more goods than the particular contract of sale, so in each of his contracts of sale the seller stipulates for the right to give a ship's delivery order. The bulk consignment can then be split up into small parcels each covered by a ship's delivery order instead of a bill of lading. Such being the commercial object of this clause, I agree with my Lord [Singleton L.J.] as to the meaning of 'ship's delivery order' in this contract. It means, I think, an order given by the seller directed to the ship, whereby the seller orders the ship to deliver the contract goods to the buyer or his order. The ship's delivery order is not as good a protection for the buyer as a separate bill of lading would be, because it gives no cause of action against the ship unless the master attorns to the buyer, and then it gives a different cause of action which may not be as favourable as a bill of lading."

Having described the general commercial purpose of the ship's delivery order, Denning L.J. then went on to hold that this was not a ship's delivery order, and therefore not good tender under this contract: " . . . the sellers did not provide a proper ship's delivery order. The document which they presented was not an order on the ship, but an order to a porter at the docks at Liverpool who had nothing to do with the ship". The effect of this decision is that it is not possible to substitute a ship's delivery order for a through bill of lading.

In fact, since *Colin & Shields* v. *W. Weddel & Co. Ltd.* it has become clear that the liability of the carrier may be greater than Denning L.J.'s remarks suggest,[62] and because the carrier is incurring a potential liability by issuing, or attorning to a delivery order, ship's delivery orders are usually given only in exchange for the bill of lading. If the carrier has a land based agent a bill of lading can be exchanged for a number of ship's delivery orders in smaller amounts, the delivery orders being used instead of the bills of lading to effect the sub-sale.[63] The delivery orders will typically be in the same terms as the bill of lading, and should state that the cargo was loaded in apparent good

61. [1952] 2 All E.R. 337, 343.
62. See further section 7.1.2.
63. As in *Cremer* v. *General Carriers S.A., The Dona Mari* [1974] 1 W.L.R. 341; [1974] 1 All E.R. 1; [1973] 2 Lloyd's Rep. 366. See further section 7.1.2.

order and condition. If the carrier has no land based agent nearby this will not usually be possible, and the best the seller can do is to issue his own delivery orders directing the shipowner to deliver a portion of the cargo to the eventual receivers. Such delivery orders confer no rights against the carrier, and cannot be stipulated as good tender in a c.i.f. contract. A seller who presents one is doing no more than promise that he will allow the goods to be delivered ex-ship.[64]

A buyer of part of an undivided bulk cargo who accepts a ship's delivery order, stating that the cargo has been loaded on board such and such a vessel on such and such a date, or indeed a bank advancing money against such a document, obtains security which is virtually as good as he would were he to have obtained a bill of lading. A ship's delivery order shares many of the features of the bill of lading. It represents the goods, operates as a receipt for the goods by the carrier, and provides evidence of the terms of the contract of carriage.

It is true that unlike a shipped bill of lading, a ship's delivery order will not usually be a document of title, although so long as it is made negotiable it could presumably become one on the principles discussed above.[65] Nor, unlike a shipped bill of lading, does a ship's delivery order come within section 1 of the Bills of Lading Act 1855.[66] It is unlikely that these differences are material, however. The carrier has undertaken to deliver the goods to the holder of the delivery order, so that in practice transfer of a ship's delivery order operates also to transfer constructive possession of the goods. Admittedly, it does not also transfer property, but since the goods are unascertained, this would be equally true of a shipped bill of lading.[67] Also, because property cannot pass, the 1855 Act will not apply in any event, whatever document is issued.[68] A *Brandt* v. *Liverpool* contract may be implied between the carrier and the holder of a ship's delivery order on exactly the same principles as it may between the carrier and the holder of a shipped bill of lading.[69]

No doubt the holder of a ship's delivery order does not obtain security comparable to that afforded to the holder of a ship's bill of lading covering specific goods, who has obtained the property in the goods in circumstances

---

64. A contract calling for such a document is therefore an ex-ship contract, and cannot be a c.i.f. contract, whatever it is expressed to be: *Comptoir d'Achat et de Vente du Boerenbond Belge S.A.* v. *Luis de Ridder Limitada, The Julia* [1949] A.C. 293; [1949] 1 All E.R. 269; 82 Ll.L. Rep. 270; 65 T.L.R. 126; 208 L.T. 215; [1949] W.N. 34.

65. See section 4.3.3.

66. Presumably this is what Denning L.J. had in mind in *Colin & Shields* v. *W. Weddel &. Co., Ltd.*, above, f.n. 60, when he said that even a ship's delivery order gave protection to the buyer which was less good than a separate bill of lading would be.

67. See section 3.3.2.

68. See further section 7.1.1. Note, however, that the first of the Law Commission's suggestions for amendment to section 1 would alter the position for bills of lading, but not delivery orders: see further, section 7.3.1.

69. This is a common law implied contract: see further section 7.1.2.

where section 1 applies. This is because of the nature of undivided bulk cargo, and in particular the passing of property therein. It is not because of the nature of the delivery order itself.

4.4.9 Commercial invoice

A c.i.f. seller must also tender an invoice. The form of the invoice, which is not defined in detail in the authorities on c.i.f. contracts, was originally set out by Blackburn J. in *Ireland* v. *Livingston*[70]:

"The invoice is made out debiting the consignee with the agreed price (or the actual cost and commission, with the premiums of insurance, and the freight, as the case may be), and giving him credit for the amount of freight which he will have to pay the shipowner on actual delivery."

In *Biddell Brothers* v. *E. Clemens Horst Co.*, Hamilton J. said that the invoice must be made out "as described by Blackburn J. in *Ireland* v. *Livingston* or in some similar form".[71]

Clearly the common law requirement is loose in the extreme, with not even a mention, for example, of any description of the goods. It would be usual for there to be additional express requirements, if not in the sale contract itself then certainly in the credit. Where the credit requires a commercial invoice, it differs from other documents in that it must comply *strictly* with the terms of the credit, whereas for other documents some leeway is allowed by the U.C.P.[72]

In a c.i.f. contract, the invoice would usually debit the buyer with the agreed price, and credit him with any freight or other charges he may have to pay the carrier at discharge (for example, if freight has not been paid in advance and a freight collect bill of lading is used).

4.4.10 Insurance requirements

A c.i.f. seller is under an obligation to insure the goods with reputable insurers against marine risks, and the buyer is entitled to the benefit of the insurance policy, covering the value of the goods for the voyage. The principles elaborated in this section apply to any contract which calls for a policy of insurance, and not just to a c.i.f. sale contract. They also apply only in the absence of any custom, or express stipulation to the contrary.

4.4.10.1 Extent of cover

In the absence of express stipulation, the seller is obliged to provide the minimum cover current in the trade. This is simply a specific application of a prin-

---

70. (1872) L.R. 5 (H.L.) 395, 406 (bottom)–407 (top). See also f.n. 52.
71. [1911] 1 K.B. 214. See also f.n. 53.
72. See further sections 5.6. and 6.3.3.

ciple which applies to any contract which simply calls for a policy of insurance, without specifying further details. *Borthwick* v. *Bank of New Zealand*,[73] for example, concerned tender to a bank under a commercial credit which called for bills of lading, invoice and insurance policy, but did not specify the exact cover required. The sellers tendered a policy which contained a clause: "To pay a total loss by total loss of vessel only." Mathew J. held that the sellers should have obtained an all risks policy, having satisfied himself that this was "the ordinary policy in business of this kind".[74] The bank should not have accepted the policy tendered, and was liable to the buyer for the consequences of so doing.[75]

The requirement to provide the minimum cover current in the trade applies equally to a c.i.f. sale contract. The seller is under no obligation, however, again in the absence of any term to the contrary, to provide more than this. If the buyer requires more comprehensive cover he should so stipulate in the sale contract, or alternatively contract on terms whereby he takes on the insurance obligation himself (e.g., c. & f.).

4.4.10.2 War risk insurance

Obviously, the terms current in a particular trade will vary between trades and routes, and over time. A common cause of litigation occurs on the outbreak of hostilities, where ships are sunk and it is discovered that the cargo is not insured against war risk. Presumably once hostilities have been under way for a time, it is more likely that the sale contract will address the matter of war risk directly.

It is unlikely at the outbreak of hostilities that provision of war risk cover will be usual in the trade, especially as the contract itself may well have been made in peacetime. In general, therefore, on the principles set out in the last section, war risk cover must be stipulated expressly in the sale contract, and if it is not the seller is at liberty to insure "free of capture and seizure" (f.c. and s.).

In *C. Groom* v. *Barber*,[76] 100 bales of Hessian cloth were shipped c.i.f., "war risk for buyer's account", on board the *City of Winchester* on 15 July 1914, and the ship was sunk by a German cruiser on 6 August, two days after the outbreak of war. The contract had been made in peacetime (8 June), for shipment in the first two weeks of July, and Atkin J. held that the seller was entitled to tender an f.c. and s. policy. A clause in the sale contract stating

---

73. (1900) 6 Com. Cas. 1. Like *Giddens* v. *Anglo-African Produce Ltd*. (1923) 14 Ll.L. Rep. 230, considered in section 3.1.1 (except that the credit here appears to be irrevocable), the bank undertook to negotiate drafts drawn by the shippers on the buyers. This form of negotiation credit is pretty-well obsolete today, except in the Middle East.

74. (1900) 6 Com. Cas. 1, 4.

75. There was a partial loss of the consignment, in respect of which by reason of the clause the plaintiff buyer could not recover.

76. [1915] 1 K.B. 316.

"war risk for buyer's account" did not mean that the seller was to effect war risk at buyer's expense, but that war risk was the concern of the buyer alone. Any other conclusion could lead to very expensive rates even in peacetime[77]:

"In a contract on c.i.f. terms the seller has, as stated by Hamilton J. in *Biddell Brothers* v. *E. Clemens Horst Co.*,[78] to arrange for an insurance on the terms current in the trade which would be available for the buyer. I am satisfied that at the time this contract was made the terms current in the trade were terms which excluded war risk; in other words that the policy would contain the f.c. and s. clause, and therefore, apart from the special terms of this contract, a policy in such terms would be in order. The finding of the appeal committee in that respect makes the matter quite certain. But in this contract there are the words 'war risk for buyer's account'. It was said that this meant that the seller was bound to take out a policy covering war risk but was entitled to charge the buyer with the expense of it. That would mean that at all times, even in times of peace, a war risk policy must be taken out at the expense of the buyer. I am satisfied that no seller or buyer contemplated such a thing, and if the buyer were charged with the expense of such a policy he would, in ordinary times of peace, be the very first person to object. To my mind these words mean that war risk is the buyer's concern, and if he wants to cover war risk he must get it done. It might be contended that the condition meant that the proper course of business was that the buyer was entitled to ask the seller, when he was taking out the usual policy, to take out one also covering war risk at the buyer's expense. If it could mean that, I am satisfied in this case that the buyer never requested the seller to take out a war risk policy on those terms. When he made his request the buyer never intended to pay the cost, and his intention was that the seller was bound to take out the policy at his (the seller's) expense. In those circumstances I am satisfied that the buyer's contention on this point fails and that the award that the policy was in order is right."

Presumably if hostilities on particular routes last long enough, the customary insurance practices may alter so as to place an obligation to take out war risk on the seller. There do not seem to be any cases where this has actually occurred. In any case it may be difficult to define the customary risk, since wars are rarely static and rates can vary significantly even during the period of hostilities (as in the Gulf war).

4.4.10.3 Insurance policy required, unless express stipulation to the contrary

Generally, the c.i.f. seller must tender the policy itself, although it is open to the parties to stipulate a certificate of insurance instead, but this must be done by an express term in the sale contract.

In *Manbre Saccharine Co. Ltd.* v. *Corn Products Co. Ltd.*,[79] c.i.f. sellers of starch during the first world war tendered documents for cargo which was aboard the *Algonquin*, a vessel which by the time of tender, to the sellers' knowledge, had been sunk by a German submarine, with the loss of all the goods aboard. McCardie J. held that in principle, c.i.f. sellers were entitled to tender documents for goods which had to their knowledge already been lost

---

77. [1915] 1 K.B. 316, 321 (bottom)–322 (bottom).
78. [1911] 1 K.B. 214. See above, f.n. 53.
79. [1919] 1 K.B. 198.

at sea. However, the buyers were able validly to reject the documents because although a letter had been tendered which declared that the goods were insured, there was included no policy or certificate of insurance. McCardie J. stated the law as follows[80]:

"Under an ordinary c.i.f. contract the vendor is obviously bound to tender a proper policy of insurance together with the other documents required . . . The policy must be tendered even if the goods have safely arrived at the time of tender . . . In the present case the defendants tendered no policy of insurance at all. They merely made the following statement in their letter of March 14, 1917: 'We hereby hold you covered by insurance for the amount of £4,322 in accordance with the terms of a policy of insurance in our possession re shipment ex s.s. *Algonquin.*' This . . . was the mere assurance that a policy had been issued, and not the policy of insurance itself. It was suggested on behalf of the plaintiffs that the letter amounted either to an equitable assignment of the insurance moneys to the extent of £4,322 or to a declaration of trust to such amount in respect of these moneys. Even if this suggestion be well founded yet there is a wide difference between an actual policy of insurance transferable to the defendants as contemplated by s.50(3) of the Marine Insurance Act, 1906, and such a letter as that of the defendants here. The plaintiffs, I hold, were clearly entitled to a policy and not to a mere assertion by the defendants that a policy existed and that the defendants would hold the plaintiffs covered."

He went on to say that the buyers were entitled to policies covering only the goods mentioned in the bills of lading and invoices[81]:

"Even if the defendants had tendered the policies actually held by them I should still have held the tender bad, for they were policies which covered a quantity of goods outside those mentioned in the bills of lading and invoices sent to the plaintiffs. In my opinion a purchaser under a c.i.f. contract is entitled to demand, as a matter of law, a policy of insurance which covers and covers only the goods mentioned in the bills of lading and invoices . . . Unless the purchaser gets a policy limited to his own interests he would become one only of those who are interested in the insurance; and he is entitled, in my view, to refuse to occupy a position which may give rise to obvious complications . . . "

In *Wilson, Holgate & Co. Ltd.* v. *Belgian Grain and Produce Ltd.*,[82] Bailhache J. went further, and held that in the absence of any custom or express stipulation in the contract a proper *policy* of insurance must be tendered under a c.i.f. contract, and that even a certificate of insurance was insufficient. McCardie J. took the same view in *Diamond Alkali Export Corp.* v. *Fl. Bourgeois*[83]:

"I have read, I believe, all the cases on the rights and obligations of buyer and seller under c.i.f. contracts . . . In all the cases a 'policy of insurance' is mentioned as an essential document. The law is settled and established. I may point out that in *Burstall* v. *Grimsdale*[84] it was expressly provided by the contract that a certificate of insurance

80. [1919] 1 K.B. 198, 204–205.
81. [1919] 1 K.B. 198, 205 (middle)–206 (top).
82. [1920] 2 K.B. 1.
83. [1921] 3 K.B. 443, 454 (middle)–455 (top). For further discussion of this case, see sections 4.3.3 and 4.4.2.
84. (1906) 11 Com. Cas. 280.

might be an alternative for an actual policy. I ventured in *Manbre Saccharine Co.* v. *Corn Products Co.* to discuss the relevant authorities . . . It seems plain that a mere written statement by the sellers that they hold the buyers covered by insurance in respect of a specified policy of insurance is not of itself a policy of insurance within a c.i.f. contract: see the *Manbre Saccharine* case. It seems plain also that a broker's cover note or an ordinary certificate of insurance are not adequate agreements within such a contract: see Bailhache J. in *Wilson, Holgate & Co. Ltd.* v. *Belgian Grain and Produce Ltd.*"

He went on to explain the main reasons for requiring a policy, rather than merely a certificate. The first was that unless the policy is tendered the buyer cannot tell whether the terms are usual and customary in the trade, as required under a c.i.f. contract[85]:

"Now the certificate is not a policy. It does not purport to be a policy . . . It is a certificate that a policy was issued . . . , and it incorporates the terms of that policy. Those terms I do not know, nor is there anything before me to indicate that the buyers knew them. The certificate does not show whether the policy was in a recognized or usual form or not. The certificate does not therefore contain all the terms of the insurance. The terms have to be sought for in two documents—namely, the original policy and the certificate. But even if this document is not a policy yet the sellers say it is 'equivalent to a policy' . . . This leads me to ask whether the document before me differs in any material respect from a policy of insurance. To begin with, I do not see how the buyer here could know whether the document he got was of a proper character (one he was bound to accept) unless he saw the original policy, and examined its conditions, whether usual or otherwise."

He then went on to say that a certificate is not legally equivalent to a policy, and cannot be assigned under the Marine Insurance Act 1906[86]:

"In the next place I feel that the certificate of insurance falls within a legal classification, if any, different to that of a policy of insurance. The latter is a well-known document with clearly defined features. It comes within definite, established and statutory legal rights. A certificate, however, is an ambiguous thing; it is unclassified and undefined by law; it is not even mentioned in Arnould on Marine Insurance. No rules have been laid down upon it. Would the buyer sue upon the certificate or upon the original policy of insurance? If he sued simply on the certificate he could put in a part only of the contract, for the other terms of the contract—namely, the conditions of the actual policy—would be contained in a document not in his control and to the possession of which he is not entitled. Thirdly, I point out that before the buyer could sue at all he would have to show that he was the assignee of the certificate . . . In what way can he become the assignee? It is vital to remember the provisions of the Marine Insurance Act 1906. Now the relevant statutory provision is s.50(3) which says: 'A marine policy may be assigned by endorsement thereon or in other customary manner.' This subsection, however, only applies, so far as I can see, to that which is an actual marine policy . . . I must therefore hold that the buyers were entitled to reject the documents upon the ground that no proper bill of lading[87] and no proper policy of insurance were tendered by the sellers in conformity with the c.i.f. contract."

85. [1921] 3 K.B. 443, 455–456. The requirements under a c.i.f. contract are set out in section 4.4.10.1, above.
86. [1921] 3 K.B. 443, 456–457.
87. Above, section 4.4.2.

Both these cases were approved by the Court of Appeal in *Donald H. Scott & Co. Ltd.* v. *Barclays Bank Ltd.*,[88] although whereas Bankes L.J. agreed with McCardie J.'s views as expressed in the second of the above passages, that the document tendered must show all the terms of the policy, he was unprepared to go as far as McCardie J. did in the last passage above, in requiring the policy to comply "with the English law relating to policies of marine insurance."[89] It may not be necessary, therefore, that the document also falls within the technical provisions of the Marine Insurance Act 1906.

There are also two further provisos. First, it may be that some American certificates of insurance may be regarded as equivalent to policies, at any rate if they contain all the terms necessary to constitute a valid policy of insurance according to English law.[90] Secondly, in none of the cases so far discussed was there any custom or express stipulation to the contrary. In *The Julia*,[91] however, Lord Porter thought that a term which *expressly allowed* substitution of a certificate of insurance for a policy would not be repugnant to a c.i.f. contract.

The rule in *Manbre Saccharine* appears to be absolute, however, so that a term allowing a seller merely to tender a letter stating that the goods were insured would probably be repugnant to a c.i.f. contract.

4.4.11 Additional shipping documents

There is no reason why additional shipping documents cannot also be stipulated, for example a certificate of quality or origin, but in a c.i.f. contract these must be capable of being obtained by the seller not later than shipment, and must not depend on the condition of the cargo at some later time. A certificate of quality on discharge, for example, could not be stipulated under a c.i.f. contract, since the seller is not responsible for the cargo after shipment.[92]

4.5 THE COMBINED TRANSPORT DOCUMENT IN PRINCIPLE

A combined transport operation usually involves at least two land legs in addition to the sea carriage, and obviously the traditional shipped bill of

88. [1923] 2 K.B. 1. The issue was not identical, however, but arose between seller and bank, not on the sale contract. The letter of credit, set out at [1923] 2 K.B. 1, 3, required tender of an approved policy of insurance, and the question was whether a certificate could be regarded as the equivalent of a policy. The Court of Appeal held that it could not.
89. [1923] 2 K.B. 1, 13.
90. *Per* Bailhache J.: [1920] 2 K.B. 1, 7, as interpreted by Bankes L.J.: [1923] 2 K.B. 1, 11.
91. *Comptoir d'Achat et de Vente Du Boerenbond Belge S.A.* v. *Luis de Ridder Limitada, The Julia* [1949] A.C. 293.
92. Treitel: "Rights of rejection under c.i.f. sales" [1984] L.M.C.L.Q. 565, at p. 565. He was commenting on the certificate of quality required in *Gill & Duffus S.A.* v. *Berger & Co. Inc.* [1984] A.C. 382; [1984] 1 All E.R. 438; [1984] 2 W.L.R. 95; [1984] 1 Lloyd's Rep. 227. See further on this case, section 6.2.2.1. On questions of ambiguity where additional documents are stipulated, see also section 6.3.2.2.

lading, covering only port-to-port shipment, is not ideally suited to this type of transaction.

Typically, the shipper will consign the goods to a forwarding agent at a collection depot inland, and usually the shipper's only direct contact will be with the freight forwarder, who will make the necessary arrangements to cover each stage. Yet although the forwarding agent usually arranges the entire operation, there is likely to be more than one actual carrier, and different carriers will usually be responsible for each section of the combined transport operation.

One possibility is for the forwarding agent simply to act as shipper's agent in arranging each stage of carriage, the other contracting party being the actual carrier for each stage. Thus there will be three separate carriage contracts with three separate carriers, made through the agency of the freight forwarder. Alternatively, the forwarding agent may contract as principal for the first stage and agent for the shipper in arranging carriage for the on stages. In this case he will issue what is called a through transport document (T.T.D.). There will still be three separate carriers, however, and three separate carriage contracts, and a through transport document is not the same as a combined transport document.

The essence of the combined (or multimodal) transport document proper is that one carrier, usually the forwarding agent, makes himself responsible for the entire operation. He may sub-contract each stage, or more commonly each stage after the initial land leg, but he contracts with the shipper as principal. He is liable in contract to the shipper if the goods are damaged on any of the three stages, although if he is sued for damage caused while the goods are in the custody of another carrier, he should be able to recoup his costs from that other carrier.[93] The only contract of carriage, however, is with the single contracting carrier, often referred to as a Combined Transport Operator (C.T.O.).

The combined transport document is therefore essentially a development of the through bill of lading,[94] except that the carriage will involve land as well as sea legs. As with a through bill, one carrier takes on responsibility for the entire enterprise, but may sub-contract each leg.

A major difficulty with combined transport operations is that different international conventions may govern each part of the operation, so that the carrier's liability varies depending on where damage to the cargo occurs. Road transport, for example, is governed by the C.M.R. Convention, adopted in the U.K. by the Carriage of Goods by Road Act 1965. The basis of, and limits to, liability, are different from those under the Hague and Hague-Visby Rules. In other words the basis of liability, limitations and time limits may vary depending on whether damage occurs during the sea carriage,

---

93. This will depend on the terms of the contract between himself and the actual carrier, and is of no concern to the shipper.
94. Above, section 4.4.7.

or over land. Further, if the goods are in a container, it may be difficult to ascertain precisely when the loss occurs. Indeed, it may even be that damage which only becomes apparent at stage 3 has been caused by an event that occurs at stage 1.

Combined transport documents can be either negotiable or non-negotiable. A negotiable transport document could presumably become a document of title by proof of custom, but it is likely that no such customs yet exist. Consequently, even a negotiable combined transport document would not transfer constructive possession or property to the holder. Combined transport documents do not fall within the Bills of Lading Act 1855, section 1, and it is difficult to see how a *Brandt* v. *Liverpool* contract could be implied on delivery of the goods at their eventual destination, since delivery is made by the actual carrier, whereas the implied contract would have to be with the contracting carrier, who will usually be the freight forwarder on the initial land leg.

It follows that a bank which advances money against even a negotiable combined transport document obtains security which is far inferior to that provided by a shipped bill of lading. A non-negotiable combined transport provides no security at all.

4.6 NON-NEGOTIABLE WAYBILLS IN PRINCIPLE

As explained above, a possible solution to the problem of the vessel arriving before the documentation is to use, instead of a bill of lading, a document which the consignee does not need to present to obtain delivery of the goods. The liner (or sea or ocean) waybill (called a "straight bill of lading" in the United States, and also sometimes called a data freight receipt or cargo key receipt) is such a document, and it can be carried on the ship itself. It is essentially similar to an air consignment note, and is not, unlike the traditional bill of lading, a negotiable document, nor need it be presented by the consignee to take delivery of the goods at destination. The carrier delivers to a named consignee, whereas under a bill of lading it is usual only to deliver against production of the original document.

Waybills and consignment notes therefore have distinct advantages for carriers. They can travel with the goods. Lengthy and complex documentary processes are avoided. Carriers do not risk the same liability to consignees. Naturally they would prefer the use of such documents to be wider, even in sea carriage. Like a bill of lading, a waybill is evidence of the carriage contract (but with the consignor only). It also constitutes a receipt for the goods by the carrier. Unlike a bill of lading, however, it can be made out by the consignor.

Obviously, waybills and consignment notes are very different from bills of lading. The similarities between them are that the waybill constitutes a receipt by the carrier, and provides evidence of the carriage contract. By comparison with the traditional bill of lading, however, waybills and consignment notes do not represent the goods, and are not documents of title. Consequently, a bank which advances money against a non-negotiable waybill obtains the security of neither property in nor constructive possession of the goods. It is true that a bank may obtain limited protection by being named consignee itself, and making its customer notify party, but there is nothing to stop the shipper from instructing the carrier to change the identity of the consignee after shipment. International conventions for carriage of goods by air, rail and road provide some protection, in requiring the shipper to produce his shipper's copy before issuing new instructions, but no such conventions are in force for sea transit.

In short, in a commercial credit the waybill is simply not a substitute for the traditional bill of lading. A bank should only accept a waybill if reimbursement is unlikely to be a problem.

The waybill also does not, of course, come within section 1 of the Bills of Lading Act 1855.[95]

On the other hand, if there is no likelihood of the goods being resold during transit, and so long as there is no problem about payment, then a traditional bill of lading is unnecessary. This would cover, for example, sales to another branch of a multi-national company, or an associated company (i.e., house to house shipments), or sales on an open account basis, where a documentary credit is not required. The International Maritime Committee has taken the view that in the great majority of cases of general cargo a bill of lading is not necessary, and that its issue should be positively discouraged. There are difficulties for carriers in this regard, in that where the Hague or Hague-Visby Rules apply, shippers are entitled to demand a bill of lading, by virtue of Articles III (3) and (7),[96] so that the carrier does not have the option of refusing to issue a bill of lading where one is demanded by the shipper. However, nothing in Article III prevents the carrier from charging a considerable amount for its issue. The International Maritime Committee recommended that shipping lines should charge a considerable amount for a bill of lading. The amount charged may operate not only to deter shippers who do not require a document of title from demanding one, but also to compensate carriers for the increased potential liability where a negotiable document is issued.

In summary, P. & O.[97] take the view that a waybill is suitable for:

"(a) 'House-to-House' shipments: that is to say shipments between associated companies or branches of multi-national companies where no Documentary Credit transaction is involved.

---

95. See further section 7.1.1.3.
96. Above, f.n. 7. Unlike the Hague-Visby Rules the Hague Rules, where applicable, are brought into force by clause paramount in a bill of lading. If no bill of lading is issued they will not operate at all, unless expressly incorporated into the carriage contract by the parties. Where the Hague Rules apply Article III can therefore easily be avoided.
97. *The Merchants Guide* (4th ed., 1987), issued by P. & O. Containers Ltd., p. 32. See also *Guide to OCL Bills of Lading*, p. 10, which is in identical terms.

(b) Open Account Sales: where goods are shipped to an agent for sale at destination on an account sale basis.

(c) Transactions between companies where the security of a Documentary Credit transaction is not required, perhaps because of trust stemming from a long trading relationship or an alternative basis of payment being arranged."

Note that it is regarded as unsuitable where a documentary credit transaction is involved.

CHAPTER 5

DOCUMENTARY REQUIREMENTS UNDER THE U.C.P.

5.1 THE U.C.P.'S APPROACH TO DOCUMENTATION

Under the 1974 revision to the U.C.P., separate provision was made for marine bills of lading,[1] combined transport documents,[2] and other shipping documents including waybills.[3] These Articles gave rise to significant difficulties, so the 1983 revision adopted a different approach. The marine bill of lading (which is defined in Article 25 as an ocean bill of lading or a bill of lading covering carriage by sea) is still dealt with separately in Article 26, but in the case of all other documents[4]: "The 1983 Revision . . . endeavours to establish the broad 'characteristics' of an 'acceptable' transport document, having in mind developments over which the banking community can have little, if any, direct control, but which it cannot ignore." In attempting to achieve this objective, the U.C.P. lumps together all other transport documents apart from the "marine bill of lading" into Article 25, where acceptable characteristics are defined.

The terminology is arguably rather confusing. It seems that the transport document in Article 25 does not necessarily mean the same as combined transport document, but includes non-negotiable waybills also. In reality, however, the requirements are clearly based primarily around the combined transport document. The main problem with Article 25, I suggest, is that too little consideration has been given to the question whether banks are wise to accept certain types of documentation at all. Non-negotiable documentation in particular affords very little security,[5] unless perhaps the bank itself is named as consignee, but no distinction is drawn in the U.C.P., for any purpose, between negotiable and non-negotiable documents.

It is in any case not altogether clear that the 1983 revision has been successful in clarifying what are the acceptable characteristics. Of the 100 or so

1. Article 19.
2. Article 23.
3. Article 24.
4. B. Wheble, *UCP 1974/1983 Revisions Compared and Explained*, I.C.C. publication No. 411 (1984), p. 46.
5. Indeed, it seems to be customary only to use non-negotiable waybills where the security of a documentary credit is not required: see, for example, section 4.6, f.n. 97.

queries which have been put to the I.C.C. Banking Commission since the 1983 revision, some 47 per cent. have concerned Articles 22–42, on documentation. A look at the *Opinions of the ICC Banking Commission 1984–1986*[6] suggests that about a quarter of all queries are on Articles 25 and 26 alone. This is probably as much due to the continued development of trade practices, as to defects in the drafting of the 1983 revision, but whatever is the true cause, no doubt we can expect further substantial change here when the U.C.P. is next revised.

Even the definition of a marine bill of lading in Article 26 has not escaped criticism. Ventris points out that[7]:

"This is a further indication that the I.C.C. is out of touch with the practices of some trades. For example, in the Articles reference is made to 'marine bills of lading', 'ocean bill of lading' or 'bill of lading covering carriage by sea' but not to 'bill of lading' alone which is the more usual document."

The U.C.P. attempts to do no more than lay down guidelines. Most of the provisions are not absolute, therefore, but take effect only "unless otherwise stipulated in the credit".

5.2 MARINE BILL OF LADING REQUIRED

Where the credit calls for a marine bill of lading, the requirements are set out in Article 26 of the U.C.P.:

"If a credit calling for a transport document stipulates as such document a marine bill of lading:

    (a) Banks will, unless otherwise stipulated in the credit, accept a document which:

        (i) appears on its face to have been issued by a named carrier, or his agent, and

        (ii) indicates that the goods have been loaded on board or shipped on a named vessel, and

        (iii) consists of the full set of originals issued to the consignor if issued in more than one original, and

        (iv) meets all other stipulations of the credit.

    (b) Subject to the above, and unless otherwise stipulated in the credit, banks will not reject a document which:

        (i) bears a title such as 'Combined transport bill of lading', 'Combined transport document', 'Combined transport bill of lading or port-to-port bill of lading', or a title or a combination of titles of similar intent and effect, and/or

        (ii) indicates some or all of the conditions of carriage by reference to a source of document other than the transport document itself (short form/blank back transport document), and/or

6. *Opinions of the ICC Banking Commission on queries relating to Uniform Customs and Practice on Documentary Credits 1984–1986*, I.C.C. publication No.434 (1987).

7. F.M. Ventris, *Bankers' Documentary Credits*, first supplement to the second edition, Lloyd's of London Press Ltd. (1985), p. 28.

> (iii) indicates a place of taking in charge different from the port of loading and/or place of final destination different from the port of discharge, and/or
>
> (iv) relates to cargoes such as those in Containers or on pallets, and the like.
>
> (c) Unless otherwise stipulated in the credit, banks will reject a document which:
>
>   (i) indicates that it is subject to a charterparty, and/or
>
>   (ii) indicates that the carrying vessel is propelled by sail only, and/or
>
>   (iii) contains the indication 'intended', or similar in qualification, in relation to
>
> the vessel and/or port of loading—unless such document bears an on board notation in accordance with Article 27(b) and also indicates the actual port of loading and/or
>
> the port of discharge—unless the place of final discharge indicated on the document is other than the port of discharge, and/or
>
>   (iv) is issued by a freight forwarder, unless it indicates that it is issued by such freight forwarder acting as a carrier, or as the agent of a named carrier."

5.2.1 Comparison between Article 26 and requirements under f.o.b. and c.i.f. contracts

5.2.1.1 Shipped bill of lading required

In many respects, the requirements under Article 26 mirror those for a clean shipped bill of lading under f.o.b. and c.i.f. sale contracts, so that usually there will be no material discrepancies between the requirements of contracts 1 and 4[8] where under a c.i.f. or f.o.b. contract, payment is by confirmed irrevocable credit to which the U.C.P. applies.

For example, Article 26(a)(ii) requires the marine bill of lading to indicate that the goods have been loaded on board or shipped on a named vessel.[9] Thus a shipped bill of lading is required, and a received for shipment bill will not do. Nor is the qualification "intended" allowed (by comparison with some parts of Article 26(c)). In this respect, therefore, the provisions of Article 26 are in line with those of c.i.f. and f.o.b. contracts.[10]

Article 27(b) is also material, in defining a shipped bill:

"Loading on board or shipment on a vessel may be evidenced either by a transport document bearing words indicating loading on board a named vessel or shipment on a named vessel, or, in the case of a transport document stating 'received for shipment' by means of a notation of loading on board on the transport document signed or initialled and dated by the carrier or his agent, and the date of this notation shall be regarded as the date of loading on board the named vessel or shipment on the named vessel."

Attention should also be drawn to Article 26(a)(i), which requires the bill of lading to have been issued on its face by a named carrier, or his agent, and 27(c)(iv), which renders unacceptable a bill of lading issued by a freight for-

---

8. See figure 1.2.

9. Notice that Article 27, discussed below, which appears to provide the contrary, does not apply where Article 26 does.

10. See section 4.4.2.

warder, unless the freight forwarder is also the carrier, or agent for a named carrier.

5.2.1.2 Claused bills of lading

The position also approximates to that in ordinary sales in that only clean bills of lading are acceptable. Article 34 provides:

"(a) A clean transport document is one which bears no superimposed clause or notation which expressly declares a defective condition of the goods and/or the packaging.

(b) Banks will refuse transport documents bearing such clauses or notations unless the credit expressly stipulates clauses or notations which may be accepted.

(c) Banks will regard a requirement in a credit for a transport document to bear the clause 'clean on board' as complied with if such transport document meets the requirements of this Article and Article 27(b)."

Paragraph (c) was added in 1983, the earlier provision[11] being otherwise identical. It had become a common practice to require bills of lading actually to bear the words "clean on board", but the I.C.C. Banking Commission took the view that "clean" is defined in Article 34(a) and "on board" in Article 27(b), and that there was no need for additional wording to be required, so long as the bill of lading complied with those provisions.

There may be a problem with Article 34(a), which defines a clean bill of lading (or other transport document) as one with no superimposed clause or notation, which declares a defective condition of the goods and/or packaging. The requirement for the clause expressly to declare a defective condition of the goods and/or the packaging is intended to prevent such "legally useless clauses (such as 'ship not responsible' when the Hague Rules apply)"[12] rendering a bill of lading unclean. Article 34(a) does not however state when the defective condition is supposed to apply.

In *The Galatia*,[13] the Court of Appeal held that a clause stating that the goods had been damaged after shipment did not render the bill of lading unclean for the purposes of tender under a c. & f. contract. In fact, the buyers had accepted the documents without prejudice to see if they would be accepted by their sub-buyers. However, when the buyers tendered the documents to the confirming bank under the sub-sale, they were rejected on the grounds that they bore a superimposed clause or notation. The commercial credit for the sub-sale was governed by the 1962 revision of the U.C.P.,

11. 1974 revision, Article 18.
12. *The problem of clean bills of lading*, I.C.C. publication No. 283 (1963, reprinted 1987), p. 4.
13. *Golodetz (M.) & Co. Inc. v. Czarnikow-Rionda Co. Inc., The Galatia* [1980] 1 W.L.R. 495; [1980] 1 All E.R. 501. See section 4.4.3.

Article 16 of which was in identical terms to Article 34(a) and (b), except that it was not divided into sub-paragraphs.[14]

The bill of lading had also been rejected earlier, by the seller's own bank, when the bill of lading was tendered by the original shippers under the f.o.b. supply contract. It follows that, if the banks were correct in rejecting on the basis of a superimposed clause declaring a defective condition of the goods, even though it related to damage after shipment, then the requirements of the U.C.P. are out of line with those of a c.i.f. contract.

Whether the banks were in fact entitled to reject was not decided in *The Galatia*, nor even considered in the Court of Appeal. At first instance, however, Donaldson J. (as he then was, and whose decision the Court of Appeal upheld) thought that in an action by seller against buyer under the sale contract, the provisions of the U.C.P. were irrelevant[15]:

> "Counsel for the buyers submits that there are two possible tests to be applied, the practical and the legal. The practical test is whether a bill of lading in this form is acceptable to banks generally as being a 'clean' bill of lading. Since 1962, virtually all banks have accepted the international rules set out in a document issued by the International Chambers of Commerce entitled Uniform Customs and Practice for Documentary Credits ('U.C.P. rules'). Rule 16[16] provides as follows:
>
>> 'A clean transport document is one which bears no superimposed clause or notation which expressly declares a defective condition of the goods and/or the packaging. Banks will refuse transport documents bearing such clauses or notations unless the credit expressly stipulates clauses or notations which may be accepted.'
>
> This definition fails to specify the time with respect to which the notation speaks. The bill of lading and any notations speak *at* the date of issue, but they may speak *about* a state of affairs which then exists or about an earlier state of affairs or both. If the rule refers to notations about the state of affairs at the time of the issue of the bill of lading or, indeed, at any other time after shipment of the 200 tonnes [damaged by fire after loading] was completed, the bill of lading is not 'clean' within the meaning of that word in the rule for the notation clearly draws attention to the cargo being damaged. If, however, it refers to notations about the state of affairs on completion of shipment, the bill of lading is equally clearly clean for it shows that the goods were in apparent good order and condition on shipment and suggests only that they were damaged after shipment . . .
>
> There is, I think, more than one answer to this 'practical test' objection. First, the contract called for cash against documents, which no doubt assumes a documentary credit. But the board has not found that it was a custom of the trade, and the contract does not provide, that the documents shall be such as to satisfy the U.C.P. rules as to 'clean' bills of lading, which rules do not have the force of law. Furthermore, if there is ambiguity as to the meaning of those rules, that ambiguity should if possible be resolved in a way which will result in the rules reflecting the position under general

---

14. The sub-buyers had another reason for wishing to reject the documents: they had not insured the goods as they were required to do under the c. & f. sub-sale contract. The facts are stated more fully in the decision at first instance: [1979] 2 All E.R. 726; [1979] 2 Lloyd's Rep. 450, on this point at [1979] 2 All E.R. 726, 736–737.
15. [1979] 2 All E.R. 726, 737–738.
16. 1962 revision.

maritime and commercial law. So construed they add nothing to the legal test which I consider hereafter.

Second, the evidence does not disclose that banks generally would reject such a bill of lading as that relating to the 200 tonnes as not being a 'clean' bill of lading or that, if they would do so, it would be for any better reason than that they were applying what they thought the U.C.P. rules required.

Third, I am not satisfied that it is right to apply a practical test, other than that in the context of merchantability of the documents to which I will return hereafter. What is really being said here is that the very fact that the buyers and two banks rejected these documents proves that they are not 'clean'. This is a proposition which I decline to accept."

Donaldson J. then went on to apply what he called "the legal test", which was that upheld by the Court of Appeal[17]: the bill of lading was clean because the superimposed clause did not qualify the statement that the goods when loaded were in apparent good order and condition.

It is surprising and unfortunate that the difficulty in *The Galatia* has not been resolved by subsequent revisions to the U.C.P. Clearly Donaldson J. was prepared to envisage that the requirements of the sale contract may differ from the requirements of the banking community: in effect, he said that since the contract of sale made no mention of the U.C.P., and since the U.C.P. does not have the force of law, if commercial practice conflicted with the U.C.P. rules, then on an interpretation of the sale contract commercial practice, rather than the U.C.P., should prevail.

Suppose that the sale contract had required payment by a commercial credit to which the U.C.P. applied. It should perhaps be re-emphasised that it follows from the autonomy of the four contracts constituting the credit,[18] that in an action by seller against buyer, only the terms of the sale contract (contract 1 in figure 1.2) are relevant. The fact that the credit is issued on U.C.P. terms should not affect interpretation of the sale contract. It would be different, of course, had the action been against one of the banks (e.g., an action on contract 4). Even so, if the U.C.P. was mentioned in the sale contract, then arguably the terms of the sale contract might be interpreted to conform with the provisions of Article 34 (of the 1983 revision), but equally arguably, a definition of clean bill of lading which took into account the condition of the goods after loading might be held to be repugnant to a contract on c.i.f., or c. & f. terms.

It is impossible to state with certainty whether the banks were indeed entitled to reject the bill of lading in *The Galatia*. From the above passage, however, it is clear that Donaldson J. thought the U.C.P. provision ambiguous, and also that in the event of ambiguity, the ambiguity should be resolved in favour of the rules being interpreted to reflect the general maritime and commercial law. This seems correct in principle. If so, Article 34 ought to be interpreted so that "clause or notation" means a clause or notation qualifying

17. See section 4.4.3.
18. See section 1.6.1.

the statement that the goods were loaded in apparent good order and condition. In that case, the U.C.P. terms would coincide with the requirements under an ordinary sale contract.

Nevertheless, the position is not clear, and one would hope that a future revision of the U.C.P. might resolve the issue.

5.2.1.3 Charterparty bill not acceptable

In some respects, the U.C.P. provisions are more stringent than the common law on sale. Article 26(c)(i) provides that bills of lading which are subject to the terms of a charterparty will be rejected unless expressly authorised by stipulation in the credit. By contrast, the position under a c.i.f. contract is that a charterparty bill of lading must be accepted, even if the charterparty is not tendered, at any rate if it is on an unamended standard form commonly used in the trade.[19] In reality, this means that charterparty bills always have to be accepted, since unless the charterparty is tendered the buyer will not know whether the charterparty is on a form commonly used in the trade, and therefore whether or not he is entitled to reject it!

One can see why banks may require greater protection than buyers, however. There is no reason why a bank should be aware of the terms of even commonly used charterparties, however, nor will it necessarily know which charterparties are used for particular trades. In any event, it is rare that a standard form charterparty is used without amendment, and the bank will certainly be unaware of the terms of any amendment. Naturally the bank does not wish its security to be affected by the terms of a document to which it has no access, and of whose terms it is unlikely to be aware. The stipulation in Article 26 is relatively easy to justify, therefore.

Nonetheless, Article 26(c)(i) is not without its problems. Charterparty bills are extremely common. Ventris notes[20]:

"In view of other startling innovations made in the 1983 Revision it is disappointing to find that the rules still make the acceptance of a charter-party bill of lading subject to the credit including its specific acceptance. Today, more and more products are shipped in bulk which means that, unless the cargo is carried in the owner's own vessel, it is carried in a chartered vessel. Having regard to the modifications made in order to accommodate container traffic[21] there seems no valid reason to continue this ban on charter-party bills of lading . . . "

A second problem is that if the requirements of the credit do not match those of the sale contract, rejection by the bank of a charterparty bill could place the buyer in breach of the contract of sale. It is important, therefore, for buyers either to protect themselves by an express stipulation in the sale con-

19. See section 4.4.6.
20. F.M. Ventris, *Bankers' Documentary Credits* (first supplement to the second edition, Lloyd's of London Press Ltd. (1985)), p. 27.
21. He is referring here to Article 25, below, section 5.3.

tract, or to request the bank to stipulate in the credit that charterparty bills will be accepted.

5.2.1.4 Full set of originals required

Another respect in which the U.C.P. provisions are more stringent than the common law on sale may be found from Article 26(a)(iii). This requires tender of the full set of originals issued to the consignor, if issued in more than one original. By contrast, under a c.i.f. sale contract, tender of one original of the set is sufficient unless the contract expressly stipulates otherwise.[22] It has long been customary for banks to demand the entire set, as a precaution against fraud, and this provision clearly makes sense. Nevertheless, buyers should make equivalent provision in the sale contract, or risk being in breach if the bank rejects tender of less than the full set.

Note also that the provision requires tender only of the full set of originals issued to the consignor. Sometimes the carrier retains an original and carries it on board, the consignor negotiating only the other two. Presumably under the present provision the bank will accept tender of the two negotiated in these circumstances.[23] This practice is by no means desirable, however, at any rate for the banking community (although it carries clear benefits for carriers, who no longer need to wait for the bill of lading to catch up with the vessel), and maybe the I.C.C. Banking Commission could be persuaded to consider this issue.

The definition of an original document is contained in Article 22(c):

"Unless otherwise stipulated in the credit, banks will accept as originals documents produced or appearing to have been produced:
    (i) by reprographic means;
    (ii) by, or as the result of, automated or computerized systems;
    (iii) as carbon copies;
if marked as originals, always provided that where necessary, such documents appear to have been authenticated."

This provision, which was added for the first time in 1983, does not allow photocopies, or telefaxed or carbon copies, of original documents to be tendered, but allows original documents to be produced in this way, so long as they are indeed marked as original documents and authenticated as such. Where bills of lading are issued in sets of three, one is usually a typed original and the others carbon copies, although all will be signed and marked "Original", so this provision caters for trade practice.

The Chairman of the I.C.C. Banking Commission states that[24]:

" 'Authentication' has been defined as 'marking a message in a physical, electronic or

---

22. Section 4.4.5.
23. Or are all three technically issued to the consignor?
24. B. Wheble, *UCP 1974/1983 Revisions Compared and Explained*, I.C.C. publication No. 411 (1984), p. 41.

any other manner which permits the receiver to assure himself that the message comes from the source indicated', as against the more limited definition of 'signature' as 'a person's name or initials or mark used in signing'."

At first sight, therefore, it would seem that a bill of lading need not be signed, but this provision is qualified by Article 27(b) (set out above), which requires shipment to be evidenced by "notation . . . signed or initialled and dated by the carrier or his agent". Thus where a shipped bill of lading is required, some form of handwritten notation is also required as evidence of shipment, so that, for example, a signature plate will not do. It has been pointed out that this can cause problems for liner shipments, where there may be up to 2,000 consignments aboard a single vessel, and therefore up to 2,000 different bills of lading. A group of experts, in written comments to the I.C.C. secretariat, was unable to suggest an immediate solution.[25]

5.2.1.5 Through bills of lading

It has been explained that through bills of lading can be good tender c.i.f. so long as they are either expressly stipulated in the contract, or customary in the trade, and provide coverage for the entire voyage.[26] The U.C.P. also provides, subject to the express terms of the credit, for tender of through bills of lading, so long as the entire voyage is covered by one bill of lading, in Article 29:

"(a) For the purpose of this Article transhipment means a transfer and reloading during the course of carriage from the port of loading or place of dispatch or taking in charge to the port of discharge or place of destination either from one conveyance or vessel to another conveyance or vessel within the same mode of transport or from one mode of transport to another mode of transport.

(b) Unless transhipment is prohibited by the terms of the credit, banks will accept transport documents which indicate that the goods will be transhipped, provided that the entire carriage is covered by one and the same transport document.

(c) Even if transhipment is prohibited by the terms of the credit, banks will accept transport documents which:

(i) incorporate printed clauses stating that the carrier has the right to tranship . . ."

Articles 29(c)(ii)–(iv), which were added in 1983, are directed primarily towards combined transport documents, and are considered below.[27] Article 29(c)(i) is necessary because nearly all bills of lading give the carrier a liberty to tranship, whether or not transhipment actually takes place.

---

25. *Opinions of the ICC Banking Commission on queries relating to Uniform Customs and Practice on Documentary Credits 1984–1986*, I.C.C. publication No. 434 (1987), pp. 27–28.
26. Section 4.4.7.
27. Section 5.3.1.4.

5.2.1.6 Sailing vessels

Under Article 26(c)(ii), a bill of lading indicating that the carrying vessel is propelled by sail only will normally be rejected. The 1974 revision covered all "shipment by sailing vessels".

This provision is aimed at what might loosely be called old-fashioned sailing vessels, of the type that were in use before the advent of steam. It is not intended to be directed at modern vessels, even if sail assisted. The reason for the change of drafting in 1983, and particularly the addition of the word "only", was because of the introduction of wind assistance to some modern powered vessels, for fuel economy reasons.[28] Clearly a bill of lading should not be rejected simply because an otherwise modern vessel was wind-assisted. Ventris points out, however, that most sailing vessels that take to the high seas are equipped with auxiliary motors,[29] so that the introduction of the word "only" may deprive the provision of all practical effect. Perhaps a suitable amendment to Article 26(c)(ii) would be something like: "indicates that the carrying vessel uses sail as its primary means of propulsion."

5.2.1.7 Short form and combined transport bills of lading

The purpose of Article 26(b)(i) is to cater for bills of lading which may be used either for port-to-port or for combined transport operations. Article 26(b)(ii) caters for short form bills of lading. Article 26(b)(iii) would cater for a combined transport operation where the credit nevertheless calls for a shipped bill of lading. The places of taking in charge and final destination could be, for example, inland container depots, far removed from the ports of loading and discharge. The meaning of Article 26(b)(iv) is obvious.

5.2.1.8 Deck cargo

Article 28 of the U.C.P. provides:

"(a) In the case of carriage by sea or by more than one mode of transport but including carriage by sea, banks will refuse a transport document stating that the goods are or will be loaded on deck, unless specifically authorised in the credit.

(b) Banks will not refuse a transport document which contains a provision that the goods may be carried on deck, provided it does not specifically state that they are or will be loaded on deck."

The risk of damage to deck cargo, especially from weather and heavy seas, is obviously increased, and "cargo which by the contract of carriage is stated as being carried on deck and is so carried" falls outside both the Hague and

---

28. B. Wheble, *UCP 1974/1983 Revisions Compared and Explained*, I.C.C. Publication No. 411 (1984), p. 49.

29. F.M. Ventris, *Bankers' Documentary Credits* (first supplement to the second edition, Lloyd's of London Press Ltd. (1985)), p. 28.

Hague-Visby Rules.[30] Containers are often carried on deck, of course, in which case specific authorisation would need to be made in the credit.

5.2.1.9 Payment of freight

There can be no uniform rules about freight prepaid and freight collect bills, since sale contracts are not themselves uniform. For example, the buyer is responsible for payment of freight f.o.b., whereas it is the seller c.i.f. and c. & f., and f.o.b. with additional duties. Article 31 accordingly provides:

"(a) Unless otherwise stipulated in the credit, or inconsistent with any of the documents presented under the credit, banks will accept transport documents stating that freight or transportation charges (hereinafter referred to as 'freight') have still to be paid.

(b) If a credit stipulates that the transport document has to indicate that freight has been paid or prepaid, banks will accept a transport document on which words clearly indicating payment or prepayment of freight appear by stamp or otherwise, or on which payment of freight is indicated by other means.

(c) The words 'freight prepayable' or 'freight to be prepaid' or words of similar effect, if appearing on transport documents, will not be accepted as constituting evidence of the payment of freight.

(d) Banks will accept transport documents bearing reference by stamp or otherwise to costs additional to the freight charges, such as costs of, or disbursements incurred in connection with loading, unloading, or similar operations, unless the conditions of the credit specifically prohibit such reference."

5.2.1.10 Statements of shipper

Article 32 provides: "Unless otherwise stipulated in the credit banks will accept transport documents which bear a clause on the face thereof such as 'shippers load and count' or 'said by shipper to contain' or words of similar effect." This provision is self-explanatory.

5.3 OTHER TRANSPORT DOCUMENTS APART FROM MARINE BILLS OF LADING

5.3.1 General requirements of the U.C.P.

Where the credit calls for any transport document, which seems to mean simply any document relating to transport, as opposed to (for example) insurance, apart from the traditional bill of lading, the general requirements are set out in Article 25:

"Unless a credit calling for a transport document stipulates as such document a marine bill of lading (ocean bill of lading or a bill covering carriage by sea), or a post receipt or certificate of posting:

---

30. Article 1(c).

(a) Banks will, unless otherwise stipulated in the credit, accept a transport document which:

    (i) appears on its face to have been issued by a named carrier, or his agent, and

    (ii) indicates dispatch or taking in charge of the goods, or loading on board, as the case may be, and

    (iii) consists of the full set of originals issued to the consignor if issued in more than one original, and

    (iv) meets all the other stipulations of the credit.

(b) Subject to the above, and unless otherwise stipulated in the credit, banks will not reject a transport document which:

    (i) bears a title such as 'Combined transport bill of lading', 'Combined transport document', 'Combined transport bill of lading or port-to-port bill of lading', or a title or a combination of titles of similar intent and effect, and/or

    (ii) indicates some or all of the conditions of carriage by reference to a source of document other than the transport document itself (short form/blank back transport document), and/or

    (iii) indicates a place of taking in charge different from the port of loading and/or place of final destination different from the port of discharge, and/or

    (iv) relates to cargoes such as those in Containers or on pallets, and the like, and/or

    (v) contains the indication 'intended', or similar in qualification, in relation to the vessel or other means of transport, and/or port of loading and/or the port of discharge.

(c) Unless otherwise stipulated in the credit in the case of carriage by sea or by more than one mode of transport but including carriage by sea, banks will reject a document which:

    (i) indicates that it is subject to a charterparty, and/or

    (ii) indicates that the carrying vessel is propelled by sail only.

(d) Unless otherwise stipulated in the credit, banks will reject a transport document issued by a freight forwarder unless it is the FIATA Combined Transport Bill of Lading approved by the International Chamber of Commerce or otherwise indicates that it is issued by a freight forwarder acting as carrier or agent of a named carrier."

It is obvious that this provision is best suited to combined transport documents.

It is not limited to combined transport documents, however, and is equally applicable to, for example, non-negotiable waybills. The new Article 25 replaces both Articles 23 and 24 of the 1974 revision. Article 23 covered specifically combined transport documents. Article 24, however, was as follows:

"Banks will consider a Railway or Inland Waterway Bill of Lading or Consignment Note, Counterfoil Waybill, Postal Receipt, Certificate of Mailing, Air Mail Receipt, Air Waybill, Air Consignment Note or Air Receipt, Trucking Company Bill of Lading or any similar document as regular when such document bears the reception stamp of the carrier or his agent."

Article 24 has disappeared in its entirety, and it must therefore be assumed that the new Article 25 is intended to cover, in addition to combined transport documents, all those documents which were previously covered by Article 24, except for postal receipts and certificates of posting, which are expressly excluded by the new Article 25.

Postal receipts and certificates of posting (if the credit calls for them) are however covered by Article 30:

"If the credit stipulates dispatch of goods by post and calls for a postal receipt or certificate of posting, banks will accept such post receipt or certificate of posting if it appears to have been stamped or otherwise authenticated and dated in the place from which the credit stipulates the goods are to be dispatched."

Ventris comments[31]: "One may wonder why the I.C.C. included in the 'credit' system goods sent by post as the applicant for the 'credit' has no means of assuring himself, as far as he can, that that which has been dispatched is in accordance with his order." Although Article 30 is not entirely new, and is at least to some extent consequential on the removal of the old Article 24, Ventris clearly has a point. If there is one criticism to be made of the 1983 revision, it is that there is nothing in Articles 25 or 30 which addresses the question how far the banking community should embrace changes in documentation imposed upon it from outside. As was explained in Chapter 4, any non-negotiable document provides little if any security for the bank, and ideally (I would suggest) a document of title should be required. The 1983 revisions, while containing certain minimum requirements, do not address at all these issues which (I would suggest) are fundamental.

5.3.1.1 Provisions which mirror those of Article 26

It is clear that the provisions of Article 25(c)(i)–(ii) are identical with Article 26(c)(i)–(ii), at any rate where part of the carriage is by sea, and have therefore already been considered in the previous discussion.[32] Also, Article 25(b)(i)–(iv) is identical with Article 26(b)(i)–(iv).[33] Articles 28, 31, 32 and 34[34] apply in identical fashion whether the transport document is a marine bill of lading or not.

Although the broad structure of Article 25 is similar to Article 26, however, in detail it is different in a number of fundamental respects, which mirror the essential differences between bills of lading and combined transport documents.

5.3.1.2 Received for shipment transport document

Article 25(a)(ii) requires the document only to evidence the dispatch or taking in charge of the goods by the carrier, and unlike Article 26 does not require evidence of actual shipment. This provision should also be considered along with Article 27(a), which reverses the pre-1983 rule in allowing for received for shipment transport documents:

---

31. F.M. Ventris, *Bankers' Documentary Credits* (first supplement to the second edition, Lloyd's of London Press Ltd. (1985)), p. 31.
32. Sections 5.2.1.3 and 5.2.1.6.
33. Section 5.2.1.7.
34. Sections 5.2.1.8., 5.2.1.9, 5.2.1.10 and 5.2.1.2, respectively.

"Unless a credit specifically calls for an on board transport document, or unless inconsistent with other stipulation(s) in the credit or with Article 26, banks will accept a transport document which indicates that goods have been taken in charge or received for shipment."

Article 27(a) is subject to the express terms of the credit, and does not apply where it is inconsistent with Article 26.[35] In other words, it applies only where a "marine bill of lading" is not called for. The traditional bill of lading must be a shipped bill. Buyers c.i.f. will presumably continue to call for "marine bills of lading" under Article 26, as will buyers f.o.b. where the seller is under an obligation to ship.

The reason for the significant change made by Article 27 is that it is almost certain that some documents will be issued before shipment. A combined transport document, for example, is usually issued by a freight forwarder at an inland freight terminal.[36] The reason is explained by the I.C.C. Banking Commission as follows[37]:

"Except in the case of a port-to-port shipment under a marine bill of lading, the majority of transport documents will indicate that cargo has been accepted for transport from 'a place of final destination'. Also, and especially in the case of combined transport, insistence on an 'on board' document is likely to hold back the document, thereby postponing the time when the beneficiary can present documents in order to secure payment, and delaying delivery of the goods at destination (with the possibility of costly demurrage) because the goods arrive before the documents."

Notice that the terminology requirement in Article 27 may not permit the wording used in *Ishag* v. *Allied Bank International*,[38] where is was stated that the goods were "at the disposal of" the carrier's agents "intended to be shipped . . . with M.S. *Lycaon* from Bremen to Douala". The document in *Ishag* would also appear to fall foul of Article 25(b)(v).

5.3.1.3 Documents issued by freight forwarders

Whereas a marine bill of lading must be issued by a carrier or his agent,[39] a combined transport document may well be issued by a freight forwarder acting as principal. This is provided for by Article 25(d), at any rate where the I.C.C. approved FIATA Combined Transport Bill of Lading (or FIATA FBL) is used. In the United Kingdom, authority to use the FIATA FBL is granted by the Institute of Freight Forwarders, acting for FIATA. Only those who satisfy stringent requirements as to financial standing, professional capacity, competence of staff and good repute are authorised, and they must

---

35. Ventris appears to have misunderstood this point: F.M. Ventris, *Bankers' Documentary Credits*, (first supplement to the second edition, Lloyd's of London Press Ltd. (1985)), p. 29.
36. See section 4.5.
37. B. Wheble, *UCP 1974/1983 Revisions Compared and Explained*, I.C.C. publication No. 411 (1984), p. 51.
38. Section 4.3.3.
39. Section 5.2.1.1.

also provide evidence that they are adequately covered for potential liability, usually by insurance.[40]

5.3.1.4 Transhipment

Article 29[41] applies equally where a marine bill of lading is not required, and of course transhipment is almost of the essence in combined transport operations. Article 29(c) was accordingly somewhat elaborated in the 1983 revision specifically to cover combined transport, given that unlike the position with the usual through bill of lading, transhipment may not necessarily take place from one vessel to another at sea, but may equally be from land to sea or vice-versa:

"Even if transhipment is prohibited by the terms of the credit, banks will accept transport documents which:
  (i) incorporate printed clauses stating that the carrier has the right to tranship, or
  (ii) state or indicate that transhipment will or may take place, when the credit stipulates a combined transport document, or indicates carriage from a place of taking in charge to a place of final destination by different modes of transport including a carriage by sea, provided that the entire carriage is covered by the same transport document, or
  (iii) state or indicate that the goods are in a Container(s), trailer(s), 'LASH' barge(s), and the like and will be carried from the place of taking in charge to the place of final destination in the same Container(s), trailer(s), 'LASH' barge(s), and the like under one and the same transport document;
  (iv) state or indicate the place of receipt and/or of final destination as 'C.F.S.' (container freight station) or C.Y. (container yard) at, or associated with, the port of loading and/or the port of destination."

5.3.1.5 Full set of originals issued to consignor

Article 25, like Article 26, requires tender of the full set of originals issued to the consignor, and the definition of original document in Article 22(c) also applies.[42] The application is slightly different here, however, especially for air waybills, where usually only one of the three originals is issued to the consignor. Obviously in such a case (always assuming that a bank is wise to accept an air waybill at all), it would be absurd to require tender of the entire set, so that only the full set of originals issued to the consignor is required.

5.4 GENERAL PROVISIONS ON DOCUMENTATION

5.4.1 Chain sales afloat, and back-to-back credits: Articles 33 and 24

Where bills of lading are used in chain sales of goods afloat, then except in the case of the first sale, the beneficiary under the credit will not be the consignor

40. See further B. Wheble, *UCP 1974/1983 Revisions Compared and Explained*, I.C.C. publication No. 411 (1984), p. 49.
  41. Section 5.2.1.5.
  42. Section 5.2.1.4.

of the goods. The same applies to back-to-back credits,[43] where the consignor is likely to be the beneficiary under the main credit, but the applicant for the credit under the second credit (which will finance the purchase of goods from the manufacturer or supplier). However, Article 21 of the 1962 U.C.P.[44] stated: "Banks may require the name of the beneficiary to appear on the bill of lading as shipper or endorser, unless the terms of the credit require otherwise." This Article was not reproduced in the 1974 revision, but nor was any provision made to the contrary, i.e., for credits to be acceptable where the beneficiary was not shipper or endorser. This created confusion, and in order to clarify the position, the present Article 33 was added in 1983: "Unless otherwise stipulated in the credit, banks will accept transport documents indication as the consignor of the goods a party other than the beneficiary of the credit." Article 24, which like 33 was added for the first time in 1983, also caters for chain sales: "Unless otherwise stipulated in the credit, banks will accept a document bearing a date of issuance prior to that of the credit, subject to such document being presented within the time limits set out in the credit and in these articles." Where cargo is purchased afloat, the bill of lading may well have been issued before the eventual buyer's credit is opened.

5.4.2 Other documents

The credit may call for documents which are not covered by Articles 25 or 26. Examples may be delivery orders,[45] certificates of quality,[46] etc. These are catered for by Article 23:

"When documents other than transport documents, insurance documents and commercial invoices are called for, the credit should stipulate by whom such documents are to be issued and their wording or data content. If the credit does not so stipulate, banks will accept such documents as presented, provided that their data content makes it possible to relate the goods and/or services referred to therein to those referred to, in the commercial invoice(s) presented, or to those referred to in the credit if the credit does not stipulate presentation of a commercial invoice."

This Article represents a considerable change from its predecessor, Article 33 of the 1974 revision. Article 33 spelt out a list of named documents (warehouse receipts, delivery orders, consular certificates, certificates of origin, of weight, of quality or of analysis, etc.), and provided that when no further definition is given, banks would accept such documents as tendered. The new Article 23 covers all documents other than transport documents, whether or not contained within the old list, but qualifies the circumstances in which they will be accepted.

The main reason for no longer limiting the documents to a specified list is that while the list may well suffice for the conventional documentary credit,

---

43. See section 2.3.5.
44. Based on a similar provision in the 1951 revision.
45. Section 4.4.8.
46. Section 4.4.11.

since 1983 the U.C.P. has also applied to standby letters of credit. The documentation for a conventional letter of credit will not usually be appropriate to a standby letter of credit,[47] so it became necessary to stipulate generally for all "documents other than transport documents".

The other major change, by contrast with the 1974, the spelling out of the conditions under which the banks will accept such documents, was probably made in response to the Court of Appeal decision in *Banque de l'Indochine et de Suez S.A.* v. *J.H. Rayner (Mincing Lane) Ltd.*[48] This case is best dealt with under the doctrine of strict compliance: see further Chapter 6.[49]

For completeness, reference ought also to be made to Article 42:

"If a credit calls for an attestation or certification of weight in the case of transport other than by sea, banks will accept a weight stamp or declaration of weight which appears to have been superimposed on the transport document by the carrier or by his agent unless the credit specifically stipulates that the attestation or certification of weight must be by a separate document."

5.5 INSURANCE REQUIREMENTS

Insurance documents are dealt with in section d.2 of the U.C.P., in Articles 35–40. Article 35 provides:

"(a) Insurance documents must be as stipulated in the credit, and must be issued and/or signed by insurance companies or underwriters or their agents.

(b) Cover notes issued by brokers will not be accepted, unless specifically authorized by the credit."

At common law, in the absence of express stipulation, a certificate of insurance is not good tender c.i.f., the buyer being entitled to require the policy, or at the very least a certificate which shows on its face the terms and conditions of the insurance policy.[50] It is probable that a brokers' cover note can never be good tender c.i.f. Under paragraph (b), cover notes may be specifically authorised by the credit, but this would only be appropriate if the sale contract was not on c.i.f. terms. If under paragraph (a) a certificate alone is specified, appropriate amendments should be made to the sale contract, if on c.i.f. terms.

Details of the extent of cover are set out in Articles 36–38:

Article 36:

"Unless otherwise stipulated in the credit, or unless it appears from the insurance document(s) that the cover is effective at the latest from the date of loading on board

47. See section 8.2.
48. [1983] 1 All E.R. 1137; [1983] 1 Lloyd's Rep. 228, on appeal from [1983] 1 All E.R. 468; [1982] 2 Lloyd's Rep. 476. It should also be borne in mind that if the instructions given to a bank are ambiguous, then as between the bank and its customer the bank can rely on any reasonable interpretation, any ambiguity being resolved in its favour: see further, section 6.3.2.2.
49. Section 6.3.4.
50. Section 4.4.10.3.

or taking in charge of the goods, banks will refuse documents which bear a date later than the date of loading on board or dispatch or taking in charge of the goods as indicated by the transport document(s)."

Article 37:

"(a) Unless otherwise stipulated in the credit, the insurance document must be expressed in the same currency as the credit.

(b) Unless otherwise stipulated in the credit, the minimum amount for which the insurance document must indicate the insurance cover to have been effected is the CIF (cost, insurance and freight . . . named port of destination') or CIP (freight/carriage and insurance paid to 'named port of destination') value of the goods, as the case may be, plus 10%. However, if banks cannot determine the CIF or CIP value, as the case may be, from the documents on their face, they will accept as such minimum amount the amount for which payment, acceptance or negotiation is requested under the credit, or the amount of the commercial invoice whichever is the greater."

Article 38:

"(a) Credits should stipulate the type of insurance required and, if any, the additional risks which are to be covered. Imprecise terms such as 'usual risks' or 'customary risks' should not be used; if they are used, banks will accept insurance documents as presented, without responsibility for any risks not being covered.

(b) Failing specific instructions, banks will accept insurance cover as tendered."

Article 38 places the responsibility very clearly on the applicant to give complete and precise instructions, in the absence of which he takes the risk that the banks will accept whatever documents are tendered, assuming (presumably) they conform with Article 35. But this is hardly satisfactory for the banks, who might also be interested in the minimum risks covered. This is another case, like Articles 25 and 30, where the U.C.P. appears to ignore the minimum requirement banks may require for their own security.

The position ties in with that for c.i.f. contracts to the extent that, if war risks cover is required, there must be an express stipulation to that effect.[51] There is also no suggestion in Articles 36–38 that less cover will be accepted than the general common law requirement, that is to say the minimum cover that is usual in the trade.

Articles 39 and 40 are detailed documentary requirements:

Article 39:

"Where a credit stipulates 'insurance against all risks', banks will accept an insurance document which contains any 'all risks' notation or clause, whether or not bearing the heading 'all risks', even if indicating that certain risks are excluded, without responsibility for any risk(s) not being covered."

Article 40:

"Banks will accept an insurance document which indicates that the cover is subject to a franchise or an excess (deductible), unless it is specifically stipulated in the credit that the insurance must be issued irrespective of percentage."

The explanation for the drafting of Article 39, which was amended slightly

---

51. Section 4.4.10.2.

in 1983, is that in 1982 Lloyd's and the Institute of London Underwriters altered their policy, such that the "all risks" clause is now headed "clause A", and like all "all risks" clauses, does indeed exclude certain risks.[52]

5.6 COMMERCIAL INVOICE

The U.C.P. provisions on the Commercial Invoice are more detailed than the common law requirements,[53] and are contained in Article 41:

"(a) Unless otherwise stipulated in the credit, commercial invoices must be made out in the name of the applicant for the credit.

(b) Unless otherwise stipulated in the credit, banks may refuse commercial invoices issued for amounts in excess of the amount permitted by the credit. Nevertheless, if a bank authorized to pay, incur a deferred payment undertaking, accept, or negotiate under a credit accepts such invoices, its decision will be binding on all parties, provided such bank has not paid, incurred a deferred undertaking, accepted or effected negotiation for an amount in excess of that permitted by the credit.

(c) The description of the goods in the commercial invoice must correspond with the description in the credit. In all other documents, the goods may be described in general terms not inconsistent with the description of the goods in the credit."

Article 41(c) is perhaps the most important provision. The invoice must correspond precisely with the requirements of the credit, whereas there is some relaxation for other documents. The question of compliance of documents is dealt with in detail in Chapter 6.[54]

5.7 ELECTRONIC DATA INTERCHANGE

Discussion so far has centred around the bankers' documentary credit, which obviously assumes the existence of documents. With present-day technology, however, there are many advantages, in both speed and cost, in moving over to a system of paperless electronic trading as far as possible[55]:

"It is widely expected that the impact of computerization will be as great as that of the industrial revolution. Computers are already providing all sorts of services at rising speed and diminishing costs. International trade data communication, however, seems to be the missing link. Yet the need is great. Not only do paper documentation and procedures represent as much as 10 per cent of goods value; they are slow, insecure, complicated and growing. The possibilities of cost reduction are in the order of 50 per cent, to the benefit of not only the main parties, but everyone involved, not least the authorities."

Although this passage places the greatest emphasis on cost savings, the

---

52. B. Wheble, *UCP 1974/1983 Revisions Compared and Explained*, I.C.C. Publication No. 411 (1984), p. 63.
53. Section 4.4.9.
54. Section 6.3.3.
55. *U.N.C.I.D. Uniform Rules of conduct for interchange of trade data by tele-transmission*, I.C.C. publication No. 452 (1988), p. 7.

speed advantages also should not be forgotten. The main reason why new forms of documentation, which are not necessarily in the interests of the banking community, have been forced upon it, are precisely because the present documentary processes are too slow, so that the vessel arrives before the shipping documents catch up. It may be that E.D.I. can resolve that problem also, if we project sufficiently far into the future.

5.7.1 Electronic transfer of messages

In fact, much of the work of documentary credits is paperless already, for example the issuance and amendment of credits, and the transfer of funds. This is already provided for by Article 12 of the U.C.P.:

"(a) When an issuing bank instructs a bank (advising bank) by any teletransmission to advise a credit or an amendment to a credit and intends the mail confirmation to be the operative credit instrument or the operative amendment, the teletransmission must state 'full details to follow' (or words of similar effect), or that the mail confirmation will be the operative instrument or the operative amendment. The issuing bank must forward the operative credit instrument or the operative amendment to such advising bank without delay.

(b) The teletransmission will be deemed to be the operative credit instrument or the operative amendment, and no mail confirmation should be sent, unless the teletransmission states 'full details to follow' (or words of similar effect), or that the mail confirmation is to be the operative instrument or the operative amendment.

(c) A teletransmission intended by the issuing bank to be the operative credit instrument should clearly indicate that the credit is issued subject to Uniform Customs and Practice for Documentary Credits, 1983 Revision, I.C.C. Publication No. 400.

(d) If a bank uses the services of another bank or banks (the advising bank) to have the credit advised to the beneficiary, it must also use the services of the same bank(s) for advising any amendments.

(e) Banks shall be responsible for any consequences arising from their failure to follow the procedures set out in the preceding paragraphs."

The view of the I.C.C. Banking Commission is that teletransmission includes telegrams, telexes and telefaxes, but not telephone conversations.[56]

Notice that article 12(c) requires wording similar to that required by Article 1 for paper documentation, if the U.C.P. is to be incorporated. As was explained in Chapter 2,[57] inter-bank electronic messages sent by S.W.I.F.T. (the Society for Worldwide Interbank Financial Telecommunications), do not state, in the manner required by Article 1, that the credit is subject to the U.C.P., but the phrase: "unless specifically stated, the Documentary Credit is issued subject to Uniform Customs and Practice for Documentary Credits, International Chamber of Commerce, Paris, France, which are in effect on the date of issue" is incorporated into the user handbook. S.W.I.F.T.'s view is that usage of the S.W.I.F.T. network by a user

---

56. *Opinions of the ICC Banking Commission on queries relating to Uniform Customs and Practice on Documentary Credits 1984–1986*, I.C.C. publication No. 434 (1987), p. 19. Note that the word "teletransmission" replaces "cable, telegram or telex" in the 1974 revision.

57. Section 2.1.2.

raises the implication that the user is adopting the standards set out in the handbook. The I.C.C. Banking Commission took the view that this was correct, but of course, no such assumptions can be made as between an issuing or advising bank and a beneficiary, or someone else outside the S.W.I.F.T. system. Communications with beneficiaries should therefore expressly incorporate the U.C.P., using the wording required by Article 1, even though there will be no such express incorporation in the S.W.I.F.T. communication between banks. It is also necessary expressly to incorporate the U.C.P. when dealing with banks outside the S.W.I.F.T. system, especially in the Middle East.[58]

Where electronic means are used, banks are protected from the consequences of error by Article 18:

"Banks assume no liability or responsibility for the consequences arising out of delay and/or loss in transit of any messages, letters or documents, or for delay, mutilation or other errors arising in the transmission of any telecommunication. Banks assume no liability or responsibility for errors in translation or interpretation of technical terms, and reserve the right to transmit credit terms without translating them."

It is perhaps unfortunate that whereas Article 12 refers to "teletransmission", Article 18 refers to "telecommunications". Presumably both mean the same.[59] There would be a good argument, in a future amendment to the U.C.P., for using the same term throughout.

5.7.2 Shipping documents in electronic form[60]

Although messages are often sent electronically, however, at present the shipping documents themselves are nearly always of a documentary form. This is not to say that electronic data interchange (E.D.I.) is unknown in sea trading. A three month trial scheme was operated as a result of the D.I.S.H. project (Data Interchange for Shipping), set up in 1985 by P. & O. Containers Ltd. and a number of other large carriers and exporters. P. & O. say that[61]: "As well as reducing paper work, other benefits of the E.D.I. system include a speed up in communications, improved overall efficiency and reduced administration costs. It also eliminates double handling of information and all risk of documentary transcription error." P. & O. also say that developments are continuing under a newly formed association. Perhaps of the greatest importance in the present context is that in October 1989, the I.C.C. Banking Commission agreed to set up a sub-committee, with a view to developing an

---

58. *Opinions of the I.C.C. Banking Commission on queries relating to Uniform Customs and Practice on Documentary Credits 1984–1986*, I.C.C. publication No. 434 (1987), p. 21.

59. See f.n. 56. "Telecommunication" replaces "cables, telegrams or telex" from the 1974 revision.

60. See, in general, *International carriage of goods: some legal problems and possible solutions* (Centre for Commercial Law Studies, 1988), Chapter 2, "The Paperless Transfer of Transport Information and Legal Functions", by Professor Kurt Grönfors.

61. *The Merchants Guide* (4th ed., 1987), p. 11.

E.D.I. credit, with appropriate rules.[62] We must presume, then, that E.D.I. is increasing in importance, and that it will eventually become the norm in international trade transactions.

So far, however, E.D.I. has only been used to replace the non-negotiable waybill.[63] Under the Atlantic Container Line's Cargo Key Receipt Scheme, for example, a computer print-out in effect takes the place of a conventional waybill. It is relatively easy to replace non-negotiable documents by E.D.I., since it is necessary to send only *information* by a computerised system. If E.D.I. is ever going to replace the document of title, however, it will be necessary to send *proof* of title.

In principle, however, there is no reason why electronic documentation could not also be used in place of a negotiable document, where for example re-sales of the cargo at sea are envisaged. The carrier would need to be informed of the identity of the ultimate receiver of the cargo, to whom he would deliver, without there being any requirement for an original document to be presented, or even to exist at all. The essential requirement is that the carrier receives reliable, and regularly updated information as to the identity of the person who is presently entitled to the goods at their destination. It is of course necessary that this information is regularly updated and speedily conveyed to the carrier, but this is possible with current technology given modern satellite communication methods, at least in peace time.

However, where today a negotiable document is required it is not the information which has to be sent to the carrier, but proof of title. E.D.I. must therefore be proof against fraud. It is probably fallacious to assume, however, given even present-day technology, that the paper document has any advantages in this regard over its electronic counterpart. Indeed, the reverse is more likely to be true, especially if adequate encryption methods or procedures are adopted. In any case, since the present system is by no means proof against fraud, the evidence suggests that commercial men are prepared to accept a certain level of fraud in order to effect speedier and less costly transactions. It will also be necessary to devise methods of authentication, the equivalent for example of the handwritten signature or stamp used on paper documents.

Other changes will also be necessary. The requirement for delivery to be against production of an original document is wholly inappropriate in the electronic age; a computer print-out can never be an original document, but is a copy of the information in the computer's own electronic record at the time when it is made. Another difficulty is that electronic documents will not be

62. At present, however, they appear reluctant to drop documentary requirements altogether, and are thinking instead of developing an electronic credit only as a collateral credit, to run alongside the conventional paper credit. With respect, this seems unduly cautious, and will raise quite difficult questions, like the interrelationship between paper and paperless systems.

63. Even P. & O., who are very much in the forefront of E.D.I. development, accept that the bill of lading is not susceptible to this approach, because it exists as a tangible document requiring surrender to obtain delivery: *The Merchants Guide*, 4th ed. (1987), p. 32.

regarded as documents of title without proof of custom, and customs take a long time to establish: legislation may well be the only solution to that particular problem.

This is looking some way into the future. The first step, however, is to make electronic communications more secure, and for universal rules of conduct and definitions to be agreed. This is the purpose of the Uniform Rules of Conduct (U.N.C.I.D.), published by the International Chamber of Commerce in 1988.

CHAPTER 6

BANKS' DUTIES REGARDING DOCUMENTS

This Chapter is concerned with the banks' duties under a documentary credit. The majority of the discussion will centre around the relationships between the confirming bank and beneficiary, and issuing bank and customer. For the purposes of discussion an irrevocable confirmed credit will be assumed, but the principles apply equally to unconfirmed credits, in which case the beneficiary's action (if any) is against the issuing bank directly. Where there are two banks, it is also sometimes necessary to consider the relationships between them.

It follows that this Chapter fleshes out discussion of the three autonomous contracts with which the banks are concerned, contracts 2, 3 and 4 in Figure 1.2.

6.1 GENERAL CONSIDERATIONS

6.1.1 Contracts autonomous but interconnected

It was explained in Chapter 1[1] that in principle the four contractual relationships in a confirmed documentary credit are autonomous. It follows therefore that in principle, the obligations of the confirming bank towards the beneficiary (contract 4 in Figure 1.2) may differ from those between the two banks (contract 3), and those between the issuing bank and its customer (contract 2). If, for example, the terms of the credit differed from the customer's instructions, the confirming bank's relations with the beneficiary would be governed by the terms of the credit (contained in contract 4), whereas the relationship between issuing bank and customer would be governed by the customer's instructions (contract 2). Article 6 of the U.C.P. states, in effect, that the beneficiary cannot avail himself of the provisions of either contract 2 or contract 3: "A beneficiary can in no case avail himself of the contractual relationship existing between the banks or between the applicant for the credit and the issuing bank."

---

1. Section 1.6.1.2.

However, there ought to be no difference between contracts 2, 3 and 4, since the terms of the credit should conform precisely to the customer's instructions. Only if one or other bank exceeds its mandate will the documentary requirements under these contracts differ. On the assumption that the same documents are stipulated in each of these contracts, it would obviously be very inconvenient if the courts held that the obligations owed under contract 4 differed from those under contracts 2 and 3. It is essential for business efficacy, for example, that a confirming bank is required to pay the beneficiary only if he can be assured of reclaiming the money paid from the issuing bank, and the issuing bank from the customer.[2]

The courts recognise this, and in reality, therefore, obligations under contracts two, three and four may be regarded as the same (unless of course the bank exceeds its instructions in the issue of the credit). This is probably what is meant by the notion that the four contracts, although autonomous, are interconnected.

It is clearly recognised, on the other hand, that the contracts constituting the credit are entirely independent of the underlying transaction (contract one, or the contract of sale). In performing their duties under the credit, banks are entirely unconcerned with whether their actions might thereby put either seller or buyer in breach of the sale contract, of whose terms they may in any case be wholly unaware. If, for example, the terms of the credit require a bank to reject documents which the buyer would be required to accept under the sale contract, then the seller's remedy is to sue on the contract of sale.[3] The bank's obligations are defined by the terms of the credit alone, and the sale contract is irrelevant. Indeed, it may even be governed by the law of a different jurisdiction to that governing the credit.[4]

The U.C.P. adopts the same principle. Article 3 provides: "Credits, by their nature, are separate transactions from the sales or other contract(s) on which they are based and banks are in no way concerned with or bound by such contract(s), even if any reference whatsoever to such contract(s) is included in the credit." The reference to "other contracts" is presumably intended to cover standby letters of credit, where the underlying transaction may be a construction, rather than sale contract.[5]

The last clause, "even if any reference whatsoever to such contract(s) is included in the credit", was added in 1983. It was not intended to have any effect on the practical handling of credits, but was a reaction to the practice of making reference in the credit itself either directly to the commercial contract, or to the invoice which will often include a reference to the commercial

2. See, for example, the statements made by Lord Diplock in *The American Accord*, below, f.n. 52.
3. As he attempted, unsuccessfully, for example, in *Soproma S.p.A.* v. *Marine & Animal By-Products Corporation*, above, section 3.1.3.
4. See section 8.3.
5. See section 8.2.

contract. Direct reference to the commercial contract is a practice which again is more likely with standby credits.[6]

6.1.2 Banks' expertise in documents not goods

A fundamental theme underlying the discussion in this Chapter is that the law assumes that whereas banks hold themselves out as experts in handling documents, they hold out no expertise in the handling of goods. If the documents do not conform, they have no way of knowing whether or not the non-conformity is material. Hence Article 4 of the U.C.P. provides: "In credit operations all parties concerned deal in documents, and not in goods, services and/or other performances to which the documents may relate." So far as the documents themselves are concerned, Article 15 provides:

"Banks must examine all documents with reasonable care to ascertain that they appear on their face to be in accordance with the terms and conditions of the credit. Documents which appear on their face to be inconsistent with one another will be considered as not appearing on their face to be in accordance with the terms and conditions of the credit."

This is unchanged from the 1974 revision.[7] It is not clear whether the duty of care extends to all documents, whether or not called for under the credit. Having examined the documents, the bank must determine from their face alone whether to accept or reject them. Article 16(b) accordingly provides:

"If, upon receipt of the documents, the issuing bank considers that they appear on their face not to be in accordance with the terms and conditions of the credit, it must determine, on the basis of the documents alone, whether to take up such documents, or to refuse them and claim that they appear on their face not to be in accordance with the terms and conditions of the credit."

The right to reimbursement also depends only on whether the documents appear on their face to conform. This is provided for by Article 16(a):

"If a bank so authorized effects payment, or incurs a deferred payment undertaking, or accepts, or negotiates against documents which appear on their face to be in accordance with the terms and conditions of the credit, the party giving such authority shall be bound to reimburse the bank which has effected payment, or incurred a deferred payment undertaking, or has accepted, or negotiated, and to take up the documents."

The theme that banks are not required to look behind the face of the documents is further strengthened by Article 17:

"Banks assume no liability or responsibility for the form, sufficiency, accuracy, genuineness, falsification or legal effect of any documents, or for the general and/or particular conditions stipulated in the documents or superimposed thereon; nor do they assume any liability or responsibility for the description, quantity, weight, quality, condition, packing, delivery, value, or the existence of the goods represented by

---

6. B. Wheble, *UCP 1974/1983 Revisions Compared and Explained*, I.C.C. publication No. 411 (1984), p. 13.
7. Article 7.

the documents, or for the good faith or acts and/or omissions, solvency, performance or standing of the consignor, the carriers, or the insurers of the goods or of any other person whomsoever."

The point that clearly emerges from these provisions is that neither issuing nor correspondent bank is interested in anything apart from whether the documents conform on their face to the credit requirements. Neither bank is interested in the condition of the goods, nor whether either seller or buyer is in breach of the sale contract.

6.1.3 Banks' expertise in documents not factual situations

A related point is that banks should not be concerned with the existence or otherwise of any other fact situation, apart from that indicated on the face of the documents themselves. Otherwise, extensive inquiries may be required, in an area where again the bank may not necessarily be assumed to have any relevant expertise.

In *Banque de l'Indochine et de Suez S.A.* v. *J.H. Rayner (Mincing Lane) Ltd.*,[8] the credit called for: "shipment to be effected on vessel belonging to Shipping Company that is a member of an International Shipping Conference." Sir John Donaldson M.R. noted that[9]:

"This is an unfortunate condition to include in a documentary credit, because it breaks the first rule of such a transaction, namely that the parties are dealing in documents, not facts. This condition required a state of facts to exist. What the letter of credit should have done was to call for a specific document which was to be acceptable to the buyer and his bank evidencing the fact that the vessel was owned by a member of a conference."

For the same reason, vague terminology should also be avoided. There are general requirements for terminology contained in Article 22(a) and (b)[10]:

"(a) All instructions for the issuance of credits and the credits themselves and, where applicable, all instructions for amendments thereto and the amendments themselves must state precisely the document(s) against which payment, acceptance or negotiation is to be made.

(b) Terms such as 'first class', 'well known', 'qualified', 'independent', 'official' and the like shall not be used to describe the issuers of any document to be presented under a credit. If such terms are incorporated in the credit terms, banks will accept the relevant documents as presented, provided that they appear on their face to be in accordance with the other terms and conditions of the credit."

The problem with terms such as those mentioned in paragraph (b) is not simply that they are vague, but that they require the bank to consider a factual situation (e.g., whether a certificate is "independent" or "official"), whereas their only concern should be with the documents themselves. The words "independent" and "official" were added in 1983.

---

8. [1983] 1 All E.R. 1137; [1983] 1 Lloyd's Rep. 228. See further below, section 6.3.4.
9. [1983] 1 All E.R. 1137, 1140e.
10. Article 22(c) is dealt with in section 5.2.1.4.

The terms in paragraph (b) are not exhaustive, and no term that is not capable of precise definition should be used.

6.1.4 Quick decision required

It must also be appreciated that banks do not have an infinite time in which to examine the documents tendered. Where the U.C.P. applies, Article 16(c) provides that: "The issuing bank shall have a reasonable time in which to examine the documents and to determine as above whether to take up or to refuse the documents." "Reasonable time" is not defined in the U.C.P., although the Working Party of the I.C.C. Banking Commission, whose recommendations led to the 1983 revisions, considered the possibility of stipulating a specific period. Bernard Wheble, President of the I.C.C. Banking Commission, wrote[11]:

"Considerable thought was given to the possibility of replacing 'reasonable time' by a specific period of time. Replies to a detailed questionnaire showed approximately equal support for the status quo and for a change. The suggestions for the specified period of time ranged from '36 hours' to '30 days' and from calendar days to banking days. It was therefore felt impossible to recommend any change."

Although it appears from this passage that some international bankers felt that up to 30 days was a reasonable period for examination of documents, this view seems somewhat extreme, and although there was no English authority on the question at the time of the 1983 revision,[12] it is now clear that the courts will interpret "reasonable time" as considerably less than 30 days (see below).

Two further points to note are that this provision applies only to the issuing bank, whereas there seems to be no good reason why it should not also apply to an advising or confirming bank. Secondly, there is no requirement, either here or anywhere else in the U.C.P., for documents to be presented in any particular language. Clearly the language of the documents may have a bearing on how long a time is reasonable, and also on who should bear the cost of translation, and the risk of inaccuracy in the translation.

Article 16(c) is elaborated on by Articles 16(d) and 16(e):

"(d) If the issuing bank decides to refuse the documents, it must give notice to that effect without delay by telecommunication or, if that is not possible, by other expeditious means, to the bank from which it received the documents (the remitting bank), or to the beneficiary, if it received the documents directly from him. Such notice must state the discrepancies in respect of which the issuing bank refuses the

---

11. B. Wheble, *UCP 1974/1983 Revisions Compared and Explained*, I.C.C. publication No. 411 (1984), p. 33.
12. There are *dicta* in McNair J.'s decision in *Bank Melli Iran* v. *Barclays Bank* [1951] 2 Lloyd's Rep. 367, 378 (col.1) from which it might be argued that the bank may retain the documents for several weeks, but even if the *dicta* indeed support this proposition, they seem out of line with later authorities, and in any case are not a decision on the U.C.P. On this case, see further section 6.3.

documents and must also state whether it is holding the documents at the disposal of, or is returning them to, the presentor (remitting bank or the beneficiary, as the case may be). The issuing bank shall then be entitled to claim from the remitting bank refund of any reimbursement which may have been made to that bank.

(e) If the issuing bank fails to act in accordance with the provisions of paragraphs (c) and (d) of this Article and/or fails to hold the documents at the disposal of, or return them to, the presentor, the issuing bank shall be precluded from claiming that the documents are not in accordance with the terms and conditions of the credit."

Article 16(f) is considered below.[13]

6.1.4.1 The Royan[14]

As was explained in the previous section, until recently there was no English authority on the question of what is a reasonable time for the examination of documents under the U.C.P. The issue arose in the Court of Appeal in *The Royan*, although unfortunately because of the way the case arose it was unnecessary for the court to set a precise limit, a clear upper limit alone being set.

The case involved the sale of a large quantity of natural butter oil shipped on four vessels, one of which was *The Royan*. Payment was to be by confirmed irrevocable credit, 90 per cent. against presentation of shipping documents and the remaining 10 per cent. sixty days after discharge, subject to the buyers' assurance that the consignment strictly complied with the specifications.[15] The credit (for a total sum of U.S.$5,390,000) was issued subject to the U.C.P. 1974 revision, Article 8 of which was in essentially the same terms as the present Article 16. It was valid until 31 October 1982 for shipment and 21 November 1982 for presentation of shipping documents.

The dispute in the case was between the confirming bank (The Sumitomo Bank Ltd.), and agents of the sellers (Rabobank). Unfortunately, however, it is necessary to set out the facts of the case in some detail in order to appreciate how the dispute between these parties arose.

6.1.4.1.1 THE FACTS

On 18 October shipping documents for the *Royan* shipment were tendered by Rabobank to Sumitomo. Sumitomo drew Rabobank's attention to the fact that the documents were not in order, primarily because of discrepancies in the sanitary certificates.[16] At Sumitomo's request,[17] Rabobank responded by issuing a guarantee, assuming full responsibility for any discrepancies and

---

13. Section 6.3.4.

14. *Co-Operative Centrale Raiffeisen-Boerenleenbank B.A. ("Rabobank Nederland")* v. *The Sumitomo Bank Ltd., The Royan* [1988] 2 Lloyd's Rep. 250.

15. On the balance of 10 per cent., see below, section 6.2.2.2.

16. "There were other discrepancies, but they play no part in the case." (*per* Lloyd L.J.): [1988] 2 Lloyd's Rep. 250, 253 (col.1).

17. "In order that we may effect payment to yourselves, please . . . issue your guarantee covering ourselves against the above discrepancies."

requesting payment. Sumitomo accordingly paid 90 per cent. in respect of the first instalment under reserve,[18] and forwarded the documents to Banque Misr, the issuing bank. Documents for the remaining three shipments were presented by Rabobank to Sumitomo on 19 and 28 October, and 5 November, and the same procedure was adopted in respect of each.

Banque Misr rejected the documents relating to the first two shipments on 18 November. It should perhaps be noted that Sumitomo's acceptance of non-conforming documents against a guarantee, and payment under reserve, in no way affected the obligations of Banque Misr, the issuing bank. This is provided for by Article 16(f) of the U.C.P., which is in essentially the same terms as Article 8(g) of the 1974 revision. Article 16(f) of the 1983 revision provides:

"If the remitting bank draws the attention of the issuing bank to any discrepancies in the documents or advises the issuing bank that it has paid, incurred a deferred payment undertaking, accepted or negotiated under reserve or against an indemnity in respect of such discrepancies, the issuing bank shall not be thereby relieved from any of its obligations under any provisions of this Article. Such reserve or indemnity concerns only the relations between the remitting bank and the party towards whom the reserve was made or from whom, or on whose behalf, the indemnity was obtained."

On 29 November (eight days after the letter of credit had expired) conforming sanitary certificates were sent in respect of all four shipments to both issuing and confirming banks, and on 30 November Banque Misr accepted the documents in respect of the first shipment. However, in respect of the second and fourth shipments they did not authorise payment until 6 January, and in respect of the third they authorised payment only on 22 December.

By the time conforming sanitary certificates were eventually tendered the credit had expired, but Lloyd L.J., who gave the only substantive judgment, took the view that an extension could be implied from the conduct of the parties, commenting that[19]: "It frequently happens that the validity of a letter of credit is extended by consent of all parties. Such consent can be implied, as well as expressed." He did not elaborate, however, on the juristic basis for the extension. Arguably this was academic in *The Royan* itself, where documents in respect of each of the four shipments were eventually accepted; it would have been far from academic if Banque Misr had wished to accept documents in respect of one or more, but not all of the shipments covered by the letter of credit. It is clear, for example, from *Cape Asbestos Co. Ltd.* v. *Lloyds Bank Ltd.*,[20] that it could not have been inferred from late acceptance of the documents in respect of the first shipment that Banque Misr had waived their rights to reject documents for the other shipments, on the ground of late tender. Suppose, however, that the extension had been by variation (i.e., amendment) of the original contract, or that the credit, although expired, had

18. Below, section 6.3.4.
19. [1988] 2 Lloyd's Rep. 250, 254 (col. 2).
20. See section 3.1.4.2.

been reinstated with a later expiry date. It has been suggested that in that case, "then acceptance of one set of documents will oblige acceptance of any other conforming sets of documents presented prior to presentation of the documents actually accepted". This is because the variation or reinstatement would alter the expiry date for the entire credit, and would not operate differentially as between each shipment. On the other hand, if the true analysis is waiver, Banque Misr would be entitled to "pick and choose".[21]

Whatever its juristic basis, the extension obviously affected not only the position of Banque Misr, but also that of Sumitomo. This aspect of the case is further considered below.[22]

There is something to be said for consideration being given, now that the U.C.P. is again undergoing revision, to the question whether late acceptance by the issuing bank of conforming documents, or acceptance by the issuing bank at any time of non-conforming documents, has the effect of varying or amending the credit.

6.1.4.1.2 THE CLAIM

Although the end result was that Banque Misr, having eventually accepted the documents in respect of all four shipments, reimbursed Sumitomo for the full amount that Sumitomo had paid under reserve to Rabobank, Sumitomo had been kept out of its money for some considerable time, and had lost interest of some U.S.$73,000. When the remaining 10 per cent. fell due under the letter of credit 60 days after discharge, Sumitomo deducted U.S.$73,000 from the further amount due to Rabobank, claiming that it was entitled to do so under the guarantee. Rabobank sued for the U.S.$73,000, claiming that Sumitomo was not entitled to set it off.

The main issue was how much of the U.S. $73,000 was due to the delays by Banque Misr in processing the documents, since obviously Rabobank ought not to be liable for Banque Misr's delay. The question in effect was therefore, how much of the delay was caused by Rabobank's tender of non-conforming documents, and how much by Banque Misr's delay in accepting them.

6.1.4.1.3 THE DECISION

The Court of Appeal held that Rabobank were responsible for the period up to 30 November, since only on 29 November were conforming documents tendered, but that losses thereafter were caused by Banque Misr's delay, for which Rabobank were not responsible. The reasoning was that since Banque Misr had all the documents, except the fresh sanitary certificate, by 12

---

21. Anthony Pugh-Thomas and Christopher Chapman, "The Effect of the Decision of the Court of Appeal in the *Rabobank* Case on the Law and Practice on Documentary Credits" [1989] 1 J.I.B.L. 30, at 31–32. They argue that reinstatement is the correct analysis, since by the time the documents in respect of the first shipment were accepted the original credit had expired, so that there was no longer any contract in existence to vary, nor any contractual term to waive.
22. See section 6.1.4.1.4.

November, a reasonable time for examining the documents had expired by 30 November at the latest.[23]

It follows that 18 days must be regarded as the outside period for examination under the U.C.P. Of course, it was unnecessary to determine what lesser period was reasonable, since until 30 November conforming documents had not been provided, and consequently Banque Misr can have been under no obligation to accept until then.[24]

It is probable, I would suggest, that even 18 days is well over what the courts would be prepared to allow. United States authority, for example, suggests up to about six but less than 10 days, and German authority no more than eight,[25] but of course what is reasonable can vary depending on the circumstances. The U.S. Uniform Commercial Code gives the issuer three business days,[26] but this seems a little strict. In any case it is arguable that what is reasonable should depend on the particular transaction, and that a longer period may be appropriate where the credit is for a very substantial sum, or the documents are either numerous or unusually complex, or in a foreign language.[27]

It may perhaps be concluded, then, that the I.C.C. Banking Commission were right not to recommend replacement of "reasonable time" in the U.C.P. by a specific period of time. Their survey suggested that five to six working days might be considered a normal acceptable period, and seven to eight might be appropriate for a more complex transaction.[28]

Nevertheless, it is clear that a bank taking up documents must do so quickly, and ought therefore not be expected to concern itself with details of any dispute between the parties to the sale contract, for example as to the condition of the goods themselves.

6.1.4.1.4 ADDENDUM: WAS THE CONFIRMING BANK PREJUDICED BY THE EXTENSION?

In *The Royan*, from the conduct of the issuing bank, Banque Misr, was implied an extension of the letter of credit in favour of Rabobank, the beneficiary. Although the point did not directly arise in the case, it has been

23. [1988] 2 Lloyd's Rep. 250, 255 (col. 2).
24. [1988] 2 Lloyd's Rep. 250, 256 (col.1). There was a further issue over payment of the remaining 10 per cent., 60 days after discharge, but that is not relevant to the present discussion. See further below, however, section 6.2.2.2.
25. See, e.g., the authorities set out by E.P. Ellinger: "Reasonable time for examination of documents" [1985] J.B.L. 406, at p. 406.
26. Professor John F. Dolan: "Documentary Credit Fundamentals: Comparative Aspects" (1989) 3 B.F.L.R. 121, 138.
27. Ellinger, *op. cit.*, [1985] J.B.L., at p. 407.
28. Ellinger notes, *ibid.* at p. 408, that a set of documents can ordinarily be perused in about one and a half hours, and a complex set in about three. He points out, however, that there are usually at least two "checkers", whose "worksheets" may have to be referred to a senior person in the department.

argued that the conduct of Banque Misr also affected the position of Sumitomo, the confirming bank.[29] In effect, so the argument goes, Sumitomo were bound by the extension, even though they were only minimally concerned in the late acceptance by Banque Misr of the late tender of conforming certificates. Indeed, Rabobank sent certificates both to Sumitomo and to Banque Misr directly.

In principle it is clearly wrong that a confirming bank can be bound by the unilateral action of the issuing bank, and I would suggest that this argument is reading too much into *The Royan*. In the case itself Sumitomo and Banque Misr were in close communication throughout, and it was in any case in Sumitomo's interest for the credit to be extended, since they had already made payments under reserve in favour of Rabobank. In other words, it might be reasonable to infer acceptance by Sumitomo as well as Banque Misr to the extension of the credit.

Where it is not possible to draw that inference, for example where the confirming bank has not paid against a credit which has expired, and has no interest in agreeing to an extension, then all that can be inferred surely is a new contract between the beneficiary and the issuing bank, with a later expiry date. Since agreement could only be inferred between the beneficiary and the issuing bank, it must also be assumed that the beneficiary has accepted the substitution of a new unconfirmed credit in place of the old confirmed credit. In that case, the position of the confirming bank is unaffected by the conduct of the issuing bank.

On the other hand, *The Royan* leaves at any rate open the possibility that a confirming bank may be prejudiced by the conduct of the issuing bank. It has been suggested that the following clause ought to be effective to protect the confirming bank in such circumstances[30]:

"The confirmation of [name of issuing bank] is given strictly subject to the terms of the letter of credit (including its date of expiration) in the form herewith. Such confirmation shall not be extended or otherwise varied except by written notice to that effect signed by [name or position of nominated officer]. No other person has the authority of [name of confirming bank] to effect any variation to such confirmation whether by words, writing or conduct.

Without prejudice to the foregoing, any communications received from the beneficiary or from the issuing bank may, after the expiration of [name of confirming bank], at the discretion of [name of confirming bank] be transmitted to the issuing bank or the beneficiary respectively strictly on the basis that the obligations of [name of confirming bank] in respect of the letter of credit have expired and that no transmission gives rise to any liability on the part of [name of confirming bank]."

This is also a matter which could usefully be clarified by amendment to the U.C.P.

---

29. Pugh-Thomas and Chapman, *op. cit.* (f.n. 21), at pp. 32–33.
30. Pugh-Thomas and Chapman, *op. cit.*, at p. 33 (col. 2).

6.1.5 Vendor of goods under a confirmed credit selling under assurance that nothing will prevent him from receiving the price

A third theme running through this Chapter is that "an elaborate commercial system" has been built up, whereby a "vendor of goods selling against a confirmed letter of credit is selling under the assurance that nothing will prevent him from receiving the price".[31] This is very important when exporting to a foreign country, especially in view of the fact that the vendor himself would often use a documentary credit to raise money to purchase or manufacture the goods, the subject matter of the contract of sale.

This is yet another argument, therefore, for banks not to be involved in any substantive disputes between the parties to the sale contract.

6.2 DOCUMENTS CONFORM BUT DOUBTS ABOUT GOODS

It should be clear from the preceding paragraphs that there are very strong arguments against banks being required to look behind the documents tendered to them, and in particular to involve themselves in disputes about the goods. Subject to a narrow fraud exception, the law has developed in accordance with these arguments: if the documents conform the bank must pay against them, and may claim reimbursement from the customer.

6.2.1 As between issuing bank and customer, or buyer and seller

The first cases were all cases either between the bank and its customer, where the customer attempted to restrain the bank from paying under the credit, or between buyer and seller, where the buyer attempted to restrain the seller from claiming under the credit. Only in 1982 did it become clear that the same position obtained between the bank and its beneficiary.

In the United States it has been clear that at least since the decision of the New York Supreme Court in *Sztejn* v. *J. Henry Schroeder Banking Corporation*[32] in 1941, where the documents appear on their face to be in accordance with the terms and conditions of the credit, a bank may only refuse to honour the credit where the seller has himself been fraudulent. Shentag J. said[33]:

"It is well established that a letter of credit is independent of the primary contract of sale between the buyer and the seller. The issuing bank agrees to pay upon presentation

---

31. *Per* Jenkins L.J. in *Hamzeh Malas & Sons* v. *British Imex Industries Ltd.* [1958] 2 Q.B. 127, 129.
32. (1941) 31 N.Y.S. 2d. 631.
33. (1941) 31 N.Y.S. 2d. 631, 633.

of documents, not goods. This rule is necessary to preserve the efficiency of the letter of credit as an instrument for the financing of trade."

In the particular case, however, the general rule did not apply because of the seller's fraud[34]:

" . . . on the present motion, it must be assumed that the seller has intentionally failed to ship any goods ordered by the buyer. In such a situation, where the seller's fraud has been called to the bank's attention before the drafts and documents have been presented for payment, the principle of the independence of the bank's obligation under the letter of credit should not be extended to protect the unscrupulous seller."

In reality, it is very rare for the fraud exception to be successfully invoked, since suspicion of fraud is not enough, whereas proof is very difficult, so that the general position usually applies. It is also now clear that the law in the U.K. mirrors that in the U.S.A. The leading U.K. authority is the decision of the Court of Appeal in *Hamzeh Malas & Sons* v. *British Imex Industries Ltd.*,[35] where Jenkins L.J. thought that[36]:

"it seems to me to be plain enough that the opening of a confirmed letter of credit constitutes a bargain between the banker and the vendor of goods, which imposes upon the banker an absolute obligation to pay, irrespective of any dispute there may be between the parties as to whether the goods are up to contract or not."

In this case, the plaintiffs, Hamzeh Malas & Sons, were c.i.f. buyers of two consignments of reinforced steel rods from the defendant sellers, British Imex Industries Ltd., payment to be effected by confirmed letters of credit in respect of each consignment. The credits were accordingly opened by the Midland Bank in London, in consideration for a confirming commission of £18, which the defendants paid.[37] Hamzeh Malas alleged that the first consignment, against which payment (of £21,468) had already been made under the first letter of credit, was "by no means up to contract quality", and in order to secure any damages which they may eventually be awarded, sought an injunction barring the defendants from claiming the price under the second letter of credit.

The court took the view that it had no jurisdiction to interfere. Sellers L.J. only agreed, however, subject to reservations about fraudulent transactions,[38] and it now seems clear that the position would be different were the seller himself fraudulent.[39]

A similar conclusion was reached by Megarry J. in *Discount Records Ltd.*

---

34. (1941) 31 N.Y.S. 2d. 631, 634.
35. [1958] 2 Q.B. 127; [1958] 2 W.L.R. 100; [1957] 2 Lloyd's Rep. 549.
36. [1958] 2 Q.B. 127, 129.
37. The full facts of the case are to be found in *British Imex Industries Ltd.* v. *Midland Bank Ltd.* [1958] 1 Q.B. 542; [1958] 2 W.L.R. 103; [1958] 1 All E.R. 264; [1957] 2 Lloyd's Rep. 591, which involved the same transaction but different parties. See also below, sections 8.1.8–8.1.10.
38. [1958] 2 Q.B. 127, 130.
39. See below, section 6.2.2.1.

v. *Barclays Bank Ltd.*[40] The plaintiffs were purchasers of a consignment of records and cassettes from a French company called "Promodisc", payment to be by confirmed irrevocable credit. Conforming documents[41] were tendered, but by then it had become clear that the cartons shipped contained largely rubbish. The plaintiffs nevertheless failed to restrain the defendant bank from paying under the credit, however, Megarry J. distinguishing *Sztein* on the grounds that no fraud was proven, merely alleged. It is not easy to prove fraud—the question of when an injunction might be obtained restraining a bank from making payment under a credit was considered by the Court of Appeal in *Bolivinter Oil S.A.* v. *Chase Manhattan Bank*,[42] where Sir John Donaldson M.R. said[43]:

"Before leaving this appeal, we should like to add a word about the circumstances in which an *ex parte* injunction should be issued which prohibits a bank from paying under an irrevocable letter of credit or a performance bond or guarantee.[44] The unique value of such a letter, bond or guarantee is that the beneficiary can be completely satisfied that, whatever disputes may thereafter arise between him and the bank's customer in relation to the performance or indeed existence of the underlying contract, the bank is personally undertaking to pay him provided that the specified conditions are met . . . If, save in the most exceptional cases, he is to be allowed to derogate from the bank's personal and irrevocable undertaking, given be it again noted at his request, by obtaining an injunction restraining the bank from honouring that undertaking, he will undermine what is the bank's greatest asset, however large and rich it may be, namely its reputation for financial and contractual probity. Furthermore, if this happens at all frequently, the value of all irrevocable letters and performance bonds and guarantees will be undermined.

Judges who are asked, often at short notice and *ex parte*, to issue an injunction restraining payment by a bank under an irrevocable letter of credit or performance bond or guarantee should ask whether there is any challenge to the validity of the letter, bond or guarantee itself. If there is not or if the challenge is not substantial, *prima facie* no injunction should be granted and the bank should be left free to honour its contractual obligation, although restrictions may well be imposed on the freedom of the beneficiary to deal with the money after he has received it. The wholly exceptional case where an injunction may be granted is where it is proved that the bank knows that any demand for payment already made or which may thereafter be made will clearly be fraudulent. But the evidence must be clear, both of the fact of fraud and as to the bank's knowledge. It would certainly not normally be sufficient that this rests on the uncorroborated statement of the customer, for irreparable damage can be done to a bank's credit in the relatively brief time which must elapse between the granting of such an injunction and an application by the bank to have it discharged."

The difference between proof of fraud, and mere allegations or suspicion, is further considered below.[45]

---

40. [1975] 1 W.L.R. 315; [1975] 1 All E.R. 1071; [1975] 1 Lloyd's Rep. 444.
41. Or at any rate, documents which were eventually accepted as conforming by an official of the plaintiffs: [1975] 1 All E.R. 1071, at p. 1073b.
42. [1984] 1 All E.R. 351; [1984] 1 Lloyd's Rep 251.
43. [1984] 1 All E.R. 351, 352.
44. See further, section 8.2., especially section 8.2.3.
45. Section 6.2.2.1.

6.2.1.1 Apparent conformity only required

Given the requirement for banks to act promptly on presentation of documents, it is not surprising that exact conformity is not required, but apparent conformity will do. The test is whether the bank has taken reasonable care to ensure that the documents conform. Only if it has not done so will it be liable to its customer, even if the documents do not in fact conform to the requirements of the credit.

Gian Singh & Co. Ltd. v. *Banque de l'Indochine*[46] concerned the purchase of a fishing vessel in Taiwan for $45,000, payment to be by irrevocable credit issued directly by the issuing bank in favour of the beneficiary. Among the "Special Instructions" was the requirement that a certificate, certifying that the vessel had been built according to specifications and was in a fit and proper condition to sail, was signed by Balwant Singh, holder of Malaysian Passport E–13276. A certificate was presented, apparently signed by Balwant Singh, and the issuing bank having checked against the signature on Passport E–13276, paid the beneficiary under the credit, and debited $45,000 from its customer's account. It later became clear, however, that both the signature and passport were forged.

The customer failed in an action against the issuing bank, claiming that it had been wrongly debited $45,000. In the Judicial Committee of the Privy Council, Lord Diplock said on the issue of conformity[47]:

"The fact that a document presented by the beneficiary under a documentary credit, which otherwise conforms to the requirements of the credit, is in fact a forgery does not, of itself, prevent the issuing bank from recovering the moneys paid under the credit. The duty of the issuing bank, which it may perform either by itself, or by its agent, the notifying bank, is to examine the documents with reasonable care to ascertain that they appear on their face to be in accordance with the terms and conditions of the credit. The express provision to this effect in Article 7 of the Uniform Customs and Practice for Documentary Credits[48] does no more than restate the duty of the bank at common law. In business transactions financed by documentary credits banks must be able to act promptly on presentation of documents. In the ordinary case visual inspection of the actual documents presented is all that is called for. The bank is under no duty to take any further steps to investigate the genuineness of a signature which, on the face of it, purports to be the signature of the person named or described in the letter of credit."

He went on to observe that the special requirement imposed on the bank the additional duty to take reasonable care to ensure that the signature on the certificate appeared to correspond with the signature of Balwant Singh, holder of passport No. E–13276, but that the onus of proving lack of reasonable care was on the customer,[49] and that this onus had not been discharged.

---

46. [1974] 1 W.L.R. 1234; [1974] 2 All E.R. 754; [1974] 2 Lloyd's Rep. 1.
47. [1974] 2 All E.R. 754, 757j–758b.
48. 1974 revision. See now article 15, set out in section 6.1.2, the text of which is identical to the old article 7.
49. [1974] 2 All E.R. 754, 758c.

6.2.2 As between confirming bank and beneficiary

6.2.2.1 The American Accord

Whereas the position has long been clear as between issuing bank and customer, it was not until *The American Accord*,[50] the leading case in the House of Lords, that the English courts were called upon to rule directly on the position as between confirming bank and beneficiary. From this case it is clear that the positions under both contracts are the same, so that only where the confirming bank can reclaim the price from the issuing bank, who can in turn reclaim from the customer, is the confirming bank under any obligation to pay the beneficiary in the first place. Obviously, any other conclusion would have created enormous practical difficulties for the banking community.

The case arose from an f.o.b. sale of plant for the manufacture of fibre-glass, payment to be by confirmed irrevocable credit. Under the terms of the credit, shipment had to take place on or before 15 December 1976. The cargo was actually shipped aboard the *American Accord* on 16 December 1976, but the bill of lading was fraudulently backdated by the loading brokers, who were not in this regard acting for the plaintiff sellers. Documents which therefore apparently conformed to the credit were tendered, but rejected by the confirming bank because of the loading brokers' fraud. It is important to note that there was no evidence that the seller was fraudulent.

The issue which directly arose, therefore, in an action by the seller against the bank, was whether a bank was entitled to refuse payment under a confirmed irrevocable documentary credit, where although the documents appeared to be in order on their face, the goods were not in fact shipped according to contract.[51] The House of Lords held that the bank was bound to pay unless fraud on the part of the seller was proved. This of course brings the contract between seller and confirming bank (contract 4) into line with that between issuing bank and buyer (contract 2). Lord Diplock observed[52]:

"It has, so far as I know, never been disputed that as between confirming bank and issuing bank and as between issuing bank and the buyer the contractual duty of each bank under a confirmed irrevocable credit is to examine with reasonable care all documents presented in order to ascertain that they appear *on their face* to be in accordance with the terms and conditions of the credit, and, if they do so appear, to pay to the seller/beneficiary by whom the documents have been presented the sum stipulated by the credit, or to accept or negotiate without recourse to drawer drafts drawn by the seller/beneficiary if the credit so provides . . .

It would be strange from a commercial point of view, although not theoretically

---

50. *United City Merchants (Investments) Ltd.* v. *Royal Bank of Canada, The American Accord* [1983] A.C. 168; [1982] 2 All E.R. 720, [1982] 2 W.L.R. 1039, [1982] 2 Lloyd's Rep 1.

51. The bank also took a second point, which was that the transaction was unenforceable because it was contrary to the exchange control regulations brought into force by the Bretton Woods Agreements Order in Council 1946. The plaintiffs' claim succeeded only to the extent that the contracts did not offend against the regulations. That issue is not relevant to the discussion in this section, however.

52. [1983] A.C. 168, 184E–185A.

impossible in law, if the contractual duty owed by confirming and issuing banks to the buyer to honour the credit on presentation of apparently conforming documents despite the fact that they contain inaccuracies or even are forged were not matched by a corresponding contractual liability of the confirming bank to the seller/beneficiary (in the absence, of course, of any fraud on his part) to pay the sum stipulated in the credit on presentation of apparently conforming documents.''

The decision applies whenever the documents appear on their face to be in accordance with the terms and conditions of the credit, and would equally apply, for example, to a bill of lading which stated, without qualification, that defective goods were shipped in apparent good order and condition. It follows, therefore, that the confirming bank may have to pay for defective goods, and that the issuing bank having reimbursed the confirming bank, can itself look for reimbursement from the buyer. Indeed, in a later case[53] the House held that even where there is no documentary credit, a c.i.f. buyer is not entitled, in the absence of proof of seller's fraud, to reject documents which conform on their face to the contractual requirements. If he does so, the seller may sue on the sale contract (contract 1) for wrongful rejection, even if the goods were not shipped according to contract.

Such a position clearly requires justification, but many justifications can in fact be advanced. First, banks should not be expected to know the terms of the sale contract, and should not be interested in disputes between buyer and seller. Secondly, whereas banks may be assumed to have the expertise to check documentation, there is no reason to suppose that they have any expertise in the goods themselves. Perhaps even more importantly, however, it is said that an elaborate commercial system has built up on the basis that a vendor of goods (who may himself be relying on the credit to raise money to purchase or manufacture the goods), selling against a confirmed letter of credit, is selling under the assurance that nothing will prevent him from receiving the price.

If the seller is himself fraudulent, then (but only then) there are obvious, and more powerful, policy considerations depriving the fraudulent seller of the right to bring an action[54]:

"To this general statement of principle as to the contractual obligations of the confirming bank to the seller, there is one established exception: that is, where the seller, for the purpose of drawing on the credit, fraudulently presents to the confirming bank documents that contain, expressly or by implication, material representations of fact that to his knowledge are untrue. Although there does not appear among the English authorities any case in which this exception has been applied, it is well established in the American cases, of which the leading or 'landmark' case is *Sztejn* v. *J. Henry Schröder Banking Corp*. This judgment of the New York Court of Appeals was referred to with approval by the English Court of Appeal in *Edward Owen Engineer-*

53. *Gill and Duffus S.A.* v. *Berger & Co. Inc.* [1984] A.C. 382; [1984] 1 All E.R. 438; [1984] 2 W.L.R. 95; [1984] 1 Lloyd's Rep. 227.
54. [1983] A.C. 168, 183G–184B.

ing Ltd. v. *Barclays Bank International Ltd.,*[55] though this was actually a case about a performance bond under which a bank assumes obligations to a buyer analogous to those assumed by the confirming bank to the seller under a documentary credit. The exception for fraud on the part of the beneficiary seeking to avail himself of the credit is a clear application of the maxim *ex turpi causa non oritur actio* or, if plain English is to be preferred, 'fraud unravels all'. The courts will not allow their process to be used by a dishonest person to carry out a fraud."

It is important to appreciate the extremity of the position, however. The fraud exception is very narrow. It must be fraud on the part of the seller, and it must be proved. Banks have to honour a credit even if they suspect fraud, if they cannot prove it (and it is very difficult to prove fraud). They even have to pay if they know that the documents tendered are fraudulent, unless they can prove that the seller was aware of the fraud. Professor Schmitthoff comments that[56]: "[banks] will not like the idea that they have to honour a credit although they know that the documents tendered are fraudulent, only because it cannot be proved, before the credit is honoured, that the seller is aware of the fraud."

6.2.2.2 The Royan and the balance of 10 per cent.

In *The Royan,*[57] 90 per cent. of the consignment value was to be paid against presentation of the shipping documents[58]: "The remaining 10 per cent. to be paid to beneficiaries within sixty days from date of completion of discharging and after assurance that consignment strictly complying for specifications mentioned in credit terms . . . " This was effectively a simple form of guarantee. If the buyers took the view that the consignment was not up to specification then they would not pay the last 10 per cent. of the purchase price. No doubt they could have achieved a similar result by demanding a performance bond in a similar amount, but retention of the final 10 per cent. was clearly simplest from their point of view. Obviously, however, the clause is open to the objection that payment of the final 10 per cent. depends on the buyer's assurance that the consignment strictly complies with the specifications in the credit, and this appears at first sight to be contrary to the principles discussed so far in this section.

In fact the buyers instructed Banque Misr to pay the remaining 10 per cent. on 5 May 1983, well over 60 days after discharge,[59] and only then did Sumitomo pay over the balance to Rabobank. In addition to the U.S.$73,000 set-off already considered, Rabobank also claimed interest on the final 10 per

---

55. See further section 8.2.3.
56. [1982] J.B.L. 319, at p. 322.
57. Above, section 6.1.4.1.
58. [1988] 2 Lloyd's Rep. 250, 256 (col.1).
59. Discharge of the first vessel took place on 26 October 1982, so that the 60 days expired on 24 December 1982.

cent. from 60 days after discharge (when they said it should have been paid) until 5 May 1983, when it was actually paid. This amounted to $4,276, and the Court of Appeal held that they were entitled to this sum. Sumitomo's argument, that they were not obliged to pay the final 10 per cent. until the Egyptian buyers had assured themselves that the goods complied with the specification, was rejected.

Lloyd L.J.'s analysis of the above clause is of considerable interest, since similar clauses are by no means uncommon. After commenting that "the meaning of the provision is obscure",[60] he said that the controlling provision was that for payment within 60 days. Were the buyers to claim within the 60 day period that the goods were not up to specification, then the final 10 per cent. would not become payable at all under the credit (although this would not of course preclude the sellers from taking proceedings on the sale contract). Were no such claim to be made within 60 days, however, then the 10 per cent. would become payable at the end of the 60 day period. No such claim had been made in the case, so that Rabobank should have been paid 60 days after discharge. Lloyd L.J. commented that had he accepted Sumitomo's argument, the buyers could have delayed indefinitely, and indeed it is difficult to see that the 60 day period could have any meaning except on Lloyd L.J.'s analysis.

An argument was also put forward, however, that this analysis offended against the fundamental principle that all parties deal in documents, not goods,[61] and Lloyd L.J. was prepared to accept that this was indeed the case. Indeed it seems at first sight to offend also against the principle that banks are not concerned with disputes between the parties to the contract of sale. In fact, however, it is by no means clear that fundamental principles are offended. All that the bank is concerned with is whether the buyer claims that the goods do not conform to specification. If so, it withholds the final 10 per cent. It is not concerned with whether the buyer's claim has any merit, and if the seller disputes his claim then he must do so under the sale contract. The bank is thus concerned neither with the provisions of the sale contract nor with the actual condition of the goods, so that fundamental principles are not in fact infringed.

This is not in any case significantly different from the position under a performance bond payable on demand,[62] where in the absence of fraud the bank must act on the buyer's claim however ill-founded. Since the clause in *The Royan* is simply another way of achieving what could have been achieved by performance bond, Lloyd L.J.'s interpretation does not seem to be open to objection.

---

60. [1988] 2 Lloyd's Rep. 250, 256 (col. 2).
61. Above, section 6.1.2.
62. See, e.g., *Edward Owen Engineering Ltd.* v. *Barclays Bank International Ltd.* [1978] 1 Q.B. 159, set out in detail in section 8.2.3.

6.2.2.3 Fraud potential

It is clear from the discussion above of *The American Accord* that the law achieves the twin objectives of promoting the negotiability of bills of lading, and insulating banks from any concern over disputes under the sale contract. Equally clearly, however, it does very little to protect buyers and banks from the consequences of frauds by sellers.

It is true that *The American Accord* position does not apply where it can be proved that the seller is fraudulent, but the onus of proof is very much on the buyer or his bank, and proof of fraud is very difficult.[63] In practice, therefore, documents which conform on their face to the contract description must be accepted, whether they actually represent goods shipped or not.

Obviously this opens up possibilities for fraud by sellers, or collusive fraud by sellers and carriers, and indeed maritime fraud is increasingly becoming a matter for concern. The most extreme form is where no goods are shipped at all, the documents tendered being forgeries. In *Etablissement Esefka International Anstalt* v. *Central Bank of Nigeria*,[64] for example, apparently conforming documents were tendered in respect of 94,000 tonnes of cement said to be aboard eight vessels, although there was considerable doubt whether the vessels ever existed at all. If the obligation to insure is on the seller (as in a c.i.f. contract) and all the documents are forgeries, then the buyer obtains nothing at all, since obviously there will be no valid insurance policy. Nor, of course, does the bank obtain any security for its advance. Even if the buyer has taken out insurance his position is no better, as insurance companies do not generally pay if no goods have ever existed, or if goods are shipped of the wrong quality or quantity.

Alternatively, cargo may be lost or stolen in the loading process, so that a bill of lading may be issued for a greater quantity than is actually loaded.[65] Or goods which have been loaded may be unloaded again after shipped bills of lading have been issued. This type of fraud usually involves collusion between seller and carrier, or between seller and master (or someone else involved in cargo-handling). Or the carrier could steal the goods for which bills of lading have been issued, sail to a different destination and re-sell them to a third party.[66]

---

63. See, e.g., the statements made in *Bolivinter Oil S.A.* v. *Chase Manhattan Bank*, above, section 6.2.1.

64. [1979] 1 Lloyd's Rep. 445 (C.A.).

65. See, for example, *V/O Rasnoimport* v. *Guthrie & Co. Ltd.* [1966] 1 Lloyd's Rep. 1, where some of the cargo was stolen after mate's receipts had been signed, but before it was loaded on board. The loading broker did not know, and issued bills of lading for the entire cargo.

66. The most extreme example occurred in *Shell International Petroleum Co.* v. *Gibbs, The Salem* [1983] 2 A.C. 375; [1983] 2 W.L.R. 371; [1983] 1 All E.R. 745; [1983] 1 Lloyd's Rep. 342, where shipowners stole an entire cargo of 200,000 tons of crude oil. Another example is *Manchester Trust* v. *Furness, Withy & Co. Ltd., The Boston City* [1895] 2 Q.B. 282, where time charterers persuaded the master to divert an entire cargo of coal destined for Rio de Janeiro to Buenos Aires, where they sold it to a third party.

Where cargo is in drums, bags, sacks or containers, it is possible for a seller to ship rubbish, and obtain clean documents because the master is unaware of what is contained inside. The goods are indeed shipped in apparent good order and condition, the requirement for a clean bill of lading. In *Discount Records Ltd.* v. *Barclays Bank Ltd.*,[67] for example, the purchasers had ordered 8,625 records and 825 cassettes. The cargo was packed in 94 cartons, but of these two were found to be empty, five were filled with rubbish or packing, and 28 were only partly filled. 275 records and 518 cassettes were actually delivered, but of the 518 cassettes only 25 per cent. were delivered to order. Nevertheless clean shipping documents were obtained and the buyer could not restrain the bank from paying under the credit. It was alleged, but not proved, that the sellers were fraudulent.

Buyers and banks can afford themselves some protection against fraud, although this is a lot more difficult in the case of chain sales. Except where there are multiple re-sales, buyers can ensure that they deal only with reputable sellers, and can demand certificates from independent survey firms that goods of the correct quality have been loaded. Buyers can also take advantage of Lloyd's Information and Lloyd's Shipping Intelligence, at least to protect themselves against no goods having been shipped. It should be possible to discover whether a ship is capable of carrying the cargo purchased, and whether it could in fact have been at the port of loading at the shipment date.

Alternatively, the buyer may insist on a performance guarantee or bond issued by a reputable bank,[68] payable in the event of default by the seller. He will then at least be compensated if the seller breaks his contract, and the bank may actively discourage fraud by demanding from the seller some form of security against the issue of the guarantee.

It is much more difficult, however, for sub-buyers in chain sales, especially of generic goods, to protect themselves. They may be sure of the honesty of their particular buyer, but will have no control over the seller from whom he buys, or earlier sellers in the chain. In any event, they will have to show that their immediate seller has been fraudulent, if they are to avoid having to pay against documents. Normally this will not be the case, the fraud having been committed by the original seller and/or carrier.

6.3 THE DOCTRINE OF STRICT COMPLIANCE

The effect of the so-called "doctrine of strict compliance" is that the beneficiary must tender the exact documents stipulated in the credit, and that the bank must accept only those exact documents. The position as between bank and beneficiary is the same as that regarding the bank's own reimbursement,

67. Above, f.n. 40.
68. See further section 8.2.2.

i.e., that between confirming and issuing bank, and between issuing bank and customer.

Most of the cases[69] concern the common law position, where the U.C.P. does not apply. The common law adopts a very strict attitude, but this is one area where the U.C.P. differs, and presumably in an attempt to prevent too many disputes over documentation, adopts a more relaxed position. The strict common law position continues to apply, however, not only where the credit is not governed by the U.C.P., but also to the commercial invoice.[70]

6.3.1 Same rules apply to contracts 2, 3 and 4

As in the previous section, although contracts 2, 3 and 4 in Figure 1.2 are theoretically autonomous, it is clear that in principle, in any situation where the confirming bank is obliged to accept documents and pay the beneficiary, it should be able to claim reimbursement from the issuing bank, which should in turn be able to claim reimbursement from its customer. The doctrine of strict compliance accordingly operates in exactly the same way in contracts 2, 3 and 4. Of course, where the action arises between beneficiary and bank the documentary requirements depend upon the terms of the credit (contract 4 in Figure 1.2, in the case of a confirmed credit), whereas an action between the bank and its customer will be determined by its mandate (contract 2). Obviously the banks should ensure that the documentary requirements in the credit are the same as those required by the customer's mandate, but subject to that obvious qualification, the doctrine of strict compliance operates similarly as between each of the three contracts.

The leading case involves contract 2, i.e, the contract between the bank and its customer. The common law position is that the issuing bank's mandate derives from the instructions of its customer (the buyer), and that it has no authority to depart from these instructions in any particular. It follows that the mandate is to accept only the exact documents stipulated in the credit. If the beneficiary or confirming bank deviates at all from tendering the required documents, not only is the issuing bank under no obligation to pay, but unless the buyer expressly permits payment, it is under a positive obligation not to pay. It is immaterial that the goods conform to the contract description.

No doubt the courts are also influenced by the other factors described earlier in the chapter. Banks must act quickly, and in any case have no way of knowing whether slight variations are material. In the leading case of *Equitable Trust Company of New York* v. *Dawson Partners Ltd.*, Viscount Sumner observed[71]:

"It is both common ground and common sense that in such a transaction the accepting

---

69. Which are numerous: no attempt has been made to set them out exhaustively here.
70. See below, section 6.3.3.
71. (1927) 27 Ll.L.Rep. 49, at p. 52, followed in numerous later cases, and approved, e.g., by Lord Diplock in *Gian Singh & Co. Ltd.* v. *Banque de l'Indochine* [1974] 2 All E.R. 754, 758h.

bank can only claim indemnity if the conditions on which it is authorised to accept are in the manner of the accompanying documents strictly observed. There is no room for documents which are almost the same, or which will do just as well. Business could not proceed securely on any other lines. The bank's branch abroad, which knows nothing officially about the details of the transaction thus financed, cannot take upon itself to decide what will do well enough and what will not. If it does as it is told, it is safe; if it departs from the conditions laid down, it acts at its own risk."

In that case, the customer, who was a c.i.f. purchaser of vanilla beans, originally required the bank to pay only against (among other things) a Dutch Government certificate certifying that the goods were sound, sweet and of prime quality. The agreement was later varied, substituting for the certificate of the Dutch Government a certificate of quality to be issued by experts who were sworn brokers, and signed by the Chamber of Commerce. The words "experts" and "brokers" were in the plural. Apparently the terms were incorrectly decoded during transmission by cable, and in the event the bank paid against a certificate issued by one broker only, and signed not by the Chamber of Commerce, but by the Batavia Trade Association. The sellers having fraudulently shipped a quantity of sticks, stones and old iron covered by only a thin layer of vanilla beans, whose sole purpose was to conceal the fraud, the bank was unable to succeed in an action against its customer for reimbursement.

As has already been observed, the doctrine applies in exactly the same way where the action is brought between bank and beneficiary. The leading common law authority on this relationship is *J.H. Rayner & Co. Ltd.* v. *Hambros Bank Ltd.*,[72] a decision of the Court of Appeal. An irrevocable sight credit required the sight drafts to be accompanied by bills of lading for "Coromandel groundnuts". The sellers tendered bills of lading for "machine-shelled groundnut kernels", which were universally understood in the trade to be identical to "Coromandel groundnuts". The bank refused payment, the seller sued and failed, the Court of Appeal reversing Atkinson J. MacKinnon L.J. took the view that the position between bank and beneficiary ought in principle to be the same as that between bank and customer. Having quoted Lord Sumner in the passage set out above from *Equitable Trust Company of New York* v. *Dawson Partners Ltd.*, he continued[73]:

"The words in that bill of lading clearly are not the same as those required by the letter of credit. The whole case of the plaintiffs is, in the words of Lord Sumner, that 'they are almost the same, or they will do just as well'. The bank, if they had accepted that proposition, would have done so at their own risk. I think on pure principle that the bank were entitled to refuse to accept this sight draft on the ground that the documents tendered, the bill of lading in particular, did not comply precisely with the terms of the letter of credit which they had issued."

Nor did he think the bank ought to be assumed to know the customs and

72. [1943] 1 K.B. 37; (1943) 74 Ll.L. Rep. 10.
73. [1943] 1 K.B. 37, 40.

customary terms of the trade, so as to know that "machine-shelled groundnut kernels" meant the same as "Coromandel groundnuts"[74]:

"A homely illustration is suggested by the books in front of me. If a banker were ordered to issue a letter of credit with respect to the shipment of so many copies of the '1942 Annual Practice' and were handed a bill of lading for so many copies of the '1942 White Book', it would be entirely beside the mark to call a lawyer to say that all lawyers know that the '1942 White Book' means the '1942 Annual Practice'. It would be quite impossible for business to be carried on, and for the bankers to be in any way protected in such matters, if it were said that they must be affected by a knowledge of all the details of the way in which particular traders carry on their business."

Similar sentiments can be found at the beginning of Goddard L.J.'s judgment[75]:

"It seems to me that Atkinson J. [whom the court reversed] has based his judgment on the consideration that the bank was affected in some way by this custom of the trade, and, secondly, that he has considered whether what the bank required was reasonable or unreasonable. I protest against the view that a bank is to be deemed affected by knowledge of the trade of its various customers . . . "

The same position obtains of course as between the banks (i.e., contract three). In *Bank Melli Iran* v. *Barclays Bank D.C.O.*,[76] a confirmed irrevocable credit (as amended) required a delivery order and other documents to be tendered for "100 new Chevrolet trucks", accompanied by a U.S.A. government undertaking confirming that the trucks were new. The trucks were in fact left in the open in Belgium before shipment, during the very severe winter of 1947.

The invoice tendered to Barclays, the confirming bank, described the trucks as "in a new condition", the U.S.A. government undertaking referred to "100 new, good" trucks, and the delivery order described the trucks as "new-good". Barclays accepted and paid against the documents, and forwarded them to Bank Melli Iran, the issuing bank. Bank Melli Iran informed Barclays that they regarded the documents as faulty, but far from rejecting them immediately they authorised Barclays to increase the credit. Six weeks later they did reject them, and sued for a declaration that Barclays were not entitled to debit them with sums paid out under the credit.

McNair J., having referred to the passage from *Equitable Trust Company of New York* v. *Dawson Partners Ltd.* set out above, held that each of the documents tendered was faulty, and that Bank Melli should not be required to accept them. Of the invoice, he felt that the phrase "in a new condition" did not mean the same as "new", at any rate when applied to a motor-vehicle. Nor did "new, good" in the undertaking necessarily mean the same as "new", because "it may have a special trade meaning in relation to motor vehicles".[77] In any case, the undertaking did not identify any particular trucks, so that it

74. [1943] 1 K.B. 37, 41.
75. [1943] 1 K.B. 37, 42.
76. [1951] 2 Lloyd's Rep. 367.
77. [1951] 2 Lloyd's Rep. 367, 375 (col. 2).

was impossible to say that it related to those covered by the invoice or delivery order. On the question of the delivery order, again McNair J. did not think "new-good" meant the same as "new", although there was some suggestion that the hyphen appeared only because of a typing error.

Clearly, then, the doctrine of strict compliance is indeed strict! McNair J. went on to hold, however, that although the documents were clearly faulty, Bank Melli Iran must, from its conduct, be taken to have accepted them. The defence of ratification operated, and Bank Melli Iran had lost its right to reject. The defence of ratification operates not unlike the doctrines of waiver and estoppel considered in Chapter 3,[78] except that it is a once and for all doctrine: ratification for a time operates as ratification altogether. In the present context, this means that once documents are taken to have been accepted, they cannot later be rejected, even if they did not conform precisely.

6.3.2 Strict compliance in practice

6.3.2.1 Same type of document required

It should be reasonably obvious from the discussion in the previous paragraph that the documents tendered must at any rate be the same type as those specified in the credit. This will apply even if the documents tendered give better protection than the credit requires. In *National Bank of South Africa* v. *Bank Italiana Di Sconto*,[79] Bankes L.J. thought that if the credit specified delivery orders, then the sellers could not tender bills of lading instead unless on its construction the credit also gave them that option.[80]

6.3.2.2 Ambiguity resolved in favour of bank

There is also a principle that the customer's mandate must be precise, and that if it is ambiguous the bank is entitled to rely upon any reasonable interpretation of an ambiguous expression. In *Commercial Banking Co. of Sydney Ltd* v. *Jalsard Pty. Ltd.*,[81] one of the documents required by the credit was a "Certificate of Inspection". The certificates tendered showed that the goods (decorative battery-operated Christmas lights) had been visually but not physically inspected, whereas in fact they suffered from serious defects which could have been discovered only by physical inspection. Lord Diplock, in the Judicial Committee of the Privy Council, held that in the absence of better particulars, "Certificate of Inspection" should bear its ordinary meaning, which required only a visual inspection. If a particular type of inspection was required then the instructions should expressly so specify[82]:

78. See section 3.1.4.
79. (1922) 10 Ll.L. Rep. 531.
80. (1922) 10 Ll.L. Rep. 531, 534. The passage is not altogether clear, because it appears to confuse the credit with the sale contract. In principle, however, this view must be correct.
81. [1973] A.C. 279; [1972] 2 Lloyd's Rep. 529.
82. [1973] A.C. 279, 285–286.

" 'Certificate of Inspection' is a term capable of covering documents which contain a wide variety of information as to the nature and the results of inspection which had been undertaken. The minimum requirement implicit in the ordinary meaning of the words is that the goods the subject-matter of the inspection have been inspected, at any rate visually, by the person issuing the certificate. If it is intended that a particular method of inspection should be adopted or that particular information as to the result of the inspection should be recorded, this, in their Lordships' view, would not be implicit in the words 'Certificate of Inspection' by themselves, but would need to be expressly stated.

It is a well-established principle in relation to commercial credits that if the instructions given by the customer to the issuing banker as to the documents to be tendered by the beneficiary are ambiguous or are capable of covering more than one kind of document, the banker is not in default if he acts upon a reasonable meaning of the ambiguous expression or accepts any kind of document which fairly falls within the wide description used."[83]

6.3.2.3 Linking of documents

An application of the principle enunciated in the last section is that if a number of documents are specified, if the buyer requires each document to contain all the particulars, he must say so expressly, otherwise it will be enough that all the documents between them (i.e., the set of documents) contain all the particulars.

The leading authority is *Midland Bank Ltd.* v. *Seymour*,[84] Seymour was an importer of feathers from Hong Kong. Payment was to be by irrevocable documentary credit, at 90 days' sight, opened by Midland Bank Ltd. in London. Unfortunately for Seymour, the sellers, Taiyo Trading Company of Hong Kong, were "a quite worthless concern who made no attempt to fulfil their contracts", and later disappeared without trace.[85] However, by shipping rubbish they were able to obtain shipping documents, against which the bank paid. When the bank claimed reimbursement Seymour cast around "to find some good reason in law for throwing the loss upon the bank rather than upon himself . . . ".[86] In so casting around, he discovered that although the shipping documents as a whole contained all the requirements of the credit, the same could not be said of each individual shipping document. So, for example, although the invoice stated that the goods were "85 per cent clean", the bill of lading did not. He also discovered that whereas the credit was "to be available at Hong Kong", valid to 15 December 1952 (later extended by agreement between the parties to 31 December 1952), acceptance of drafts by the bank took place in London after 31 December 1952.[87]

---

83. Lord Diplock cites *Midland Bank Ltd.* v. *Seymour*, a case dealt with in detail in the following section.
84. [1955] 2 Lloyd's Rep. 147.
85. [1955] 2 Lloyd's Rep. 147 (*per* Devlin J.) at p. 150 (col. 1).
86. [1955] 2 Lloyd's Rep. 147 (*per* Devlin J.) at p. 153 (col. 2).
87. Seymour also counterclaimed against the bank, in respect of failure to pass on supplemental information received in the course of its enquiries, but the counterclaim is irrelevant to the present discussion.

Devlin J. began with a general statement of the doctrine of strict compliance[88]:

"There is, of course, no doubt that the bank has to comply strictly with the instructions that it is given by the customer. It is not for the bank to reason why. It is not for it to say: 'This, that or the other does not seem to us very much to matter.' It is not for it to say: 'What is on the bill of lading is just as good as what is in the letter of credit and means substantially the same thing.' All that is well established by authority. The bank must conform strictly to the instructions it receives."

The problem for Seymour was that the instructions were ambiguous, in that they did not clearly state whether each document must contain all the particulars, or that it was enough that all the documents between them (i.e., the set of documents) must contain all the particulars. Making it clear that any ambiguity would be resolved against Seymour, Devlin J. concluded that on the construction of this particular documentary credit, it was enough that the set contained the particulars, and there was no additional requirement that each document must. It follows that if the customer requires the particulars to be included in each of the shipping documents he should expressly so state.

However, even where the customer does not so stipulate, there is a second principle which applies whenever a set of documents is required, namely that the particulars in the various documents in the set must be consistent between themselves, "otherwise they would not be a good set of shipping documents".[89] In the particular case, however, there was no inconsistency between the documents in the set, so that the bank had acted in accordance with the instructions in the credit, and had not exceeded its mandate.

Devlin J. also held that the bank had not exceeded its authority by accepting drafts in London rather than Hong Kong because, again on the construction of the credit, the naming of Hong Kong was additional and not exclusive, so that acceptance in London was permitted as well. However, by accepting drafts after the expiry date the bank was prima facie in breach, but even on this point the defence claim failed because on the evidence, Seymour had instructed the bank to accept the drafts after the expiry date.

6.3.3 Strict compliance and the U.C.P.

The U.C.P. relaxes the strict rules of the common law, at any rate to a limited extent. Article 41(c) provides: "The description of the goods in the commercial invoice must correspond with the description in the credit. In all other documents, the goods may be described in general terms not inconsistent with the description of the goods in the credit." This provision is unchanged from Article 32(c) of the 1974 revision, and indeed earlier versions of the U.C.P. were to similar effect. The common law doctrine continues to apply in its full

---

88. [1955] 2 Lloyd's Rep. 147, 151 (col. 2).
89. [1955] 2 Lloyd's Rep. 147, 153 (col. 1).

stringency to the commercial invoice, but in the case of other documents, a description in general terms will suffice.

An earlier version of the U.C.P. provision was considered by McNair J. in *Soproma S.p.A.* v. *Marine & Animal By-Products Corporation.*[90] The facts of this case have already been set out in Chapter 3.[91] It will be recalled that the buyer agreed to buy a quantity of Chilean fish full meal from the seller c. & f. Payment was to be by documentary credit, to which the U.C.P. (1951 revision) applied.

Documents were tendered which did not conform to the credit in a number of respects. The bill of lading described the goods as "Fishmeal", not "Fish Full Meal", was marked "freight collect", not "freight prepaid", and named the confirming bank as consignee, rather than being issued to order. A quality certificate was also tendered certifying a minimum protein content of 67 per cent., rather than 70 per cent. as required. The buyers instructed the bank to reject the documents, and the bank did so. The sellers sued the buyers on the contract of sale.

McNair J. held that the buyers were entitled to require the bank to reject, and by implication that had the issue arisen between seller and bank, the bank would have been entitled to reject. The common law position was clear enough, but the question was what was the effect of the U.C.P. The provision before McNair J. was virtually identical to the present Article 41(c). He held that if the only fault had been the description in the bill of lading as "Fishmeal", the tender would have been valid[92]:

"I now turn to a number of . . . points taken as to the sufficiency of the credit. First, it was said there was an inconsistency between the description of the goods in the invoice, namely, '*Chilean Fish Full Meal*', and the description of the goods in the bill of lading, namely '*Chilean Fishmeal*', and reliance was placed upon (1) *Midland Bank Ltd.* v. *Seymour*,[93] for the statement that the documents must be mutually consistent, and (2) upon *J.H. Rayner & Co. Ltd.* v. *Hambro's Bank Ltd.*, for the proposition that the description of the goods in the shipping documents—in that case the bills of lading—must conform with the description of the goods in the letter of credit. In the present case the letters of credit as stated above incorporated the 'UNIFORM CUSTOMS AND PRACTICE FOR COMMERCIAL DOCUMENTARY CREDITS' which by Art. 33 provide as follows:

'The description of the goods in the Commercial Invoice must correspond with the description in the credit. Wherever the goods are described in the remaining documents, description in general terms will be acceptable.'

I have already set out earlier in this judgment the findings of the Board of Appeal . . . as to the meaning and effect of the terms 'Fish Full Meal' and 'Fish Meal' and their conclusion that the invoice specifically states 'Fish Full Meal', and anyone in the trade seeing a bill of lading would not expect to see a more specific description than 'fishmeal' and could not reasonably object to such a description. In my judgment, so far as concerns the [first] tender under the letters of credit, the bill of lading contained a sufficient general description to comply with Art. 33, the invoice having described

90. [1966] 1 Lloyd's Rep. 367.
91. Sections 3.1.3, 3.1.4 and 3.2.2.
92. [1966] 1 Lloyd's Rep. 367, 389 (col. 2).
93. [1955] 2 Lloyd's Rep 147, 153.

the goods in accordance with the letters of credit. There was no clause corresponding with Art. 33 in *Rayner's* case . . . "

However, the U.C.P. did not cure the faults in the certificate of quality and the certificate of analysis[94]:

"The next point to be taken was as to the inconsistent statements as to the protein content . . . [McNair J. stated the relevant facts] . . . [It] is in my judgment plain that the two documents relied upon by the buyers in their rejection, namely, the shippers' certificate of quality and the certificate of analysis, did not constitute valid shipping documents under the letter of credit as was in fact acknowledged by the sellers when, on making their second tender direct to the buyers, they instructed the Italian bank to withdraw these documents and to substitute in their place an analysis certificate signed by themselves dated Oct. 16 and a quality certificate also so signed and dated without any certificate as to protein content. In my judgment, the documents so tendered were not a good tender against the letter of credit."

It was also clear, of course, that there is nothing in the wording of what is now Article 41(c) that was capable of curing the other discrepancies in the bill of lading, namely that it was not made out to order, and that it was a freight collect bill. The argument as to whether these were acceptable tender rested on the common law alone.[95]

Article 41(c) allows for the description of the goods, in all documents apart from the commercial invoice,[96] to be described in general terms not inconsistent with the description of the goods in the credit. In *Banque de l'Indochine* v. *J.H. Rayner Ltd.*,[97] however, the Court of Appeal held that this provision (or rather the equivalent provision of the 1974 revision) gave no latitude as to identification. In the particular case there were defects in an EUR certificate and a certificate of origin, and in respect of these U.C.P. did not alter the common law position, requiring *exact* compliance. The documents did not exactly comply, and could therefore be rejected. Sir John Donaldson M.R. said[98]:

"There is, in my judgment, a real distinction between an identification of 'the goods', the subject matter of the transaction, and a description of those goods. The second sentence of art. 32(c)[99] gives latitude in description, but not in identification. For example, the EUR certificate or certificate of origin could identify 'the goods' by reference to marks on the bags or by reference to a hold in the vessel which they occupied provided that no other goods were in the hold. Having so identified 'the goods' they

94. [1966] 1 Lloyd's Rep. 367, 389 (col.2)–390 (col.1).
95. They were not: see section 3.1.3.
96. But the description in the invoice must be accurate. In *Kydon Compania Naviera S.A.* v. *National Westminster Bank, The Lena* [1981] 1 Lloyd's Rep. 68, a standby letter of credit, to which the 1962 revision of the U.C.P. applied, was provided to finance the acquisition of a ship. The description of the ship in the invoice did not correspond in a number of respects, including discrepancies regarding gross and net register tonnage, and Parker J. held that the bank was entitled to reject the documents tendered on these and other grounds. On this case see further section 8.4.3.
97. [1983] 1 All E.R. 1137; [1983] 1 Lloyd's Rep. 228.
98. [1983] 1 All E.R. 1137, 1143 b–c.
99. The 1974 version of what is now Article 41(c), and identical with it.

could then describe them as 'sugar' simpliciter since this description is not inconsistent with 'E.E.C. White Crystal Sugar Category No. 2., Minimum Polarisation 99.8 degrees Moisture Maximum 0.08 per cent'. But however general the description, the identification must, in my judgment, be unequivocal. Linkage between the documents is not, as such, necessary, provided that each directly or indirectly refers unequivocally to 'the goods'. This seems to me to be the proper and inevitable construction to place on art. 32(c) [1974 revision] if the specified documents are to have any value at all."

It is probably because of this case that banks are no longer required to accept documents apart from transport documents as tendered, without further qualification.[100] Article 23 of the 1983 revision provides:

"When documents other than transport documents, insurance documents and commercial invoices are called for, the credit should stipulate by whom such documents are to be issued and their wording or data content. If the credit does not so stipulate, banks will accept such documents as presented, provided that their data content makes it possible to relate the goods and/or services referred to therein to those referred to, in the commercial invoice(s) presented, or to those referred to in the credit if the credit does not stipulate presentation of a commercial invoice."

The condition is essentially similar to that laid down by Sir John Donaldson M.R., and removes any possible inconsistency between Articles 23 and 41(c).

6.3.4 Possible response of banks to non-conforming documents

Supposing documents are tendered to a confirming bank, which are, in its view, non-conforming. There is some doubt, however, beneficiary taking the view that they conform. This situation is by no means uncommon: in some 60 per cent. of all credit transactions there is some doubt about the conformity of the documents.

The bank can obviously reject the documents, but then it runs the risk of being sued by the beneficiary. Furthermore, the value of documentary credits to merchants would quickly diminish if banks routinely rejected documents on the slightest doubt as to their validity. An alternative is to pay, taking an indemnity from the beneficiary in respect of any loss or damage resulting from the deficiency in the documentation. That may put the bank into difficulty if the issuing bank does not make reimbursement. If there is a deficiency in the documents it must sue on the indemnity to recover its money from the beneficiary, but if it transpires that there is no deficiency it must proceed instead against the issuing bank. Since whether there is a deficiency is a matter of doubt, this is very unsatisfactory from the bank's point of view. Also, of course, protracted litigation could keep it out of its money for a considerable period.

The solution is to make a payment under reserve. The confirming bank did this in *Banque de l'Indochine* v. *J.H. Rayner Ltd.* At first instance,[101] Parker J. held that this entitled the confirming bank to demand its money back if the

100. Article 33 (1974 revision)—see further section 5.4.1.
101. [1983] 1 All E.R. 468; [1982] 2 Lloyd's Rep. 476.

documents were rejected by the issuing bank, but only if the discrepancies were a valid reason for not making payment in the first place. The Court of Appeal's view was that this would mean that the confirming bank had, by paying under reserve, laid itself open to the possibility of becoming involved in legal proceedings. They did not think that this accorded with the commercial reality of the situation, and held instead that where payment is made under reserve, the sellers are obliged to pay the money back on demand if the issuing bank rejects the documents, either on its own initiative or on the buyer's instructions, for reasons which include at least one of the discrepancies relied on by the confirming bank for making payment only under reserve in the first place. Whether the discrepancies are good reasons in law for refusing to make payment is irrelevant.

In the event, the discrepancies relied on by the issuing bank (on the instructions of the buyer) were sufficiently serious as to entitle the confirming bank to have rejected them in the first place. The confirming bank was therefore entitled to demand its money back on either analysis. Parker J.'s decision was accordingly affirmed, but on other grounds.

The issuing bank has the same choices as the confirming bank, of course, the issue in this case being whether the buyer will accept the documents.

The U.C.P. makes clear, by Article 16(f), that payment under reserve, or against an indemnity, by a confirming bank, does not affect the obligations between issuing bank and buyer (i.e., contract 2). It affects contract 4 only, i.e., the relationship between confirming bank and beneficiary:

"If the remitting bank draws the attention of the issuing bank to any discrepancies in the documents or advises the issuing bank that it has paid, incurred a deferred payment undertaking, accepted or negotiated under reserve or against an indemnity in respect of such discrepancies, the issuing bank shall not be thereby relieved from any of its obligations under any provisions of this Article. Such reserve or indemnity concerns only the relations between the remitting bank and the party towards whom the reserve was made or from whom, or on whose behalf, the indemnity was obtained."

CHAPTER 7

THE RELATIONSHIP BETWEEN THE BANK AND THE CARRIER

Where a bank takes a bill of lading as security for an advance under a documentary credit, that security is considerably weakened unless the bank also has a cause of action against the sea carrier, if the goods represented by it are lost or damaged on the voyage. There are two possibilities, an action on the contract of carriage, and if the carrier has been negligent, an action in tort.

It would be fair to say that from the point of view of the banking community the law in this regard has never been satisfactory, and over the last two or three years has significantly worsened. It is also clear that the impetus for law reform has been largely dissipated, and it is unlikely that there will be significant change in the foreseeable future.

7.1 ACTION ON THE CONTRACT OF CARRIAGE

The difficulty arises from the fact that in a normal commercial credit transaction the bank will not be party to an express contract with the carrier. The contract of carriage is usually made by the shipper of the goods, and the bank's action, if any, depends on its possession of the bill of lading. The same difficulty, of course, usually affects buyers of goods under a typical c.i.f. or f.o.b. contract.

At common law, although transfer of the bill of lading might, given the necessary intention, also transfer the property in the goods,[1] it did not also transfer contractual rights and liabilities, at any rate as a matter of law. In the Exchequer decision of *Thompson* v. *Dominy*,[2] the plaintiff indorsees for

---

1. *Lickbarrow* v *Mason* (1794) 5 Term Rep. 683; 101 E.R. 380.
2. (1845) 14 M. & W. 403. The case may perhaps be regarded as an early statement, at least in this context, of the privity of contract doctrine. In *Sewell* v. *Burdick* (1884) 10 App. Cas. 74, Lord Blackburn commented at p. 91:

> "Some attempts had been made to say that the contract in a bill of lading might, under some circumstances at least, be transferred to an assignee in a manner analogous to that in which the contract in a bill of exchange was transferred by the indorsement of the bill of exchange; but I think that since the decision of *Thompson* v. *Dominy* in 1845, it has been undisputed law that under no circumstances could any one not a party to the contract from the beginning sue on it in his own name. Any action on the contract at common law must be brought in the name of an original contractor, and no action could be brought on the contract against one who was not liable to be sued as an original contractor."

value of a bill of lading sued the carrier for alleged short delivery, but failed on the grounds that the transfer of a bill of lading does not enable the transferee to bring an action in his own name on the carriage contract. It follows that at common law at least, a bank cannot sue a sea carrier in contract merely by virtue of taking a bill of lading as security.

Nevertheless there are two methods, in theory at least, by which a bank, which is not a party to the original contract of carriage, might nevertheless acquire rights under it. The first is section 1 of the Bills of Lading Act 1855. The second is the common law *Brandt* v. *Liverpool* doctrine.

7.1.1 Bills of Lading Act 1855, section 1

The Bills of Lading Act 1855, section 1, and the relevant part of the Preamble,[3] enact:

"Whereas by the custom of merchants a bill of lading of goods being transferable by indorsement the property in the goods may thereby pass to the indorsee, nevertheless all rights in respect of the contract contained in that bill of lading continue in the original shipper or owner and it is expedient that such rights should pass with property . . .
1. Every consignee of goods named in a bill of lading, and every indorsee of a bill of lading to whom property in the goods therein mentioned shall pass, upon or by reason of such consignment or indorsement shall have transferred to and vested in him all rights of suit and be subject to the same liabilities in respect of such goods as if the contract contained in the bill of lading had been made with himself."

Clearly the intention of the legislature was to reverse *Thompson* v. *Dominy*, or at any rate to mitigate against some of the effects of that decision. So, for example, in c.i.f. and most f.o.b. sales, where the seller makes the contract of carriage, the section is probably intended to pass rights and liabilities under that contract to the buyer, and indeed will often have that effect.[4] There are difficulties over the operation of this section, even as between seller and buyer, but they are beyond the scope of this book.

7.1.1.1 Sewell v. Burdick[5]

However, since the House of Lords decision in *Sewell* v. *Burdick*, it has usually been assumed that section 1 does not operate in favour of a bank who holds a bill of lading merely as pledgee. Machinery shipped by one Nercessiantz aboard the respondent's vessel ("*Zoe*") was landed at Poti (a Black Sea port) and warehoused in a Russian custom-house. Nercessiantz disappeared, and accordingly under Russian law, the cargo was sold to pay custom-house duty and charges. The sale realised no more than was sufficient for that pur-

---

3. The remainder of the preamble relates only to other sections of the Act, which is set out in full in Appendix B.
4. For a general review of the operation of the section, see, e.g., Todd, "Contracts with consignees and indorsees" [1984] 3 L.M.C.L.Q. 476.
5. (1884) 10 App. Cas. 74.

pose. The connection between the appellants, who were bankers in Manchester, and the goods was that they had taken bills of lading, indorsed in blank, as security for a £300 advance to Nercessiantz. They did not claim delivery of the cargo, however, in order to realise their security, and indeed could not have done so. The respondents were unable to claim freight from Nercessiantz, and claimed it instead from the appellants, on the basis that as holders of bills of lading they became liable under the Act.[6]

It is perhaps not surprising, in view of the fact that the appellants had not received (and were unable to receive) any benefit from their security, that the House of Lords held them not liable for freight under the Act. In all the discussions for reform of section 1, it has not been seriously argued that the actual decision should be reversed.[7] The reasoning of at any rate a majority of their Lordships goes well beyond the facts of the case, however, and would prevent *any* bank merely by way of taking a bill of lading as security for a pledge *either suing or being sued* on the bill of lading contract. This clearly covers commercial credits, although there was only a simple pledge in *Sewell* v. *Burdick* itself, the decision presumably pre-dating modern international banking practices.

The reasoning of Lords Blackburn, Bramwell and FitzGerald was essentially that it did not follow from *Lickbarrow* v. *Mason*[8] that a bank as pledgee obtained the entire legal property in the goods in order to trigger the section. As pledgee a bank obtains only a special property in the goods, and not the general property, so that generally section 1 is inapplicable in this situation.[9]

On this reasoning, a bank as pledgee never, merely by virtue of holding the bill of lading, becomes liable for bill of lading freight. It clearly follows that it can never sue under the Act either, since the test for transfer of rights and imposition of liabilities is the same. Obviously, if the bank does not by virtue of indorsement of the bill in its favour obtain even special property as pledgee,[10] then the position is even clearer.

It is now fairly clear that this is indeed the position, but before leaving *Sewell* v. *Burdick* altogether, it is necessary also to consider alternative interpretations, which are less extreme in their effect.

6. Section 1 depends on property in the goods passing "upon or by reason of . . . consignment or indorsement". The respondents claimed that by virtue of the decision in *Lickbarrow* v. *Mason*, note 1, above, the transfer of the bills of lading to the bank had also transferred the entire legal property in the goods to them, as required by the section.
7. Although this would be a side effect of the proposals of the Law Commission, Working Paper No. 112 (1989): *Rights to Goods in Bulk*, paras. 4.21–4.22. See f.n.s 42–43, below. It is clear, however, that these proposals were at best advanced somewhat tentatively by the Commission.
8. Above, f.n.s 1 and 6.
9. E.g., Lord Blackburn (1884) 10 App. Cas. 74, at pp. 95 and 102–103, Lord Bramwell at p. 104, and in particular Lord FitzGerald at p. 106. Lord Blackburn also took the view that the position of a mortgagee would be similar, at p. 98, although without finally deciding the point (at p. 103).
10. As in *Sale Continuation* v. *Austin Taylor*, sections 2.4.2 and 3.3.

7.1.1.1.1 THE JUST AND CONVENIENT APPROACH

The reasoning of the Earl of Selborne L.C. was different in some respects from that of the other judges in *Sewell* v. *Burdick*,[11] and until recently it may have been possible to argue that the effect of that case was less extreme than the conclusion in the previous paragraph. On the application of section 1 he said:

"[I]t seems to provide for those cases only in which the property so passes, as to make it just and convenient that all rights of suit under the contract contained in the bill of lading should be 'transferred to' the indorsee, and should *not* any longer 'continue in the original shipper or owner.' One test of the application of the statute may perhaps be, whether, according to the true intent and operation of the contract between the shipper and the endorsee, the shipper still retains any such proprietary right in the goods, as to make it just and reasonable that he should also retain rights of suit (the word is *suit*, not *action*) against the shipowner, under the contract contained in the bill of lading. If he does, the statute can hardly be intended to take from him those rights, and transfer them to the indorsee, neither is the indorsee subjected to the shipper's liabilities."[12]

Although this reasoning is here used to limit the operation of section 1, it suggests the possibility of a "just and reasonable" approach to the interpretation of the section. This could lead to a less rigid approach than that of the other judges in the case, in that although it was not just and reasonable to transfer rights of suit (and hence liabilities) in the particular case, it might well be in different circumstances.

For example, *Sewell* v. *Burdick* was a case of a straightforward pledge, where at the time of indorsement the pledgor clearly retained a proprietary interest in the goods, whereas in a normal documentary credit transaction, there is no good reason why, after documents have been tendered, the shipper (who has after all sold the goods and been paid for them) should retain any rights of suit, and it could perhaps be argued therefore that they should pass to the bank holding the bill of lading. On this argument, it does not necessarily follow from *Sewell* v. *Burdick* that a bank as pledgee can *never* rely on section 1, merely that it was not just and reasonable for the bank to be sued on the carriage contract in the particular case before him.

The just and reasonable interpretation of section 1 has now been rejected, as part of the *ratio*, by the Court of Appeal in *The Aramis*.[13] It is not a banking case, but the decision has important ramifications for the banking community. The case involved the sale to two plaintiffs of undivided shares in a bulk cargo; Unigrain, whose agents had presented a bill of lading (No. 5), and Van der Valk, whose agents had presented a bill of lading (No. 6). Each bill

---

11. Although he also alluded to the distinction between general and special property: (1884) 10 App. Cas. 74, at p. 78.
12. (1884) 10 App. Cas. 74, at pp. 84–85. The italics are those of Lord Selborne. The quotations are from the section itself.
13. *Aramis (cargo owners)* v. *Aramis (owners), The Aramis* [1989] 1 Lloyd's Rep. 213.

of lading represented a consignment of a little over 200 tonnes of Argentine linseed expellers. The consignments were part of an undivided bulk, being mixed also with other consignments of Argentine linseed expellers, destined for other receivers.

The vessel proceeded to Rouen, where part of the cargo was discharged in favour of other receivers, and thence to Rotterdam, where the cargo destined for the plaintiffs was supposed to be discharged. The trial was conducted without oral evidence or full discovery, so that the facts found were rather sparse, but it seems that no cargo was discharged in respect of bill of lading No. 5, and only 11,550 kilos in respect of bill of lading No. 6. Since it was accepted that no linseed expellers remained on board when the vessel left Rotterdam, the reason for the shortage was either that the full cargo had not been originally loaded, or because of over-discharge at Rouen.

The main part of the case is on the *Brandt* v. *Liverpool* doctrine,[14] but there are also important statements to be found on section 1. Unigrain had no possible claim under section 1, since none of their cargo at all was discharged, so that no property could have passed to them. Van der Valk's case was stronger, since at least some of their cargo had been delivered, and they also attempted an alternative argument, based on section 1.

Van der Valk's difficulty was that property in a share of an undivided bulk cargo cannot pass until the bulk is divided, which typically (and in this case) occurs on discharge.[15] Clearly therefore property had not passed upon or by reason of consignment or indorsement, as required by a literal interpretation of section 1, or indeed during the voyage at all, but Van der Valk argued that it was "just and convenient" that the right of suit should pass under the section, where the only reason for property not passing was that the goods formed part of a larger bulk.

In making it clear that if property does not pass at all, the section cannot operate,[16] the Court of Appeal in *The Aramis* also rejected the "just and reasonable" approach. The reasons were first, that the speeches of the other members of the House gave no hint that considerations of justice and reasonableness have any role to play, secondly that Lord Selborne's language, and in particular use of the word "perhaps",[17] was not the language of decision, and thirdly that in the view of Bingham L.J. the legislative intention was plain from the statutory language used.

It must be assumed, therefore, that since the bank does not obtain the

---

14. See section 7.1.2, below.
15. See section 3.3.3.
16. [1989] 1 Lloyd's Rep. 213 at p. 218 (cols.1 and 2). Hence section 1 will never operate where the sale is of an unascertained part of an undivided bulk cargo, except for the very unusual circumstances that occurred in *Karlshamns Oljefabriker* v. *Eastport Navigation, The Elafi* [1982] 1 All E.R. 208. After discharge of parts of the bulk to various buyers en route, all that remained was destined for the same buyer, and property passed (on the voyage) by process of exhaustion.
17. "One test of the application of the statute may *perhaps* be . . . " above, f.n. 11, and text thereto.

general property in the goods, section 1 does not operate however just and reasonable it would be for it to do so.

7.1.1.1.2 FORM OF INDORSEMENT OF BILL OF LADING

It is necessary to consider also another distinction drawn by the Earl of Selborne, in his attempt not to lay down a general rule in *Sewell* v. *Burdick*. He laid great stress on the particular facts of the case, taking the view for example, that there may be reason for distinguishing between personal indorsement and indorsement in blank[18]:

"So long as it remains in blank it may pass from hand to hand by mere delivery . . . It would be strange if the Bills of Lading Act has made a person whose name has never been upon the bill of lading and who (as between himself and the shipowner) has never acted upon it, liable to an action by the shipowner upon a contract to which he was not a party."

Perhaps Lord Selborne took the view, then, that had the bank taken a personal indorsement the result in *Sewell* v. *Burdick* might have been different, and by the same token that a bank which takes a personal indorsement under a commercial credit might be able to rely on the Act. However, Lord Selborne did not elaborate on the distinction, and it has never been taken in any subsequent case.[19] It cannot be assumed that this was the basis of the decision.

However, there is something to be said for the view that the Act cannot apply in any case where the bill of lading is indorsed in blank, so maybe this should be seen as an *additional* reason for the decision. A bill of lading which is indorsed in blank can pass from hand to hand by mere delivery, just like a bearer bill, and it would indeed be strange if liability to pay freight, and other liabilities under the carriage contract, could be imposed by transfer of a bill of lading in so informal a manner. If liabilities are not imposed, then nor of course are rights of suit transferred. Another reason why the Act may not apply where the bill is blank indorsed is that because it is transferred by mere delivery, property does not pass upon or by reason of consignment or indorsement. The same is of course also true of bearer bills.

7.1.1.1.3 SUPPOSE THE PLEDGEE TAKES DELIVERY

Lord Selborne also thought that the decision in *Sewell* v. *Burdick* might have been different if the pledgee had taken delivery,[20] but it is not entirely clear whether, in his view, liability in this case would have depended on the 1855 Act itself, or on an implied contract under what later became the *Brandt* v.

18. (1884) 10 App. Cas. 74, at p. 83.
19. In *Sewell* v. *Burdick* itself Lord Blackburn doubted its validity: (1884) 10 App. Cas. 74, at p. 93.
20. (1884) 10 App. Cas. 74, at pp. 86–88.

Liverpool[21] doctrine. Atkin L.J. in *Brandt* v. *Liverpool* itself thought this distinction wrong.[22] Scrutton L.J. in the same case thought Lord Selborne must have been thinking of the earlier common law, in other words the common law implied contract which later became generally known as the *Brandt* v. *Liverpool* doctrine.[23]

7.1.1.1.4 CONCLUSION ON *SEWELL V. BURDICK*

At the end of the day, then, even if from the speech of the Earl of Selborne can be gleaned the possibility of a less rigid approach, his views have found little favour subsequently, and it has been almost universally assumed that the case turns on the distinction between general and special property drawn by Lords Blackburn, Bramwell and FitzGerald.[24] It makes no difference whether the bill of lading is indorsed in person or in blank, or whether or not the bank takes delivery of the goods.

7.1.1.2 Narrow and wide views of the section

The decision in *Sewell* v. *Burdick* depends, then, on the nature of the property obtained by the bank as pledgee. It does not obtain the general property, and of course may not on indorsement obtain any property at all, if the general property has already been passed to the buyer. A bank might, however, obtain the general property in the goods if it realises its security, for example if the buyer goes bankrupt or disappears. Can section 1 be triggered by the bank eventually obtaining the general property in the goods?

One situation can easily be disposed of. If the bank does not obtain general property until after the completion of the voyage,[25] then the bank's position would be exactly analogous to that of Van der Valk in *The Aramis*. It will eventually obtain the general property in the goods, but since the voyage has by now ended property clearly cannot pass on indorsement of the bill of lading, or by reason of it. It may be "just and reasonable" for rights of suit to pass, but if *The Aramis* is correct those criteria will carry no weight.

It is possible that the buyer goes into liquidation before the voyage is completed, in which case *The Aramis* is no longer directly analogous. Also, of course, a bank which releases documents in exchange for a trust receipt may thereupon become equitable owner of the goods while they are still at sea. Usually there will be a gap between indorsement and the passing of the

---

21. *Brandt* v. *Liverpool Brazil & River Plate S.N. Co.* [1924] 1 K.B. 575. In this case a bank who held a bill of lading as security successfully sued the carrier in contract, not on the basis of the 1855 Act but on an implied contract. That the Earl of Selborne may have been thinking of the implied contract doctrine is borne out at (1884) 10 App. Cas. 74, at p. 87.

22. [1924] 1 K.B. 575, at p. 598.

23. *Ibid.*, at p. 596.

24. This view is strongly fortified by the view taken of the case, in particular by Mustill L.J., in *Enichem Anic S.p.A.* v. *Ampelos Shipping Co. Ltd., The Delfini* [1990] 1 Lloyd's Rep. 252, 268-275, noted by Treitel [1990] L.M.C.L.Q. 1.

25. As in *Sewell* v. *Burdick* itself, of course.

general property to the bank, or between indorsement and the bank becoming equitable owner on the terms of the trust receipt, but this is not necessarily fatal to the operation of section 1, at any rate where indorsement is part of the causal chain leading to the passing of general property to the bank. It is not an essential part of the causal link where the bank obtains equitable property under a trust receipt, since the buyer may declare himself trustee for the bank at any time, whether or not the bank has ever held the shipping documents. Where the bank obtains special property on indorsement, and general property on the bankruptcy of the buyer, however, indorsement is an essential part of the causal link: had the bank never become holder of the bill of lading, property could not have passed to it, even though it is not the immediate cause, that being the liquidation of the buyer.[26]

The problem here is that even on the widest interpretation of section 1, the parties to the transaction must intend the property to pass. It is difficult to see how any of the parties in a documentary credit (i.e., seller, buyer and the bank as holder of the bill of lading) can intend that *general* property pass to the bank, since that will occur only if the buyer cannot pay, and this is obviously unlikely to be an intended consequence.

The wide view of section 1 is that taken by Carver, *Carriage by Sea*[27]: "It appears then that the property need only pass from the shipper to the consignee or indorsee under a contract in pursuance of which goods are consigned to him under the bill of lading, or in pursuance of which the bill of lading is indorsed in his favour." This view contrasts with a narrow and literal interpretation of the section, as adopted by Scrutton on Charterparties[28]: "If the property in the goods passes otherwise than upon or by reason of consignment or indorsement the rights of suit do not pass to the receiver." Even if the Carver view is correct, the contract to which he refers in the passage is presumably the sale contract, and it is clear that there is never an intention to pass general property to the bank under the sale contract. In any case, however, since the decision of the Court of Appeal in *The Delfini*,[29] the wider Carver view of section 1 can no longer be sustained.

---

26. The position is analogous to *The Elafi*, above, f.n. 16, where property passed by process of exhaustion, some time after indorsement. *The Elafi* has been approved by the Court of Appeal in *The Delfini*, above, f.n. 24, which adopted what was otherwise a narrow interpretation of section 1. Mustill L.J. said, for example, at p. 274 (col.1):

"Section 1 presents two alternative situations in which the contract is transferred to the endorsee. The first is where the property passes 'upon' the endorsement (and delivery of the document) . . . The second is where the property passes 'by reason of' the endorsement. This must signify something different, since the expression is 'upon or by reason of' not 'upon and by reason of'. In my judgment it means that although the endorsement of the bill is not the proximate occasion of the passing of property, nevertheless it plays an essential causal part in it."

27. 13th ed., para. 98.
28. 19th ed. (1984), p. 27.
29. *Enichem Anic S.p.A.* v. *Ampelos Shipping Co. Ltd., The Delfini* [1990] 1 Lloyd's Rep. 252.

In conclusion, it is unlikely after *The Aramis* and *The Delfini* that a bank as pledgee will ever be able to use section 1.

7.1.1.3 Importance of type of document used

It is in any case clear that section 1 can only be relied upon, whether by a buyer or a bank, if a shipped bill of lading is used. Presumably no other documentation was commonly used in 1855. Even a received for shipment bill of lading will not suffice, still less a delivery order, combined transport document or waybill. Section 1 is simply not drafted so as to deal with the current revolution in documentation.

Even where a shipped bill of lading is issued, for section 1 to operate it must still be valid as a document of title when it is indorsed, and property thereby passes. It has already been noted that in the oil trade the documentation may take months or even years to catch up,[30] and bills of lading may well be negotiated after the cargo has been discharged. This is what happened in *The Delfini*, and at first instance Phillips J. held that the bill of lading had ceased to be effective as a transferable document of title when the cargo was discharged. Hence the ultimate receiver (who claimed short delivery) could not rely on section 1, primarily on the grounds that indorsement and transfer of the bill of lading could not be instrumental in conferring upon the indorsee either proprietary or possessory title.[31] The decision of the Court of Appeal was on wider grounds,[32] but exactly the same result was reached by Phillips J. in *The Sirina*,[33] for the same reasons that he had adopted in *The Delfini*.

7.1.2 The *Brandt* v. *Liverpool* doctrine

Because a bank as pledgee cannot generally rely on section 1, it is forced to fall back on the common law *Brandt* v. *Liverpool* doctrine. This doctrine is really a device to avoid the deficiencies of the Bills of Lading Act, and in particular its dependence on the passing of property. It works by implying a new contract between receiver and carrier: on delivery of the cargo against tender of a bill of lading or ship's delivery order, a contract is implied that delivery will be on the terms of the bill of lading or ship's delivery order.[34] Its operation depends on whether the facts support the implication of a new contract, but where they do, many of the difficulties of the 1855 Act are avoided. For

---

30. Section 1.2.
31. [1988] 2 Lloyd's Rep. 599, 607 (col. 2). He adopted the reasoning of Mustill J. in *The Elafi*, f.n.s 16 and 24, reasoning which was later approved by the Court of Appeal in *The Delfini*.
32. Above, f.n. 29.
33. *Conoco U.K. Ltd.* v. *Limni Maritime Co. Ltd., The Sirina* [1988] 2 Lloyd's Rep. 613.
34. In *Brandt* v. *Liverpool* itself, the shipowner delivered the goods against presentation of the bill of lading, and the receiver (a bank as pledgee) paid the freight. The Court of Appeal was prepared to imply a fresh contract between receiver and carrier, on the terms of the bill of lading.

example, *Brandt* v. *Liverpool* contracts have been implied (in the case itself) in favour of a bank which had advanced money against the security of a bill of lading, and by a purchaser of part of an undivided bulk cargo.

Such common law contracts have been implied since even before the 1855 Act, but the authority which gives the doctrine its name is the Court of Appeal decision in *Brandt* v. *Liverpool, Brazil & River Plate S.N. Co.*[35] Zinc ashes were shipped in a damaged condition, but the shipowner nevertheless issued a bill of lading stating that they were shipped in apparent good order and condition. Subsequently, the cargo had to be unloaded and reconditioned, at a cost of £748, and re-shipped on another vessel, being forwarded late to its destination.

The bill of lading was indorsed in favour of the plaintiff pledgees (a bank), who advanced money on it in good faith. When the second vessel arrived at its destination, the indorsees presented the bill of lading, paid the freight and (under protest) the sum of £748, which the shipowner demanded, and took delivery of the cargo.

The indorsee bank sued the shipowners for damages due to delay (the general value of the cargo having fallen), and for repayment of the £748. As pledgees they had no action based on the Bills of Lading Act 1855, but they succeeded on the basis of a common law implied contract. By the acts of presenting the bill of lading, payment of the freight and delivery of the cargo, a contract was implied between the indorsees and shipowners on the terms of the bill of lading.[36]

The doctrine was extended to cover ship's delivery orders in *The Dona Mari*.[37] The implied contract was on delivery order terms, of course, since no bill of lading was tendered. It is important to note that the delivery order was issued by the carrier. Merchants' delivery orders will not suffice. In *The Wear Breeze*,[38] none of the documents, which included delivery orders, was issued by the shipowner, and it was assumed (though not clearly held) that the buyer had no contract action.

7.1.2.1 *Offer, acceptance and consideration for the implied contract*

In order to be able to imply a contract, it is necessary to be able to infer offer, acceptance and consideration. In *Brandt* v. *Liverpool* itself the payment of freight (and other charges) constituted the consideration for the implied con-

---

35. [1924] 1 K.B. 575.
36. The shipowners tried to avoid liability for the damage which occurred before shipment, but were estopped from so pleading by virtue of the statement in the bill of lading that the goods were shipped in apparent good order and condition.
37. *Cremer* v. *General Carriers S.A., The Dona Mari* [1974] 1 W.L.R. 341; [1974] 1 All E.R. 1.
38. *Margarine Union G.m.b.H.* v. *Cambay Prince Steamship Co., The Wear Breeze* [1969] 1 Q.B. 219.

tract, moving from the receiver of the cargo. The consideration moving from the carrier was delivery of the cargo, on the terms of the bill of lading.[39]

The difficult areas are in finding acceptance by the shipowner of an obligation to deliver on bill of lading terms, and consideration moving from the receiver. In *Brandt* v. *Liverpool* itself, neither of these presented any difficulty: the shipowner had actually delivered the goods, and so could be taken to have accepted the undertaking, and the consideration moving from the receiver had been payment of the freight (and the £748 reconditioning cost). Also, the bill of lading was presented in exchange for the discharge of the goods from the ship.

Clearly, if freight is paid by the shipper (freight is commonly prepaid for dry-cargo shipments, but not for tankers), it will be more difficult to find any consideration, and if delivery is not actually made, it will be more difficult to infer acceptance, in which case it may be impossible to infer a *Brandt* v. *Liverpool* contract. It may also be more difficult to imply a contract where the goods are not delivered against production of an original bill of lading, but for example against a bank indemnity.

In principle, however, the freight and delivery requirements should not be regarded as being set in concrete. They are merely among the conditions under which acceptance and consideration may be inferred. If acceptance and consideration can be inferred in other ways, then their absence need not be crucial.

In recent years it had begun to look as though the courts were prepared to recognise the fictitious nature of the *Brandt* v. *Liverpool* device, and perhaps even to bend the rules of offer, acceptance and consideration somewhat in order to extend its scope. In *The Elli 2*,[40] the doctrine was invoked although the receiver did not pay freight, and it was assumed that a contract could be implied, notwithstanding that the evidence did not make clear whether the buyer tendered the bills of lading in exchange for the goods, or whether on occasions he gave a guarantee or undertaking that they would be forthcoming as soon as they came into his possession.

A quantity of cement was sold c.i.f. Jeddah to the defendant receiver (Mr. Bamaodah). Bills of lading incorporating charterparty terms were issued and signed and sent to the receiver, but it was not clear whether he presented those against discharge or merely guaranteed that he would produce them later. In an *ex parte* application to serve the defendant out of the jurisdiction, the shipowners claimed demurrage due under the charterparty. The Court of

39. It is of no consequence that he probably has to deliver the cargo anyway, under his existing obligations towards the shipper. However, in *The Eurymedon* [1975] A.C. 154, the Privy Council affirmed, as part of the *ratio* of the case, that consideration for a new contract can include the performance of obligations already owed under an existing contract. On this case see further below.

40. *Ilyssia Compania Naviera S.A.* v. *Ahmed Abdul Qawi Bamadoa, The Elli 2* [1985] 1 Lloyd's Rep. 107.

Appeal held that there was at least a good arguable case[41] that shipowners were entitled to demurrage on the basis of a *Brandt* v. *Liverpool* contract, although this was not a case to which the Bills of Lading Act 1855, section 1, clearly applied.[42]

In principle, so long as agreement can be inferred, it should make no difference what is the nature of the consideration, nor whether or not the documents are actually exchanged for the goods.[42a] In reality there are no consideration difficulties in *The Elli 2*, as demurrage was paid.[42b] But the question was said to depend on the circumstances of each particular case, and no rigid rules were laid down requiring financial consideration. Ackner L.J. said[42c]:

"It is common ground that the implication of [a *Brandt* v. *Liverpool* contract] is a matter of fact to be decided on the circumstances of each case. Indeed, that is made clear by *Brandt*'s case. Mr. Gross [for the defendant] accepts that although one usually finds that freight has been paid, this is not essential, nor was it to be expected in Mr. Bamaodah's case since he had no obligation for freight."

Similar views are echoed by May L.J.[42d]:

"Nevertheless, I agree that the boundaries of the doctrine are not clear. I would not expect them to be so. As the question whether or not any such contract is to be implied is one of fact, its answer must depend on the circumstances of each particular case— and the different sets of facts which arise for consideration in these cases are legion. However, I also agree that no such contract should be implied on the facts of any given case unless it is necessary to do so: necessary, that is to say, in order to give business reality to a transaction and to create enforceable obligations between parties who are dealing with one another in circumstances in which one would expect that business reality and those enforceable obligations to exist . . . "

Not that it is easy to think of non-financial consideration in this context.[43]

---

41. For the purposes of the application, under Rules of the Supreme Court, Order 11, rule 1(1)(f), it was only necessary for the owners to show a good arguable case that there was an implied contract, governed by English law. On the issue of whether English law applied, see further section 8.3.2.

42. The problem was essentially the same as in *The Delfini* and *The Sirina*, above, section 7.1.1.3, namely that because the bill of lading may not have arrived before discharge, that it may not still have been able to be enforced as a document of title when it was indorsed. Since the case succeeded on the basis of *Brandt* v. *Liverpool*, however, the Court of Appeal did not decide the section 1 point: [1985] 1 Lloyd's Rep. 107 (*per* Ackner L.J.) at p. 112 (col. 2); (*per* May L.J.) at p. 115 (col.1).

42a. A possible difficulty is that the receiver, not having received the bill of lading, may not know the terms of the implied contract into which he is entering, he had had previous dealings with the carrier in *The Elli 2* itself. This would also not be a fatal objection if the bill of lading was on a standard form commonly used in the trade.

42b. At least, that was the result of the case. Neither freight not demurrage appears to have been paid voluntarily by the receiver.

42c. [1985] 1 Lloyd's Rep. 107, 111 (col. 2).

42d. [1985] 1 Lloyd's Rep. 107, 115 (col. 2).

43. One possible argument is that the receiver could provide consideration by agreeing, on taking delivery, to be bound by either liabilities or exemption clauses in the bill of lading. The problem is that the receiver is not giving anything up; indeed, his position is improved from being unable to sue at all, to being able to sue subject to the exemption clauses.

In order to invoke the doctrine where neither freight nor other charges are paid by the receiver it might be necessary to recognise the artificial nature of the doctrine, and stretch the rules of offer, acceptance and consideration to suit commercial convenience.

Until recently it appeared that the courts were prepared to go down this route. Indeed, in the above passage May L.J. suggested that a contract could be implied in order to give business efficacy to a transaction. A far stronger authority is *The Eurymedon*,[44] where stevedores negligently damaged the consignees' cargo while unloading it from the vessel. They wished to rely on the one-year time bar in the bill of lading contract, but the problem was that neither they nor the consignees were party to that contract, which had been made between shipper and carrier. There was a *Himalaya* clause in the bill of lading, which purported to extend the benefits of the bill of lading contract to the stevedores, but that was of no assistance to the stevedores without more, since they were not party to the bill of lading contract. The Privy Council avoided the difficulty, which would have been commercially very inconvenient, by implying a unilateral contract between the plaintiff and defendant. It was a highly artificial contract. The shipper, by contracting on the terms of that particular bill of lading, was taken to be making an offer to the stevedores that, if they unloaded his goods,[45] he would extend to them the benefit of the bill of lading time bar, and other bill of lading exemptions. The stevedores accepted by unloading the goods. It cannot possibly have been the intention of either shipper or stevedores to enter into such a contract, the only terms of which were the clauses protecting the stevedores in the bill of lading. But Lord Wilberforce said[46]:

"The whole contract is of a commercial character, involving service on one side, rates of payment on the other, and qualifying conditions as to both. The relations of all parties to each other are commercial relations entered into for business reasons of ultimate profit . . . It is only the precise analysis of this complex of relations into the classical offer and acceptance, with identifiable consideration, that seems to present difficulty, but this same difficulty exists in many situations of daily life, e.g., . . . bankers' commercial credits.[47] These are all examples which show that English law, having committed itself to a rather technical and schematic doctrine of contract, in application takes a practical approach, often at the cost of forcing the facts to fit uneasily into the marker slots of offer, acceptance and consideration."

It is clear from this passage that Lord Wilberforce was prepared to bend the normal rules of offer, acceptance and consideration precisely in order to

44. *New Zealand Shipping Co. Ltd. v. A.M. Satterthwaite & Co. Ltd., The Eurymedon* [1975] A.C. 154.

45. Similar offers were also made to all other servants, agents and independent contracts employed or engaged by the carrier, the offer being accepted by them performing their contractual duties.

46. [1975] A.C. 154, 167.

47. Presumably the difficulty in the case of bankers' commercial credits is that of finding a contract between confirming bank and beneficiary, under a confirmed irrevocable letter of credit. See further section 8.1.

arrive at a commercially convenient solution. It is also noteworthy that although the main issue there was not the implication of a *Brandt* v. *Liverpool* contract, it was necessary to bind the consignee, as well as the shipper, to the implied contract with the stevedores. The Privy Council was prepared to assume that he was bound on the basis of a *Brandt* v. *Liverpool* contract, although freight appears to have been prepaid by the shipper.[48]

7.1.2.2 *The Aramis*[49]

Any hope that the *Brandt* v. *Liverpool* doctrine might be extended outside the "technical and schematic . . . slots of offer, acceptance and consideration" have been seriously dashed by the recent decision of the Court of Appeal in *The Aramis*.

In *The Elli 2* the cargo was delivered, albeit not necessarily against production of a bill of lading, and some payment, albeit not of freight, was made by the receiver. In *The Aramis*[50] there was no payment of freight or anything else, and at any rate in respect of one of the plaintiffs, none of the cargo was delivered. The Court of Appeal held that the *Brandt* v. *Liverpool* doctrine could not be invoked, and although this is probably not surprising on the facts, the judgment of Bingham L.J. lends no succour to the view that the courts may bend the rules of offer and acceptance in order to extend the doctrine.

Although bills of lading were presented, and delivery of the cargo requested, neither plaintiff paid freight or other charges. Unigrain faced the additional difficulty that none of their cargo at all was discharged. Both plaintiffs' main argument was based on the *Brandt* v. *Liverpool* doctrine, and in both cases it failed. The Court of Appeal took the view that, in order to be able to imply a contract, it is necessary to be able, as a matter of fact, to make the inference that the parties intended to make a contract. It must be possible, in other words, to infer offer and acceptance (the case does not appear to turn on the lack of consideration). The Court of Appeal was unable to do this in *The Aramis*, since the parties behaved in exactly the same way as they would have behaved in the absence of a contract. The receivers tendered the bills of lading, and the ship's agents accepted them, but that will always be the case, and therefore this conduct alone cannot form the basis for inferring a contract. As Bingham L.J. observed[51]:

" . . . it would in my view be contrary to principle to countenance the implication of a contract from conduct if the conduct relied upon is no more consistent with an intention to contract than with an intention not to contract. It must, surely, be necessary to identify conduct referable to the contract contended for or at the very least conduct inconsistent with there being no contract made between the parties to the effect con-

---

48. Unfortunately, there was very little discussion of this aspect of the decision.
49. *Aramis (cargo owners)* v. *Aramis (owners)*, *The Aramis* [1989] 1 Lloyd's Rep. 213.
50. The facts are set out above, section 7.1.1.1.1.
51. [1989] 1 Lloyd's Rep. 213, 224 (col. 2).

tended for. Put another way, I think it must be fatal to the implication of a contract if the parties would or might have acted exactly as they did in the absence of a contract."

The facts were perhaps rather unusual. Neither plaintiff paid freight or other charges. Unigrain faced the additional difficulty that none of their cargo at all was discharged. Perhaps it would indeed be difficult to infer a contract on these facts. However, Bingham L.J.'s statement is in wider terms, and its effect may be to make it very difficult to infer a *Brandt* v. *Liverpool* contract in the absence of freight or other charges being paid by the receiver.

At the very least, the effect of Bingham L.J.'s statement is that the doctrine will only operate when the parties *change their positions* in such a way as to lead to the inference of an implied contract. It is not enough, for example, merely for the receiver to tender a bill of lading and take delivery of the goods. A change of position is required, and it is difficult to see what will suffice in the absence of payment by him of freight or other charges.[52] Yet with dry cargoes freight is usually prepaid, which will deprive banks of any cause of action against the carrier in nearly all dry cargo cases.

It is also clear from *The Aramis* that a real (rather than fictitious) contract must be implied, and that the courts will not artificially extend the doctrine in order to reach a commercially just solution. Elsewhere in his judgment, Bingham L.J. said[53]: "One cannot cast principle aside, and simply opt for a commercially convenient solution." It is possible that Bingham L.J.'s remarks are wrong. Certainly his remarks contrast strikingly with those of Lord Wilberforce in *The Eurymedon*, who quite clearly *was* prepared to bend the normal rules of offer, acceptance and consideration precisely in order to arrive at a commercially convenient solution. It is also difficult to see how, in *The Eurymedon*, either consignee or stevedores changed their positions one iota to justify implying a contract between them.[54] Professor Treitel argues that the Court of Appeal could have implied a contract in *The Aramis* "without violation of legal principle".[55]

Even if the approach taken by Bingham L.J. is wrong, however, it cannot be challenged short of litigation to the House of Lords. For the time being at least, therefore, the development of the *Brandt* v. *Liverpool* doctrine has been severely curtailed by *The Aramis*, and this decision is obviously not generally in the interests of the banking community.

In fact the *Brandt* v. *Liverpool* doctrine has never been entirely

---

52. As in *Brandt* v. *Liverpool* itself. See also *Cremer* v. *General Carriers S.A., The Dona Mari* [1974] 1 W.L.R. 341.

53. [1989] 1 Lloyd's Rep. 213, 225 (col. 2).

54. Nor indeed, was there any clear change of position in *The Elli 2*, since demurrage was paid only as a result of the court action. There was however a previous course of dealing, and demurrage had previously been paid by the receiver (see *per* Ackner L.J.: [1985] 1 Lloyd's Rep. 107, 110 (col. 2), so this may be a ground for distinguishing between the two cases.

55. [1989] L.M.C.L.Q. 162. See also Law Commission, Working Paper No. 112 (1989): *Rights to Goods in Bulk*, page 34, f.n. 91.

satisfactory,[56] and certainly amendment to section 1 is a better solution than an artificial extension of the *Brandt* v. *Liverpool* doctrine, such as was argued unsuccessfully in *The Aramis*. Indeed, the decision in *The Aramis* was apparently influenced by the knowledge that the Law Commission were considering reform of section 1,[57] since at the end of his judgment Bingham L.J. said[58]:

" . . . it may fairly be said that the modern prevalence of undivided bulk cargoes calls for a new, commercially workable, solution. I agree. But the solution is, in my view, to be found in an amendment of the 1855 Act along the lines now under consideration by the Law Commission, rather than in the implication of a contract where the grounds for such implication do not exist."

7.2 TORT ACTIONS AGAINST CARRIERS

7.2.1 Property requirement

Even if the bank has no action against the carrier in contract, it may be able to bring an action in tort for negligence, assuming it can be proved. The House of Lords recently held in *The Aliakmon*[59] that in order to sue in negligence, at least in this type of case, it is necessary for the plaintiff to have property in the goods at the time that they were damaged.

Property in this context means either legal ownership or a possessory title to the property concerned at the time when the loss or damage occurred. Although Lord Brandon does not elaborate upon this, it would seem that "possessory title" encompasses the special property which the bank obtains as pledgee on the principles of *Sewell* v. *Burdick*. Thus a bank which obtains special property on indorsement can sue the carrier in tort.

If under the sale contract, however, property passes from seller to buyer before the documents are pledged, the bank will not obtain any legal property, but may later obtain equitable property by virtue of a trust receipt.[60] It is also clear from *The Aliakmon*, however, that equitable ownership on its own does not give the bank a cause of action[61]:

"My Lords, under this head [equitable ownership] Mr. Clarke put forward two propositions of law. The first proposition was that a person who has the equitable ownership of goods is entitled to sue in tort for negligence anyone who by want of care causes them to be lost or damaged without joining the legal owner as a party to the action. [The second proposition is not relevant to the present discussion] . . .

---

56. Another situation, for example, where the doctrine could not apply would be if the vessel were totally lost at sea, because then there could be no question of delivering cargo on any terms.

57. See below, section 7.3.

58. [1989] 1 Lloyd's Rep. 213 at p. 225 (col. 2). Similar sentiments can be found in *The Delfini*, above, f.n. 24, where a narrow interpretation was taken of section 1.

59. *Leigh & Sillivan Ltd.* v. *Aliakmon Shipping Co. Ltd., The Aliakmon* [1986] A.C. 785; [1986] 2 W.L.R. 902; [1986] 2 Lloyd's Rep. 1.

60. See sections 2.4.1 and 3.3.4.1.

61. [1986] A.C. 785, 812A–E.

In my view, the first proposition cannot be supported. There may be cases where a person who is the equitable owner of certain goods has already a possessory title to them.[62] In such a case he is entitled, by virtue of his possessory title rather than his equitable ownership, to sue in tort for negligence anyone whose want of care has caused loss of or damage to the goods without joining the legal owner as a party to the action: see for instance *Healey* v *Healey*.[63] If, however, the person is the equitable owner of the goods and no more, then he must join the legal owner as a party to the action, either as co-plaintiff if he is willing or as co-defendant if he is not. This had always been the law in the field of equitable ownership of land and I see no reason why it should not also be so in the field of equitable ownership of goods."

7.2.2 Exemption clauses in the bill of lading

In *The Aliakmon* itself, the action was brought by buyers to whom property had not passed, and who therefore failed. Nor did they have an action under either the Bills of Lading Act, section 1 nor under *Brandt* v. *Liverpool*, and the result of the case was that they therefore had no action at all against the carrier.

The buyers argued that this was a most unsatisfactory situation, and that the courts should, on grounds of policy, allow recovery in negligence in this situation, although they did not have property in the goods when they were damaged. One of the reasons for the refusal of the House to extend recovery in tort was that since there was no contract between the buyers and the carrier, if the cargo-owner was able to sue in tort the carrier would have been unable to rely on any exemption clauses, time bars or damages limitation clauses written into the bill of lading. The contract of carriage incorporated the Hague Rules, which give the carrier the benefit of excepted perils, package limitation and a one-year time bar. There was no sound policy, in Lord Brandon's view, in extending recovery in tort if the effect would be to deprive the carrier of the benefits he would have under the Hague Rules. The buyers argued that, in principle, the duty of care in tort could be limited by reference to the Hague Rules, but the House of Lords held that the duty of care in tort could not be limited by clauses contained in a contract to which the plaintiffs were not party[64]:

"[Counsel] for the buyers submitted that your Lordships should hold that a duty of care did exist in the present case, but that it was subject to the terms of the bill of lading. With regard to this suggestion Sir John Donaldson M.R. said in the present case[65]:

'I have, of course, considered whether any duty of care in tort to the buyer could in some way be equated to the contractual duty of care owed to the shipper, but I do not see how this could be done. The commonest form of carriage by sea is one on the terms of the Hague Rules. But this is an intricate blend of responsibilities

---

62. For example, a bank which already has special property releasing the documents in return for a trust receipt.
63. [1915] 1 K.B. 938.
64. [1986] A.C. 785, 817H—818C.
65. [1985] Q.B. 350, 368.

and liabilities (Article III), right and immunities (Article IV), limitations to the amount of damages recoverable (Article IV, r. 5), time bars (Article III, r. 6), evidential provisions (Article III, rr. 4 and 6), indemnities (Article III, r. 5 and Article IV, r. 6) and liberties (Article IV, rr. 4 and 6). I am quite unable to see how these can be synthesized into a standard of care.'
I find myself suffering from the same inability to understand how the necessary synthesis could be made as the Master of the Rolls."

The essential problem was that unless the buyers were party to a contract, by virtue of either section 1 or *Brandt* v. *Liverpool*, then any tort action they might have would be at large, and not subject to the time bar, package limitation and other exemptions and limits on liability in the contract of carriage.

In the present context, however, the bank will commonly have a possessory title to the goods and be able to sue in tort, but will not be privy to the contract of carriage unless *Brandt* v. *Liverpool* applies. In that case, precisely the difficulty alluded to in *The Aliakmon* arises. The bank's tort action is not limited by any provisions of the contract of carriage to which it is not party. The carrier will be unable to rely on the terms of the Hague Rules, or any other provision in the contract of carriage protecting him.

The Hague Rules were amended in various respects by the Brussels Protocol in 1968, and the amended Hague-Visby Rules were adopted by the U.K. legislature in the Carriage of Goods by Sea Act 1971, which was brought into force executively in 1977, when 20 contracting states had signed. It was arguable until recently that the drafting of the Hague-Visby Rules was sufficiently different to enable the carrier to rely on their provisions even where the plaintiff was not party to the contract of carriage.

7.2.3 The privity doctrine and the Hague-Visby Rules

The bill of lading in *The Aliakmon* incorporated the Hague Rules, and it is clear that had the tort action succeeded the carrier would have been unable to rely on the Hague Rules exemption clauses. Where the Hague-Visby Rules apply it might be thought that Article IV *bis*, which was added by the Visby amendments, allows the carrier to rely on the exemption clauses where the buyer sues in tort, whether or not he is also a party to the carriage contract. The relevant part is para. 1 of Article IV *bis*: "The defences and limits of liability provided for in these Rules shall apply in any action against the carrier in respect of loss or damage to goods covered by a contract of carriage whether the action be founded in contract or in tort." Anthony Diamond Q.C. suggests that article IV *bis* allows the carrier to rely on the Rules "even if the carrier is being sued by someone who is not a party to the bill," although his argument is not backed by authority.[66] It may be thought relevant that section 1 (2) of the Carriage of Goods by Sea Act 1971 provides: "The provisions of

66. [1978] L.M.C.L.Q. 225, 249.

the Rules, as set out in the Schedule to this Act, shall have the force of law." Arguably, this subsection gives the Rules an independent force, so that they do not work only by incorporation into a carriage contract.

On the other hand, there is a clear assumption elsewhere in the Act, and in the Rules themselves, that they work by incorporation into the carriage contract. For example, Article II provides:

"Subject to the provisions of Article VI, under *every* contract of carriage of goods by sea the carrier, in relation to the loading, handling, stowage, carriage, custody, care and discharge of such goods, shall be subject to the responsibilities and liabilities, and entitled to the rights and immunities hereinafter set forth."

It is clearly assumed here that the responsibilities and liabilities, rights and immunities referred to are incorporated into the carriage contract, and have no independent force.

If this is the correct analysis, the Hague-Visby Rules apply only by incorporation into the carriage contract, and so do not help the carrier in a tort action *by a third party to that contract* (e.g., the buyer in *The Aliakmon*). In the view of Professor Treitel,[67] the effect of Article IV *bis* is merely "that a person *who is party to the contract of carriage* cannot improve his position by disregarding the contract of carriage and suing in tort" (my italics).

This issue, which until recently was unresolved, has now been settled by the Court of Appeal in *The Captain Gregos*.[68] The purchasers of a cargo of crude oil claimed that a quantity of their cargo had been stolen by the carrier, and wished to sue the carrier in tort. The carrier claimed the benefit of the one year time bar in Article III (6) of the Hague-Visby Rules, which were incorporated into the two bills of lading issued in respect of the cargo. The case arose by way of originating summons, the carrier as plaintiff seeking a determination that he could rely on the one year limitation period.

The cargo-owners advanced two main arguments. First, the time bar contained in Article III (6) did not apply on its construction to theft of cargo, or misdelivery by the carrier. Secondly, even if it did, the cargo-owners were not party to the carriage contract, and so were not bound by any of the provisions of the Hague-Visby Rules. It is the second argument that concerns us here. At first instance, Hirst J. took the view that on its construction, Article III (6) did not apply to theft or misdelivery of the cargo, so did not need to decide on the second argument. Had Hirst J.'s reasoning stood on the construction issue it would have had far-reaching consequences for carriers, but the Court of Appeal has now taken the opposite view. It follows that the Court of Appeal had to address itself to the second argument, and it concluded that the drafting of the amended Hague-Visby Rules made no difference.

---

67. [1986] L.M.C.L.Q. 294, 304.
68. *Cia Portorafti Commerciale S.A.* v. *Ultramar Panama Inc., The Captain Gregos* [1990] 1 Lloyd's Rep. 310 (C.A.), upholding in part [1989] 2 All E.R. 54; [1989] 2 Lloyd's Rep. 63.

Hirst J. did not need to decide this, since in his view the carrier was unable to succeed on the construction of the Rules. The Court of Appeal in *The Captain Gregos* therefore had to decide the issue as if sitting as a court of first instance. They effectively took the Treitel line, and held that the position was the same under the Hague-Visby as under the Hague Rules: if the cargo-owners were not party to the carriage contract, none of the provisions of the Hague-Visby Rules applied. Insufficient argument was heard on the issue *whether* the cargo-owners were party.[69]

In the Court of Appeal Bingham and Slade L.JJ. went into some considerable degree of detail over the Visby amendments to the Hague Rules. After setting out the issues, Bingham L.J. continued[69a]:

"The shipowners' argument was in essence very brief. They could rely on the time bar in Article III rule 6 because the Rules have the force of law and apply to any bill covered by Article X,[70] as these bills admittedly were. Article IV *bis* rule 1 expressly provides that the Rules shall apply in any action against the carrier in respect of loss or damage to goods covered by a contract of carriage whether the action be founded in contract or in tort. It would frustrate the purpose of an international convention if its application were to depend on questions of privity to which (as we know) different legal systems may yield different answers. The issue of a bill of lading to which the Rules apply is a necessary but also a sufficient condition of the right of shipowner or cargo-owner to rely on the Rules, even though neither is a party to the bill. Reliance was place in particular on views expressed by Mr. Diamond Q.C. in his article on 'The Hague-Visby Rules'[71] and on *Gillespie Bros v. Roy Bowles Ltd.*,[72] . . . where Lord Denning M.R. cited Article IV *bis* rule 1 to show how a non-party could become bound.

The cargo-owners' response was even briefer. The effect of the Act is to give statutory force to a mandatory contractual regime. The language of the Act and the Rules shows that they were intended to regulate the rights and duties of the parties to the bill of lading contract, not non-parties. That was what Mr. Mustill Q.C. thought in 1972. The issue of a bill of lading was a necessary but not itself a sufficient, condition of the application of the Rules.

We are again (no doubt unavoidably) obliged to resolve this issue without the help which the decisions or opinions of foreign judges or jurists might have given us. I have not for my part round it an easy question. I am particularly concerned at the risk that idiosyncratic legal rules on privity might yield different results in different countries. But on balance I prefer the cargo-owners' argument for three main reasons:

---

69. [1990] 1 Lloyd's Rep. 310, 316 (col. 2). The argument would have turned on section 1 of the Bills of Lading Act 1855 and the *Brandt* v. *Liverpool* doctrine.

69a. [1990] 1 Lloyd's Rep. 310, 317 (col. 2), 318 (col. 1).

70. "The provisions of these Rules shall apply to every bill of lading relating to the carriage of goods between ports in two different States if:
    (a) the bill of lading is issued in a contracting State, or
    (b) the carriage is from a port in a contracting State, or
    (c) the contract contained in or evidenced by the bill of lading provides that these Rules or legislation of any States giving effect to them are to govern the contract,
whatever may be the nationality of the ship, the carrier, the shipper, the consignee, or any other interested person."

71. [1978] 2 L.M.C.L.Q. 225, 248–249.

72. [1973] Q.B. 400, 412.

(1) As section 1(4) of the Act[73] and Articles I(b)[74] and X of the Rules in particular make clear, the bill of lading is the bedrock on which this mandatory code is founded. A bill of lading is a contractual document with certain commercially well-known consequences when endorsed and transferred. It is not clear to me why the code should treat the existence of a bill of lading as a matter of such central and overriding importance if the code is to apply with equal force as between those who are not parties to the contract which the bill contains or evidences.

(2) Much of the language in the Act and the Rules suggests that the code is intended to govern the relations between the parties to the bill of lading contract. Section 1(4) speaks of applying the Rules to a contract. Article I(a)[75] defines the carrier as including the party who enters into a contract of carriage with a shipper. Article I(b) speaks of regulating relations between a carrier and a holder of a bill or similar document of title. Most significantly of all, Article II defines the application of the Rules 'under every contract of carriage'. Articles V[76] and VI[77] are concerned with agreements between contracting parties. Article X applies the Rules to the bill of lading, not the carriage. If it had been intended to regulate relations between non-parties to the bill of lading contract, it is hard to think the language would not have been both different and simpler.

(3) Whatever the law in other jurisdictions, the general principle that only a party to a contract may sue on it is well-established here. If the draftsmen of the 1924 or 1971 Acts had intended the respective rules to infringe that principle or appreciated that that was their effect, I think they would have sought to make that clear in the Acts. It would be strange if so fundamental a principle were to be so inconspicuously abrogated.

73. "Subject to subsection 6 below, nothing in this section shall be taken as applying anything in the Rules to any contract for the carriage of goods by sea, unless the contract expressly or by implication provides for the issue of a bill of lading or any similar document of title."

74. " 'Contract of carriage' applies only to contracts of carriage covered by a bill of lading or any similar document of title, in so far as such document relates to the carriage of goods by sea, including any bill of lading or any similar document as aforesaid issued under or pursuant to a charter-party from the moment at which such bill of lading or similar document of title regulates the relations between a carrier and a holder of the same."

75. " 'Carrier' includes the owner or the charterer who enters into a contract of carriage with the shipper."

76. "A carrier shall be at liberty to surrender in whole or in part all or any of his rights and immunities or to increase any of his responsibilities and liabilities under these Rules, provided such surrender or increase shall be embodied in the bill of lading issued to the shipper. The provisions of these Rules shall not be applicable to charter-parties, but if bills of lading are issued in the case of a ship under a charter-party they shall comply with the terms of these Rules. Nothing in these Rules shall be held to prevent the insertion in a bill of lading of any lawful provision regarding general average."

77. "Notwithstanding the provisions of the preceding articles, a carrier, master or agent of the carrier and the shipper shall in regard to any particular goods be at liberty to enter any agreement in any terms as to the responsibility and liability of the carrier in respect of such goods, or his obligation as to seaworthiness, so far as this stipulation is not contrary to public policy, or the care or diligence of his servants or agents in regard to the loading, handling, stowage, carriage, custody, care and discharge of the goods carried by sea, provided that in this case no bill of lading has been or shall be issued and that the terms agreed shall be embodied in a receipt which shall be a non-negotiable document and shall be marked as such.

Any agreement so entered into shall have full legal effect.

Provided that this article shall not apply to ordinary commercial shipments made in the ordinary course of trade, but only to other shipments where the character or condition of the property to be carried or the circumstances, terms and conditions under which the carriage is to be performed are such as reasonably to justify a special agreement."

In reaching this conclusion I recognise the unattractiveness to carriers of exposure to claims by non-parties to bills not subject to limits in time or amount. But the notion that bill of lading terms may be held to regulate relations between those who were not parties to the bills was, as I understand, specifically disavowed by Lord Donaldson M.R. and the House of Lords in *The Aliakmon*.[78]

I would accordingly determine this second issue in the cargo-owners' favour. The fate of the appeal as a whole cannot be determined until the remaining questions are ruled upon."

Slade L.J.'s views are shorter, but essentially similar[78a]:

"As to the second issue falling for our decision, I think that the wording of Articles II and VI, already quoted by Bingham L.J., lend very strong support to his conclusion and to the cargo-owners' argument. Article II, read by itself, gives rise to no rights or obligations. It does no more than state the scope and purpose of all the succeeding Articles. However it clearly shows that the purpose of those succeeding Articles is, subject to the provisions of Article VI, to define (a) the responsibilities and liabilities to which the carrier shall be subject 'under every contract of carriage of goods by sea', and (b) the rights and immunities to which the carrier shall be entitled under every such contract. Article VI, however, gives the shipper and the carrier the liberty, within the limits stated in that Article, to enter into an agreement by way of variation of the responsibilities, liabilities, rights and immunities which would otherwise attach to the carrier by virtue of the preceding Articles.

These provisions, in my judgment, by themselves show fairly clearly that the purpose of all the Articles is to govern the relationship of the parties to the contract under a contract of carriage of goods by sea. For these and the other reasons given by Bingham L.J., I too would determine the second issue in the cargo-owners' favour."

It is clear, therefore, that the problems alluded to in *The Aliakmon*, whereby a cargo-owner or bank who is not party to the carriage contract, by suing in tort can avoid contractual exemption clauses, have equal force where the Hague-Visby Rules are incorporated into the carriage contract. It cannot be said that the position is satisfactory.

7.3 REFORM

7.3.1 Law Commission Working Paper No. 112 (1989): Rights to Goods in Bulk

The Law Commission, with the publication of their Working Paper No. 112 (1989): *Rights to Goods in Bulk*, have recently considered the possibility of amending section 1. Even apart from banking interests, however, many will probably feel that the recommendations of the Commission, after some four years' work, are a disappointment, and go nowhere far enough.[79] Certainly

---

78. Above, f.n. 65.

78a. [1990] 1 Lloyd's Rep. 310, 319 (col. 1).

79. The report nevertheless contains an excellent review of the law relating to bulk cargoes. It is also stated (para. 6.1) that "[t]he paper is circulated for the purpose of consultation and invites comments, criticisms and alternative suggestions", so that even if this is a missed opportunity, it may not be the last chance to look at section 1.

they do little to protect the interest of banks who take up shipping documents as security under a commercial credit.

The reason for this may be that the Commission was originally approached in response to a particular problem, and although its report deals exhaustively with that problem, it does not consider the wider ramifications of section 1. They were originally approached by an international commodity trade association, which was uneasy about the decision of the Commercial Court in Rotterdam in *The Gosforth*.[80] In that case, innocent sub-purchasers of part of a bulk cargo failed in a claim to property in the goods, although they were holders of delivery orders for their share of the cargo, and had paid against documents. Because property had not passed to them, however, they lost out to an unpaid seller three stages back in the chain, about whom they had (presumably) no knowledge.

Obviously this was very unsatisfactory in the context of chain sales, since sub-buyers need to be assured that their rights will be unaffected by whatever has occurred previously to the goods (about which they will have no knowledge), and no doubt *The Gosforth* gave rise to much concern among traders. It has to be said, however, that it was an application of well-established law, and that nobody should have been surprised by the decision, which was entirely in line with existing and well-known principles.[81]

Although no issue arose on the carriage contract in *The Gosforth*, in considering the passing of property the Law Commission could hardly avoid considering section 1, since it ties in passing of contractual rights and liabilities under the bill of lading with the passing of property.

In considering section 1, however, the Commission considered only *The Gosforth* situation, i.e., the problems of undivided bulk cargoes, so it is perhaps not surprising that no recommendations for a root and branch reform appear in their report. It is also clear that most of the report has no direct bearing on the issues considered in the present chapter. Only those aspects which are directly relevant are discussed here.

Three alternative proposals on section 1 were made by the Commission,[82] none of which is particularly radical, the Commission apparently taking the view that limited reform would "undoubtedly give rise to fewer difficulties than would a more comprehensive reform",[83] a debatable position perhaps. The first proposal[84] was to amend the Act so that rights of suit should be transferred, and liabilities imposed, not only where property *has* passed upon or by reason of consignment or indorsement, but also where the only reason it

---

80. Unreported, 20.02.85, noted [1986] L.M.C.L.Q. 4. See also Law Commission, Working Paper No. 112 (1989), paras. 3.4–3.6.
81. The reason that property had not passed was because, as part of an undivided bulk cargo, the goods were unascertained. See further, section 3.3.3.
82. Paras. 4.15-4.25. There are also proposals on section 16 of the Sale of Goods Act 1979 (paras. 4.4-4.14), which are beyond the scope of this book.
83. At para. 4.16.
84. At paras. 4.15–4.20.

has not done so is because the goods to which the bill of lading related were part of a larger bulk. This was one of the unsuccessful arguments advanced in *The Aramis*. This proposal affects bulk cargoes alone, and has no direct relevance to the banking community.

The second proposal of the Commission was to remove the link between section 1 and the passing of property at all. This more radical proposal would transfer contractual rights and liabilities to *all* consignees and indorsees, and were this proposal adopted a bank would have a contractual action against the carrier. However, the proposal, which was advanced very tentatively, would also reverse the actual decision in *Sewell* v. *Burdick*, so that the bank would also become liable for freight merely by virtue of holding the bill of lading. As it stands, therefore, this second proposal is unlikely to be acceptable as a solution to the particular problem discussed in this chapter.[85]

The third proposal was not to change the existing law.[86] Given the amount of criticism which has been generated by section 1 in recent years this proposal is surprising to say the least. The Law Commission make the point, however, that the parties themselves can overcome the problems of the section, although the extent to which this is practical in reality is, I would suggest, debatable. They referred[87] to extract from the speech of Lord Brandon in *The Aliakmon*[88]:

"In this situation the persons who had a right to sue the shipowners for loss of or damage to the goods on the contract contained in the bill of lading were the sellers, and the buyers, if properly advised, should have made it a further term of the variation that the sellers should either exercise this right for their account . . . or assign such right to them to exercise for themselves. If either of these two precautions had been taken, the law would have provided the buyers with a fair and adequate remedy for their loss.

These considerations show, in my opinion, not that there is some *lacuna* in English law relating to these matters, but only that the buyers, when they agreed to the variation of the original contract of sale, did not take the steps to protect themselves which, if properly advised, they should have done. To put the matter quite simply the buyers, by the variation to which they agreed, were depriving themselves of the right of suit under s.1 of the Bills of Lading Act 1855 which they would otherwise have had, and commercial good sense required that they should obtain the benefit of an equivalent right in one or other of the two different ways which I have suggested."

It is important to bear in mind the context of these remarks. *The Aliakmon* involved an international sale (c. & f.) of a quantity of steel coils, the original contract later being varied because the buyers could not pay. Because of the

---

85. The proposal (at paras. 4.21–4.22) also leaves many questions unanswered, such as the position of shippers and intermediate purchasers, and does nothing to extend the section to documents other than the traditional shipped bill of lading.

86. Paras. 4.23–4.25.

87. At pages 35–36.

88. [1986] A.C. 785, 819 C–F. The same passage (or at least the sentiment expressed therein) is alluded to by all three judges in the recent Court of Appeal decision in *The Delfini*, f.n. 24 above, where in an ordinary c.i.f. sale contract section 1 was interpreted so narrowly that it did not apply.

terms of the re-negotiation, property in the coils never passed to the buyers (or if it did, not until long after the damage had occurred). Thus the 1855 Act could not apply, and on the facts nor did *Brandt* v. *Liverpool*. The coils were damaged at sea through the carrier's negligence.

As has already been explained, the House of Lords held that the buyers had no action in tort either, for negligence, since property had never passed to them. An argument put on behalf of the buyers was that under a rational system of law the buyers ought to have an action. This was rejected by Lord Brandon partly on the grounds that they ought themselves to have ensured that they had the right to sue. This is the context of the above quote.

How far these remarks of Lord Brandon are realistic in the general case is, I would suggest, open to doubt. It should be remembered that he was dealing with a one-off sale, where multiple re-sales were not envisaged, and there was a lengthy process of re-negotiation with lawyers involved on both sides. I would suggest that for the buyers to take an assignment from the sellers would be difficult where, for example, multiple re-sales are envisaged. Indeed, an unbroken chain of assignments back to the original shipper. In the case of banks the position is further complicated by the fact that because of the uncertainties attendant upon the operation of section 1, the bank may be unsure from whom it is appropriate to take the assignment, seller or buyer. It will be the buyer if section 1 operates: the seller otherwise. If the seller is the party who can sue, there is the further difficulty that neither issuing nor confirming bank (under a confirmed irrevocable credit) typically negotiates with the seller. One possible way around the difficulty might be to require tender of a document assigning rights along with the shipping documents, but even this is not much good if the seller's rights are automatically transferred to the buyer under section 1. Nor is it much good, in a chain sale, unless the immediate seller has rights to assign. He may only have such rights if there is an unbroken chain of assignments back to the original shipper.

It is perhaps ironic that whereas in *The American Accord*[89] the House of Lords strove to maximise the free negotiability of the shipping documents, only some three years later in *The Aliakmon* they appear to be striving with equal stringency in the reverse direction.

7.3.2 Principles for reform

It would be fair to say that the Law Commission did not specifically address to problems of banks as pledgees, and it may perhaps be appropriate, therefore, to address those problems here. It is not intended to discuss all the problems of section 1, however.

So far as banks are concerned, a major problem with section 1 is its dependence on property. There seems little reason in logic for this dependence to exist, and it almost certainly arises merely from the historical accident that the

89. See section 6.2.2.1.

legislature was concerned only to reverse the reasoning in *Thompson* v. *Dominy*,[90] at a time when modern banking practices simply did not exist. Removal of tto enable any holder of a bill of lading (and perhaps other shipping he link between section 1 and property would undoubtedly be a first step, documents) to use the section, subject perhaps to other conditions.

What should those conditions be? Arguably, as at present, banks should not be subjected to liabilities merely because they hold bills of lading, so that merely to remove the property link does not suffice; on the other hand, there is no reason why they should not be bound by exemption clauses if they sue carriers. Nor is it easy to see why they should enjoy rights of suit unless they choose to realise the security in the shipping documents. Perhaps the answer would be only to transfer rights of suit to banks, and subject them to liabilities, if they accept delivery of the goods (whether or not they also pay freight or other charges).

In the meantime, banks would be well advised to protect themselves as best they can as suggested by Lord Brandon in *The Aliakmon*.[91]

90. Above, f.n. 2.
91. Above, f.n. 88.

CHAPTER 8

RESIDUAL ISSUES

The purpose of this chapter is to deal with issues which, though clearly relevant to a study of documentary credits, do not fall easily within the structure set out in the rest of the book.

8.1 RELATIONSHIP BETWEEN BANK AND BENEFICIARY

Although it is now clear that there is a contractual relationship between the confirming bank and beneficiary for a confirmed irrevocable credit (contract 4 in figure 1.2), and between the issuing bank and beneficiary for an irrevocable unconfirmed credit, this has by no means always been clear. Indeed, one of the problems of the early varieties was to establish the existence of any legal relationship at all between bank and beneficiary.

Various theories have been advanced as to the nature of the legal relationship between bank and beneficiary.[1] Some of them today look fairly bizarre, and I suspect would never have been advanced at all but for the fact that the early form of credit was quite different from the modern documentary credit. This section therefore examines the historical development of the commercial credit, the problems in establishing a legal relationship between bank and beneficiary, and the difficulties of the present contractual analysis.

For simplicity, and because the issues are the same whether or not the credit is confirmed, this section will assume an unconfirmed irrevocable credit, where the issue is the relationship between seller and issuing bank directly, unless the context otherwise requires. Where the credit is confirmed, identical issues arise as between seller and confirming bank.

8.1.1 The early letter of credit

The modern form of commercial credit, where the bank addresses a letter of credit directly to the beneficiary, did not come into general use until the last

---

1. For a detailed discussion of the various theories, many of which are derived originally from American jurisprudence, see, e.g., A.G. Davis: "The Relationship Between Banker and Seller under a Confirmed Credit" (1936) L.Q.R. 225.

quarter of the last century. Before then the bank did not correspond directly with the beneficiary at all, and naturally there were difficulties in establishing any legal relationship between these parties. Yet until recently, writers used arguments developed from the old cases in an attempt to explain a completely different type of transaction.

The earliest forms of credit, which were used in the early and middle parts of the nineteenth century, took the form of an arrangement between the bank issuing the credit (issuing bank) and the intended purchaser of the goods, who would have been a customer of the bank. Assuming either that sufficient funds had been deposited with the bank in advance, or that the bank had sufficient confidence in the solvency of its customer, it would allow him to draw bills of exchange on the bank up to a certain amount, the bills to be valid for a certain period of time. The bills would then be given by the customer to the seller, the idea being that the seller as holder would present them to the bank for payment. Effectively, the seller would be negotiating bills of exchange drawn on the bank by the purchaser.

8.1.2 No undertaking made directly by bank to seller

Once the seller had become holder of the bills of exchange, he could ship the goods, reasonably secure in the knowledge that he could look to the bank for payment against the bills, and would not have to take the risk of the purchaser's inability to pay. No doubt a reputable bank generally would pay against the bills, but it was much more difficult to establish a legal obligation: the problem was that the bank dealt directly only with its customer (who would typically be the purchaser), undertaking to honour drafts drawn by him. At no stage did the bank issuing the credit give any undertaking directly to the seller. Generally speaking, therefore, the seller (or beneficiary) obtained no *legally enforceable* rights against the bank, but was dependent on the bank's reputation, unbacked by legal sanction.

The banking community is inclined to argue that legally enforceable rights are unnecessary so long as the bank is reputable, but they can become important in the event of bankruptcy of one or other of the parties.

8.1.3 An early form of credit: Re Agra and Masterman's Bank[2]

An arrangement which was similar to an early commercial credit came before the Court of Appeal in *Re Agra and Masterman's Bank* in 1867, the issue squarely before the court being whether there was any legal relationship between the beneficiary and the issuing bank, and if so what it was. The beneficiary was not in fact a seller under an international sale contract, but the principles would have been equally applicable had he been.

It is important to appreciate that the arrangement in *Re Agra*, while being

2. (1867) L.R. 2 Q.B. 391.

similar to commercial credits in use at that time, was entirely dissimilar to today's documentary credit. Theories which were discussed in this case continued to be advanced until long after this type of credit had become obsolete, however, creating a great deal of unnecessary confusion in the subject.

Agra and Masterman's Bank gave its customer, Dickson, Tatham & Co., a letter of credit in the following terms:

"You are hereby authorized to draw upon this bank at six months' sight, to the extent of £15,000 sterling, and such drafts I undertake duly to honour on presentation. This credit will remain in force for twelve months from this date, and parties negotiating bills under it are requested to indorse particulars on the back hereof. [There followed instructions as to what the bills must specify]."

Dickson, Tatham & Co. drew bills under this letter of credit for £6,000. These bills were then sold to the Asiatic Banking Corporation, indorsing them in their favour. Asiatic Banking Corporation intended to present them to Agra and Masterman's Bank. This would have been a fairly typical arrangement at this time. The issuing bank (Agra and Masterman's Bank) dealt only with its customer, Dickson, Tatham & Co. It had no direct relationship with the Asiatic Banking Corporation (the beneficiary under the credit), whose only relationship was again with Dickson, Tatham & Co. Only in later forms of credit did the issuing bank enter into a direct contractual relationship with the beneficiary under the credit.

In *Re Agra* itself, Dickson, Tatham & Co. do appear to have been purchasers of property from the Asiatic Banking Corporation, and they seem simply to have sold the bills of exchange to Asiatic in order to obtain an advance.[3] It is easy to see, however, how a credit of this nature could have been used in an international sale of goods. The bank's customer, as purchaser, would negotiate bills of exchange drawn on the bank, not in favour of another bank as in *Re Agra*, but in favour of the seller of the goods.

Agra and Masterman's Bank, which was in the process of being wound up, stopped payment under the bills before the Asiatic Banking Corporation presented them, and the Asiatic Banking Corporation (or rather, its official liquidator, since it too, was being wound up[4]) claimed against Agra and Masterman's. Their problem was, of course, that they had received no undertaking directly from Agra and Masterman's. Agra and Masterman's had given a direct undertaking only to Dickson, Tatham & Co. The lack of a direct undertaking from Agra and Masterman's Bank in favour of the Asiatic Banking Corporation was essentially the reason for the dispute in the case, since without such an undertaking it was difficult to infer the existence of any contract between the parties.

Nevertheless Asiatic won, various theories being advanced as to the nature of the relationship between themselves and Agra.

3. The exact nature of the transaction does not appear from the report.
4. Banks would appear to have been by no means as secure then as they are today!

8.1.4 Assignment of customer's contract[5]

Sir H.M. Cairns L.J. thought the terms of the credit were in fact sufficient to found a contract between Asiatic and Agra,[6] but also took the alternative view that even had the only contract been between Agra and Dickson, Tatham & Co., the benefit of that contract had been assigned in equity to Asiatic.[7]

The problem with this argument is that equitable assignment of a chose in action is usually subject to the equities existing between the existing parties to the contract (i.e., Agra and Dickson, Tatham & Co.). Since Dickson, Tatham & Co. owed to Agra more than the amount in the bills of exchange, there should not have been anything of any value to assign to Asiatic. This aspect of *Re Agra* must therefore be wrong. The same difficulty would arise with a modern credit if it were argued that the buyer assigned to the seller the benefit of his contract with the bank. Unless the bank had already been put in funds by the buyer there would be nothing of value to assign.

Even if the bank had already been put in funds, the assignment reasoning in *Re Agra* was further weakened by the decision of the House of Lords in *Citizens Bank of Louisiana* v. *First National Bank of New Orleans*.[8] The facts were similar to those in *Re Agra* in that bills of exchange drawn on the Bank of Liverpool were sold by the drawer (the First National Bank of New Orleans) to third party purchasers, one of whom was the Citizens Bank of Louisiana. The evidence for assignment was somewhat stronger than in *Re Agra*, however, since the First National Bank had represented to the Citizens Bank of Louisiana that the bills would certainly be paid, since they were drawn expressly against funds to a much larger amount already remitted to the Bank of Liverpool. The assets of the First National Bank having been put into the hands of a receiver, the Citizens Bank of Louisiana claimed that they, rather than the receiver, were entitled to the funds represented by the bills, held by the Bank of Liverpool. They claimed that the benefit of the contract between the First National Bank and the Bank of Liverpool had been assigned to them, but the House of Lords took the opposite view.[9]

---

5. On this theory see, for example, the discussion in H.C. Gutteridge and Maurice Megrah, *The Law of Bankers' Commercial Credits* (7th ed., 1984), pp. 32–33, and E.P. Ellinger, *Documentary Letters of Credit* (1970), pp. 56–62. However, none of these writers argues for the theory.

6. See below, section 8.1.6.

7. (1867) L.R. 2 Q.B. 391, 397. Notice that assignment must be equitable at this time, since assignment of choses in action at common law was not generally possible until it was provided by the Judicature Act 1873, s.25(6), which was re-enacted by the Law of Property Act 1925, s.136(1). On assignment in general, see G.H. Treitel, *The Law of Contract* (7th ed., 1987), Chapter 16.

8. (1873) L.R. 6 H.L. 352.

9. There was also an argument based on estoppel. This failed, following the well-known case of *Jorden* v. *Money* (1854) 5 H.L.C. 185, because the nature of the representation by the First National Bank was a representation of intention and not of fact.

It is clear that the decision turns entirely upon its facts,[10] so it cannot be said that the benefit of the drawer's contract can never be assigned. It is also clear, however, that for assignment to operate, there must be a specific appropriation of part of the funds of the issuing bank. No doubt it would be possible to operate a commercial credit in that way, so long as the bank had already been put in funds, but equally obviously it is not the way in which a modern documentary credit operates.

We can therefore conclude that the assignment theory is a non-starter, and cannot explain the relationship between bank and beneficiary in a conventional documentary credit.

Another argument that has sometimes been advanced is that there is a novation, rather than an assignment. The difference between assignment and novation is that for a novation the original drawer drops out of the picture, leaving only a contract between bank and beneficiary. Quite apart from the difficulties of evidence, which would surely be even greater than they are with assignment, another problem would be that the drawer would be released from any obligation towards the bank, or in the context of a modern documentary credit, that the buyer would be released from his liability to pay for the goods.[11]

We may reasonably conclude that novation also is a non-starter as a theory to explain a modern credit.

8.1.5 Independent equity

To return again to *Re Agra*, where it will be recalled that Asiatic won although they were not the original drawers of the bills, and despite the fact that the letter of credit had not been issued to them, Sir G.J. Turner L.J.'s reasoning differed from that of Sir H.M. Cairns L.J. His view was that since Agra and Masterman's Bank had issued the bills in the full knowledge that they would be negotiated, and had indeed, in the second part of the letter of credit, issued instructions directly to those to whom the bills would be negotiated, and that since Asiatic made advances upon the bills on the strength of the credit, Asiatic had a claim in equity against Agra. The claim in equity, he said, was independent of any contractual claim.[12]

This reasoning is clearly wrong. The only possible claim in equity would have to be based on some form of estoppel, and indeed the facts are consistent with an estoppel, since Agra and Masterman's had made a representation upon which Asiatic had relied to its detriment.[13] Estoppel cannot be used as a

---

10. See, e.g., the statement to that effect of Lord Chelmsford: (1873) L.R. 6 H.L. 352, 366.
11. See, e.g., Gutteridge and Megrah, *op. cit.*, at pp. 33.
12. (1867) L.R. 2 Q.B. 391, 395.
13. Although it might be argued, on the basis of *Citizens Bank of Louisiana* v. *First National Bank of New Orleans* (above) that the representation by the Agra and Masterman's Bank was a representation of intention and not of fact.

cause of action, however,[14] so that in the absence of a contractual cause of action, Asiatic's claim ought to fail.

This was indeed recognised in the later case of *Union Bank of Canada* v. *Cole*.[15] The facts of this case, which were similar to those in *Re Agra*, are set out in greater detail below, but *Re Agra* was distinguished, the Court of Appeal taking the view that there was no legally enforceable relationship between bank and beneficiary. Brett L.J. said of *Agra*[16] "And I think that in the case of *Agra and Masterman's Bank* there would have been no equity if there had not been a contract at law, and the question in law and equity is the same."

Another possibility would be for the bank to constitute itself trustee of the purchase money for the beneficiary. It was made clear as long ago as *Morgan* v. *Larivière*,[17] however, that the trust analysis is inappropriate. This case is considered in detail below.

8.1.6 Contractual offer to all the world

Yet another line of reasoning advanced in *Re Agra*, again by Sir H.M. Cairns, L.J., was that the terms of the credit were sufficient to found a direct contract between Asiatic and Agra, on the basis that the terms of the letter constituted a contractual offer to all the world, which anybody could accept by tendering the drafts.[18] Although the authorities relied upon in the case were old contractual reward cases,[19] had the case been decided a few decades later a better analogy would have been with the well-known case of *Carlill* v. *Carbolic Smoke Ball Co.*[20] During a serious influenza epidemic in London, in which many people were killed, a manufacturer of a smoke ball advertised that he would pay £100 to anyone who used the smoke ball in the prescribed manner, and contracted influenza. Mrs. Carlill did, and was able to sue for £100. The smoke ball manufacturer had made an offer to the world which had been accepted by Mrs. Carlill. The reasoning is almost identical with that of Sir H.M. Cairns in *Re Agra*. It is noteworthy that the Carbolic Smoke Ball Co.'s offer was unilateral, in that Mrs. Carlill did not undertake to do anything at all, acceptance by her being using the smoke ball in the prescribed manner, and contracted influenza.

Given the overwhelming criticisms that can be advanced of the other lines of reasoning advanced in *Re Agra*,[21] if the case is correct it must depend on the contractual offer to all the world. It is now clear that this reasoning

---

14. *Combe* v. *Combe* [1951] 2 K.B. 215.
15. (1877) 47 L.J.C.P. 100. See further below, section 8.1.6.
16. (1877) 47 L.J.C.P. 100, 109 (col. 2).
17. (1875) L.R. 7 H.L. 423. See further below, section 8.1.7.
18. (1867) L.R. 2 Q.B. 391, 396–397.
19. For example *Williams* v. *Cowardine* (1833) 5 C. & P. 566; 4 B. & Ad. 621; 1 E. & E. 295.
20. [1893] 1 Q.B. 356.
21. Above, sections 8.1.4 and 8.1.5.

depended on the precise terms of the letter of credit. It was addressed to anyone at all negotiating bills under it, and made clear that the bank would accept the bills from anyone in whose favour they had been negotiated, and make payment to him. Had the letter of credit been addressed to the bank's customer alone, it could not have acted to create a legal relationship with anyone else.

In *Union Bank of Canada* v. *Cole*,[22] the facts were similar to those in *Re Agra*, except that the credit was issued expressly to the bank's customer, and not to anyone else negotiating bills under it. As in *Agra* the bills of exchange were sold to a third party, but the third party was held by the Court of Appeal unable to sue on them. In distinguishing *Re Agra*, Cotton L.J. said[23]: "If the document was, on the face of it, addressed to all persons whatever, it no doubt would make a contract at law between the giver of the document and any one who might act upon it." Similar sentiments were expressed by Brett L.J., who also accepted that there could be a contract if the person in whose favour the bill is to be drawn has authority given to him by the bank, such as express authority in writing.[24]

In *Union Bank of Canada* v. *Cole* the plaintiffs (the purchasers of the bills) had to argue a direct contract between themselves and the bank, and not an assignment of the undoubted contract between the bank and the original drawer of the bills. This was because the credit addressed to the drawer required clean bills of lading to be tendered, and the drawer did not comply with this condition. The plaintiffs therefore had to argue a new contract in order to avoid the conditions, so that an assignment argument could not work. They failed on the simple basis that the letter of credit was addressed to the drawer alone, and could not therefore constitute an offer to anyone else.

Documentary credits today are usually issued to a *named beneficiary*, and not to all the world, and the reasoning in *Cole* suggests that the offer contained in the credit cannot be relied upon by anyone else. Unless the benefit of the credit is expressly assigned, therefore, or the credit itself made transferable,[25] only the beneficiary named in the credit can present documents under it. Although the transaction in *Cole* is now obsolete, the case survives as authority for that proposition.

The reasoning in *Re Agra* also survives to this extent. It is clear that the letter of credit constitutes a *unilateral* offer which can be accepted by whoever it is addressed to (in that case anyone negotiating bills under it, more usually today the named beneficiary) performing the terms of the credit. The modern analysis is still based on the unilateral contract. The problems of this are considered in detail below.[26]

22. (1877) 47 L.J.C.P. 100.
23. (1877) 47 L.J.C.P. 100, 110 (col. 2).
24. (1877) 47 L.J.C.P. 100, 108 (col. 2).
25. See section 2.3.4.
26. See sections 8.1.8–8.1.11.

8.1.7 Direct offer to beneficiary: Morgan v. Larivière [27]

During the latter part of the nineteenth century it became usual for the bank issuing the credit to contact the beneficiary directly, so as to create a *direct* relationship between them. An early example is *Morgan* v. *Larivière*, in which the House of Lords also considered the nature of this relationship. In the light of the very clear comments made in that case, which unlike the cases considered so far concerned an essentially modern form of credit, it is perhaps surprising that arguments continued to rage over the nature of the relationship for another century.

Larivière had agreed in November 1870 to supply the French Minister of War with 20 million ball cartridges, no later than 10 January 1871, for use as ammunition. No doubt influenced by the military situation in France at the time, Larivière required a secure method of payment. Accordingly Morgan, the London financial adviser to the French Government, wrote to Larivière as follows:

the"Gentlemen, we are instructed by M. Joulin [for the French Government] to advise you that a special credit of £40,000, equivalent to one million of francs, has been opened with us in your favour, and that it will be paid to you rateably, as the goods are delivered, upon receipt of certificates of reception [acceptance], issued by the French Ambassador or by M. Joulin. We shall require receipts in duplicate for the payment or payments as made, and the surrender of this letter on the final payment under it being made."

This arrangement is quite different from that in *Re Agra and Masterman's Bank*. There the bank dealt only with its customer, and had no direct relationship with the beneficiary, whose only relationship was with the buyers. In *Morgan* v. *Larivière*, by contrast, the bank gave an undertaking directly to the beneficiary under the credit. This undertaking was enforceable directly by the beneficiary, and was independent both of the original sale contract, and of the relationship between Morgan and its customer, the French government.

Another difference between *Morgan* v. *Larivière* and *Re Agra and Masterman's Bank* is that in the earlier case the letter was addressed to anyone in the world to whom the bills of exchange had been negotiated, whereas in *Morgan* v. *Larivière* the letter of credit was addressed to a specific beneficiary. It is sometimes said that the credit in *Re Agra* is a *general* letter of credit, whereas that in *Morgan* v. *Larivière* is a *special* letter of credit. Modern credits are nearly always of the latter type.

Under the terms of the credit, payment was not made until the goods were delivered and accepted by the buyer, and indeed in the case itself Larivière did not succeed in obtaining full payment, in an action against Morgan. He had not delivered sufficient cartridges in time, and so was unable to obtain the

27. (1875) L.R. 7 H.L. 423.

necessary certificates of acceptance from the French government. He argued, however, that the effect of the letter of credit was to constitute Morgan trustee of the £40,000 for Larivière, or to effect an equitable assignment of the sum. This argument, if successful, would have enabled Larivière to avoid the contractual conditions.

The decision of the House of Lords is important in holding that the rights of Larivière against Morgan were contractual, and depended on the terms of the undertaking alone. There was no room for the intervention of equity.[28] Indeed, it is usually difficult to construe a trust from the nature of the transaction itself[29]:

"In the case of irrevocable credits the banker seldom receives the amount of the credit in advance from the buyer. In most cases he obtains reimbursement from the buyer only after tendering to him the documents of title. Moreover, in an irrevocable documentary credit the banker promises to pay the amount of the draft not out of funds remitted by the buyer, but out of his own funds."

In other words, it is difficult to see how the bank can be trustee of the fund for the beneficiary, since it is not normally put in funds by the customer until after payment has been made. It might be theoretically possible for the bank to declare itself trustee of a part of its own funds, but clear words would be required since the courts are reluctant to infer the assumption of the onerous obligations of trusteeship in their absence.[30] Even if the bank had already been put in funds, evidence would be required that the settlor (in this case the purchaser, whose money it is) intended to give it to the bank on trust for the beneficiary, and that the bank accepted the obligation of trusteeship. Of course, such an arrangement is theoretically possible, but it bears little relation to a modern documentary credit, or indeed to any other kind of credit.

From this case onwards it has been clear, then, that in a modern form of credit the relationship between bank and beneficiary depends on contract alone, and that the contract is made directly between these two parties. It is not based on an assignment, or novation, or independent equity. Recent cases have elaborated upon the contractual relationship, and the very real difficulties are considered further below.[31]

---

28. It is usually said that this decision casts doubt on *Re Agra and Masterman's Bank*, but this may be going too far. *Re Agra and Masterman's Bank* was not mentioned in *Morgan* v. *Larivière*, and in any case it is not clear whether the equitable intervention in the earlier case depended on the existence of a trust, or of an equitable assignment of the fund, as opposed to the contract between the bank and its customer. What is clear, however, is that where the credit is by way of an express undertaking by the bank to the beneficiary, as in *Morgan* v. *Larivière*, but not *Re Agra and Masterman's Bank*, the relationship between bank and beneficiary is determined solely by the terms of the undertaking, and there is no room for the intervention of equity.

29. E.P. Ellinger, *Documentary Letters of Credit* (1970), p. 71.

30. See, e.g., *Jones* v. *Lock* (1865) L.R. 1 Ch. App. 25, where Lord Cranworth L.C. said that an irrevocable intention to part with the property must be shown, and that it must be by way of trust not gift.

31. Section 8.1.10.

8.1.7.1 Differences between Morgan v. Larivière and the commercial credit today

Morgan v. *Larivière* is much more akin to a modern commercial credit than *Re Agra and Masterman's Bank*, but still differs in a number of respects from a modern commercial credit. Payment was not made until after delivery of the goods. Whereas this be acceptable in a sale between a single seller and a single buyer, particularly in the bulk commodity trade it is far more common for the cargo to be re-sold many times before it arrives at its destination, and it is essential that payment can be made before the cargo is delivered. Also, in *Morgan* v. *Larivière* payment depended on receipt of certificates of reception issued on behalf of the French government, or purchaser. If the purchaser refused to issue the certificates, the seller did not get paid. Obviously, any system which depends for its efficacy on the whim of the purchaser is hardly satisfactory from the seller's viewpoint, and there ought to be *independent* evidence that the seller has performed. This was of course later provided by the use of the shipped bill of lading.[32]

In *Morgan* v. *Larivière*, it was not clear whether the French government had deposited £40,000 in advance to enable Morgan to pay Larivière, or whether the arrangement was for Morgan to claim later reimbursement from the French government for any money advanced.[33] Today's credit usually allows the purchaser not to pay until he has himself re-sold the goods, the bank advancing the money subject to later reimbursement.[34] In a modern credit, therefore, the bank is required not only to provide security for the seller to enable him to despatch the goods in the sure knowledge that he will be paid, but also to finance the transaction for the buyer. Yet at any rate with an ordinary commercial customer a bank may well be unwilling actually to loan money under an arrangement like *Morgan* v. *Larivière*, since it obtains no security. Again, this difficulty is resolved today by transferring a shipped bill of lading, or other document of title, to the bank.

8.1.8 Present-day unilateral contractual analysis

In *United City Merchants* v. *Royal Bank of Canada, The American Accord*, Lord Diplock thought it "trite law" that in a confirmed irrevocable letter of credit, the relationship between confirming bank and seller was contractual, and that the contract (i.e., contract 4) was autonomous.[35] Given the discussion in the foregoing sections, it came as a surprise to many writers that the nature of the relationship was "trite law". Even well before 1982, however, a conventional contractual analysis was the only analysis that could fit the facts

---

32. See section 1.4.
33. The report (at p. 424) states "No actual deposit of money appeared to have been made . . . "
34. See section 2.4.
35. See section 1.6.

of the modern documentary credit. It is clear, incidentally, that Lord Dip-lock's remarks apply only to a modern irrevocable credit, where there is an undertaking made directly by the bank to the beneficiary. His analysis depends on this undertaking, and his reasoning would not necessarily apply to the older variety of credit like that discussed in *Re Agra and Masterman's Bank*.[36]

The detailed mechanics of contract 4 are still by no means clear, however, because it is unnecessary for seller and bank to agree terms, and the seller does not make any promise to the bank (as opposed to the buyer) that he will perform. It should also be remembered that neither bank acts for the seller, so that they are unlikely to enter into an express contract. If the seller pays a confirming commission in advance, then no problems arise, because an enforceable agreement can be inferred between the parties as from that moment. But confirming commissions are by no means universal, indeed, they are rare where multiple re-sales are envisaged. The assumption that is made for present purposes is that no confirming commission is paid. Usually the seller is merely notified of the opening of the credit, and may not respond at all, except to ship the goods and tender the shipping documents.

In addition to making it clear that the relationship between confirming bank and beneficiary is contractual, Lord Diplock also made it clear that con-tract 4 is autonomous. It follows that it cannot depend on one of the other contracts constituting the credit. Even if an assignment or novation could theoretically form the basis of a contract between a bank and a beneficiary, Lord Diplock's remarks preclude the possibility, in a modern confirmed irre-vocable credit, that the basis of contract 4 is an assignment or novation of con-tract 2. Various other contractual analyses that had previously been advanced are also scotched by the autonomy requirement, for example, the so-called "seller's offer theory". On this theory the seller, through the agency of the buyer, enters into a contract with the bank. The seller's offer is made by entering into the contract on terms calling for payment by confirmed irrevoc-able credit. The difficulty is that the terms of contract 4 now depend on the agency agreement contained in contract 1 (the sale contract). On this theory therefore, contract 4 cannot be autonomous, as Lord Diplock requires.[37]

Another theory that must now be discarded is that the beneficiary obtains rights as a third party under the contract between buyer and bank.[38] But not only would this contract also fail to be autonomous, but it has become clear in recent years that the privity of contract doctrine prevents a third party from enforcing another's contract.[39]

Clearly, then, none of these old theories will do. Still less will the argument

---

36. Above, section 8.1.6.
37. Although Gutteridge and Megrah still favour this theory, primarily on the grounds that it avoids the problems discussed below: *op. cit.*, at pp. 33–34.
38. E.P. Ellinger, *op. cit.*, pp. 49–56.
39. *Beswick* v. *Beswick* [1968] A.C. 58.

work that the bank's responsibility to pay is accepted as part of mercantile law, and requires no further justification. It follows from *The American Accord* that the correct analysis is contractual, and that a contract must be found directly between seller and confirming bank, not made through the agency of any other party.

The only analysis that works is that the opening of the credit must constitute an offer by the confirming bank. Since the seller makes no promise to do anything at this stage it must be a unilateral offer (i.e., binding only one party, the bank). It is exactly the same as the example favoured by contract textbook writers, where X offers to pay Y £100 if Y walks from London to York. Y makes no promise to walk to York, but if he does so, he can claim the £100. In the present context, walking to York is tendering conforming shipping documents, so by tendering the documents the seller accepts the unilateral offer, and so can sue the bank should it fail to pay as promised. This indeed occurred in *The American Accord* itself.[40]

An analysis along these lines was suggested by Donaldson J. in *Elder Dempster Lines Ltd.* v. *Ionic Shipping Agency Inc.*[41]: "The best explanation of the legal phenomenon constituted by a banker's letter of credit is that it is an offer which is accepted by being drawn upon." From the time when the documents are tendered, and the bank accepts them, there are no problems on this analysis in inferring the existence of a contract between the seller and the confirming bank, but it is more difficult to infer the existence of any contract between them before then. This problem is considered in detail in the next section.

8.1.9 The problem of irrevocability: why does it matter?

If the documents are actually tendered then, on the above theory, the seller has accepted the unilateral offer made by the bank. It is not clear, however, that any contract is made before then. The problem arises if the bank revokes its offer at an earlier stage, in other words if a bank purports to revoke an irrevocable credit before the documents are tendered. This is like the question, again favoured by contract textbook writers, whether X can revoke when Y has set off, and reached Doncaster.

This would not be a problem if the assignment or trust theories discussed above[42] applied. In that case the bank's undertaking would be irrevocable from the moment of assignment, or in the case of a trust from the moment the

40. The analysis is also similar to the offer to all the world reasoning in *Re Agra and Masterman's Bank*, considered in section 8.1.6, except that the offer is made to a named beneficiary, and not to anyone else.

41. [1968] 1 Lloyd's Rep. 529, 535 (col. 2). The case actually concerns a standby letter of credit, but the analysis is equally applicable to a documentary credit. The seller failed in *Elder Dempster* because the documents did not conform, and because they were tendered after the credit expired.

42. See sections 8.1.4, 8.1.5 and 8.1.7.

trust is declared. Were the seller a beneficiary under a trust, he would enjoy enforceable rights regardless of whether he had performed, or even begun to perform. Similarly, irrevocability would not be a problem on the other analyses discussed in the previous section. It is now clear, however, that none of these theories can apply to the modern commercial credit.

The usual response of the banking community is that this question is academic, since no reputable bank would attempt to revoke an irrevocable credit. Usually it is indeed academic, but cases have sometimes arisen where banks have refused to pay on the instructions of the buyer,[43] or because of an order of a foreign court or government.[44] The existence of a contract, and in the second case the law of which state governs it, then take on some importance. It may also be that if a bank got into serious financial difficulties it would examine closely the extent of its legal obligations.[45]

Lord Diplock also points out (albeit in a different context) in *The American Accord* that even if the bank will in fact pay, beneficiaries rely on the existence of a *legal*, and not merely a moral claim[46]:

"Counsel sought to evade the difficulties disclosed by an analysis of the legal consequences of his broad proposition by praying in aid the practical consideration that a bank, desirous as it would be of protecting its reputation in the competitive business of providing documentary credits, would never exercise its right against a seller/beneficiary to refuse to honour the credit except in cases where at the time of the refusal it already was in possession of irrefutable evidence of the inaccuracy in the documents presented. I must confess that the argument that a seller should be content to rely on the exercise by banks of business expediency, unbacked by any legal liability, to ensure prompt payment by a foreign buyer does not impress me . . . "

Another point that should be made is that the same principles of law have to apply whether or not the bank is reputable. Indeed, there is no reason in theory why a commercial credit needs to be issued by a bank at all, and indeed the undertaking was not always issued by a bank in the earlier cases.

In any case, a bank need not necessarily have to revoke a credit which is clearly irrevocable for the issue to come before the courts. Suppose, for example, that an issuing bank believes that an unconfirmed credit is also

43. E.g., the *Urquhart Lindsay* case considered below, section 8.1.3.1. See also *Power Curber International Ltd.* v. *National Bank of Kuwait S.A.K.*, discussed in section 8.3.1.3, below.
44. E.g., *Libyan Arab Foreign Bank* v. *Bankers Trust Co.*, discussed in section 8.3.1.3, below.
45. It has also been said that if the bank went into liquidation the liquidator would certainly examine its contractual obligations: Ellinger, *op. cit.*, p. 43. See also the Sixth Interim Report of the Law Revision Committee, 1937 (Cmnd. 5449), paras. 22 and 45. In practice, however, this would never be an issue. The situation would arise only if the bank went into liquidation before tender of documents by the seller. In that case, it is unlikely that the seller's best course of action would be to tender the documents and attempt to keep any contract with the bank alive, since then at best it would receive only a proportion of the price from the bank. A better approach would be either to short-circuit the credit and sue the buyer directly for the price, or (if the market has risen) to treat the bank's insolvency as a ground for repudiating the sale contract, on the principles discussed in section 3.2.3, and re-sell at the new higher market price.
46. [1983] A.C. 168, 185 F–G.

revocable, and that it therefore has the right to revoke.[47] The beneficiary takes the view that the credit is irrevocable, so the dispute is over *whether* it is revocable or irrevocable. However, if this issue came before the courts, then the question would also inevitably arise whether the bank could also revoke even if its assumption were wrong, and the credit was in fact irrevocable as the beneficiary argues.

Another argument is sometimes advanced that if the matter came before the courts, it is inconceivable that they would allow the irrevocability of the credit to be compromised by legal niceties. The law would have to fit around commercial practice. This argument may well have been sound a few years ago, but in the light of *The Aramis*,[48] it does not seem that the law is presently inclined to bend much in this direction.

8.1.10 When does an irrevocable credit become irrevocable?

The essential problem is up to what stage a bank can revoke an irrevocable credit. It could obviously be very inconvenient for a seller if a bank could revoke an irrevocable credit at any time before documents are tendered, on the grounds that no contract yet exists, especially if the seller by then has expended money in making shipping arrangements. It would also deprive the seller of the advantages of an irrevocable credit. The precise question has never been decided in the present context, but if it were to come before the courts, the principles of the general law of contract would apply.

It should be remembered that the seller's position is altered from the very moment when he receives notification of the credit, because his obligations under the sale contract are conditional upon such notification.[49] Also, after that time he is obliged to seek payment in the first instance from the confirming bank, and cannot sue the buyer directly.[50] The ideal position, therefore, which incidentally obtains in the United States, is that the bank should be unable to revoke at any later time (i.e., not at all). There is an even stronger argument that the bank should be unable to revoke once the seller has relied upon the opening of the credit, perhaps by spending money on the preparation of the goods.

Before any contract can come into existence, an offer must have been made and accepted, and consideration must move from both parties. The opening of the credit constitutes the offer, so that the problems concern acceptance and consideration. Since the discussion in the cases relates only to the question of consideration, I shall deal with that first.

---

47. As in the *Cape Asbestos* case, section 2.3.1.
48. See section 7.1.2.2.
49. See section 3.1.4.
50. See section 3.2.2.

8.1.10.1 Consideration

Since the seller makes no promise to the bank that it will perform, there may perhaps be consideration difficulties until the moment the documents are tendered, but it seems to be accepted at the very least that consideration may be provided as soon as the seller starts to perform.

The closest the English courts ever came to discussing the issue was in *Urquhart Lindsay & Co.* v. *Eastern Bank Ltd.*,[51] in the Commercial Court. It is the case which originally established that the credit constituted an independent contract between bank and seller, whose terms were not dependent on those of the sale contract.

The defendant bank opened a credit in favour of the plaintiff sellers, to the extent of £70,000, "this to be considered a confirmed irrevocable credit". The credit was intended to cover a number of shipments of machinery by instalments, as agreed in the contract of sale. Except for the top limit of £70,000, the credit required the bank to pay the amounts of the sellers' invoices without qualification.

The plaintiffs shipped two instalments under the sale contract and the bank paid under the terms of the credit. The buyers disputed the amount on the third instalment, claiming that the sellers had, in their invoices, added to the price originally quoted under the contract. In fact, the sale contract allowed the sellers to increase the price to cover increases in wages and cost of materials, and the sellers claimed to be doing no more than this. Nevertheless, the buyers instructed the bank not to pay more than what they claimed was the original price. The bank followed the buyers' instructions, very unfortunately, in Rowlatt J.'s view.[52] The sellers refused to part with the shipping documents except against the full price claimed, and sued the bank for breach of contract. The bank claimed that their contract with the plaintiff sellers had to be qualified by the terms of the sale contract, and this was rejected by Rowlatt J.[53]:

"In my view the defendants [bank] committed a breach of their contract with the plaintiffs when they refused to pay the amount of the invoices as presented. [The bank] contended that the letter of credit must be taken to incorporate the contract between the plaintiffs and the buyers; and that according to the true meaning of that contract the amount of any increase claimed in respect of an alleged advance in manufacturing costs was not to be included in any invoice to be presented under the letter of credit, but was to be the subject of subsequent independent adjustment. The answer to this is that the defendants undertook to pay the amount of invoices for machinery without qualification, the basis of this form of banking facility being that the buyer is taken for the purposes of all questions between himself and his banker or between his banker and the seller to be content to accept the invoices of the seller as correct. It seems to me that so far from the letter of credit being qualified by the contract of sale, the latter must accommodate itself to the letter of credit. The buyer having authorized his

51. [1922] 1 K.B. 318; (1921) 9 Lloyd's Rep. 572.
52. [1922] 1 K.B. 318, 322.
53. [1922] 1 K.B. 318, 322–323.

banker to undertake to pay the amount of the invoice as presented, it follows that any adjustment must be made by way of refund by the seller, and not by way of retention by the buyer."

Today it would seem to be self-evident that the contract between bank and seller is autonomous, and hence does not incorporate any terms from the sale contract, but in 1922, when this case was decided, the law was still at an early stage of its development. The only sentence with which one would take issue today is the phrase: "It seems to me that so far from the letter of credit being qualified by the contract of sale, the latter must accommodate itself to the letter of credit." This is clearly wrong—the terms of the sale contract are also independent from those of the credit (unless perhaps such a term can be implied into the sale contract, to bring it into line with the credit).

In order to establish the existence of an independent contract between seller and bank, it was necessary to find consideration for it. This is why the case is relevant to the present discussion. Rowlatt J. said[54]:

"There can be no doubt that upon the plaintiffs acting upon the undertaking contained in this letter of credit consideration moved from the plaintiffs, which bound the defendants to the irrevocable character of the arrangement between the defendants and the plaintiff; nor was it contended before me that this had not been the position when the circumstances giving rise to this action took place."

The consideration moving from the seller, then, is acting upon the undertaking. This is ambiguous, in that it may mean completing performance (i.e., tendering the documents to the bank), and of course in the case itself documents in respect of two shipments had already been tendered before the dispute arose. But a more natural interpretation of acting upon the undertaking is probably beginning to perform, (e.g., beginning to manufacture the goods, or make arrangements for their shipment), in which case there are no problems about consideration at any rate from then onwards.

8.1.10.1.1 THE OTHER ISSUE IN URQUHART LINDSAY

The other issue that arose in *Urquhart Lindsay* was as to the measure of damages. It is not central to the present discussion, but is included here because it is an important point in its own right.

The bank argued that they had merely undertaken to pay money, and that the amount of damages for non-payment of money is only the amount of the money itself. The sellers argued that the position was the same as if the buyers had themselves refused to pay for the goods, and that in a sale by instalments this entitled the sellers to cancel the entire transaction. Thus, the sellers were able to treat the non-payment of the one instalment as a ground for throwing up the entire sale contract, so as to release them from any obligations not merely under this particular shipment, but under any further shipments as

54. [1922] 1 K.B. 318, 321 (bottom).

well. This is what they chose to do. Their loss was therefore their loss of profit on the entire transaction, not merely non-payment for one shipment. Undoubtedly they could have recovered this in an action against the buyers.[55]

The action was instead brought against the bank, but Rowlatt J. thought that the position was exactly equivalent, and that the refusal by the defendants to pay on this instalment constituted a repudiatory breach of the entire credit contract, just as surely as a refusal by the buyers to pay on an instalment constituted a repudiatory breach of the entire sale contract. The sellers had accepted this breach as bringing the credit contract to an end, and were entitled to damages on that basis. They could therefore claim loss of profit on the entire transaction. After setting out the position where the action is taken against the buyer,[56] Rowlatt J. continued[57]:

"I confess I cannot see why the refusal of the bank to take and pay for the bills with the documents representing the goods is not in the same way a repudiation of their contract to take the bills to be presented in the future under the letter of credit; nor, if that is so, why the damages are not the same."

The most likely interpretation of the view taken in *Urquhart Lindsay*, then, is that at any rate once the seller has started to perform, there are no further difficulties about consideration. There are still difficulties, however, over the period between notification of the credit and the first steps of the seller's performance.

8.1.10.1.2 BANKERS' IRREVOCABLE CREDITS EXCEPTION TO CONSIDERATION DOCTRINE

An alternative approach is that commercial credits constitute an exception to the consideration doctrine. For example, Professor Treitel writes[58]:

"As in the case of other unilateral contracts, steps taken in the performance would be enough, e.g. beginning to manufacture the goods . . . Or the seller might provide consideration by forbearing to sue the buyer for the price. But the bank would not, on this view, be bound before the seller had acted, or forborne, in some such way. The widely held commercial view is that the bank is bound as soon as the seller is notified of the credit. If (as seems probable) this view also represents the law, it constitutes a clear exception to the doctrine of consideration."

Unfortunately, there is no authority for this proposition. Exceptions to established contractual doctrines would be less likely to succeed in the light of the Court of Appeal decision in *The Aramis*, decided two years after the

---

55. See further section 3.1.6.
56. See further section 3.1.6.
57. [1922] 1 K.B. 318, 324 (top).
58. G.H. Treitel, *The Law of Contract* (7th ed., 1987), p. 117. His footnote reads: "*Cf.* in the United States, U.C.C. s.5–105."

above passage was published. It may be possible, however, to reconcile "the widely held commercial view" with the consideration doctrine.

8.1.10.1.3 DEXTERS LTD. V. SCHENKERS LTD.[59]

It is arguable that the seller provides consideration even before commencement of performance, indeed as soon as notification takes place, by virtue of coming under an obligation from then to perform the sale contract. This appears to have been accepted in *Dexters Ltd.* v. *Schenkers Ltd*. The main issue was very similar to that in *Urquhart Lindsay* itself, namely that the bank argued that the contract between themselves and the seller should incorporate the terms of the contract of sale. Greer J. rejected this contention, following Rowlatt J. in *Urquhart Lindsay*. The contract between seller and bank is an independent contract in its own right. As in the earlier case, it was argued that there was no consideration for the new contract, but Greer J. thought that the seller provided consideration as soon as he had received notification of the credit[60]:

"[The sellers] received from [the purchasers] the wherewithal to implement their guarantee—the promise they were giving. Now it is clear that, until they got a form of banker's credit which would comply with the terms of the contract, plaintiffs [sellers] were not bound to send the goods forward at all; and therefore, not having got the bankers' credit until there was a substituted arrangement for some other credit elsewhere, they were under no obligation to anybody to send forward the goods. Therefore, it is quite clear there was full and ample consideration for this undertaking, and I am not surprised that Mr. Wallington withdrew the contention which appears in the pleadings that there was no consideration. It seems to me that the document means this: 'As soon as we get the documents we will be in a position to take possession of the goods; and though we do not promise to pay on presentation of the documents and only promise to pay on receipt of the goods at Rotterdam, still, our promise is to pay upon receipt of the goods which are mentioned in the documents, upon the presentation of which the purchaser has to pay.' "

In principle that argument seems correct, in which case consideration is not a problem: the seller provides consideration from the moment of notification of the credit.

8.1.10.2 *Acceptance*

Whether or not consideration is problematic, however, acceptance certainly is. When does the seller/beneficiary accept the bank's offer? As explained above, the notification to the seller must be an offer to enter into a unilateral contract, and on conventional contractual theory an offer can be revoked at any time up to acceptance. On the assumption made for the purposes of this section, that no confirming commission is paid, it is arguable that the seller

---

59. (1923) 14 Ll.L.Rep. 586.
60. (1923) 14 Ll.L.Rep. 586, at p. 588 (col. 2).

does not accept until he tenders the documents. Certainly he makes no promise to the bank that he will perform (though of course, he can be sued by the buyer if he does not). It is quite possible to argue, therefore, that the bank can revoke at any time before then. This would be a very undesirable conclusion.

On the other hand there are also general contract authorities, which are not however conclusive, that once the seller relies on the offer it cannot be revoked. If they are correct the bank could not revoke once the seller started to prepare the goods for shipment.[61] This conclusion is more desirable, but still not perfect. It is clear on any view that inaction cannot constitute acceptance, so that the very earliest point at which the seller could be taken to have accepted is when he starts to perform. Thus, the bank could revoke between notification and that time. The seller's position is altered from the moment of notification, however, so the ideal position is irrevocability from that point. It is clear that under the normal rules of offer and acceptance, that position is unattainable.[62]

8.1.10.3 Application of U.C.P.

As has been explained in Chapter 2,[63] where the U.C.P. applies, Article 10(d) states that: "undertakings [to open an irrevocable credit] can neither be amended nor cancelled without the agreement of the issuing bank, the confirming bank (if any) and the beneficiary." The problem is that the U.C.P. does not have the force of law in the U.K., but is incorporated by contract.[64] Since the problem is precisely whether there is a contract or not, it follows that Article 10 can make no difference. Nor, in the absence of legislation giving the U.C.P. the force of law in the United Kingdom, could it affect the issue, whatever it said.

---

61. In a book of this nature, space does not permit a discussion of detailed academic arguments from the general law of contract. Those who wish to pursue the matter should consult Treitel, *op. cit.*, pp. 30–34.

62. It is sometimes argued that the *dictum* of Jenkins L.J. in *Hamzeh Malas & Sons* v. *British Imex Industries Ltd.*, set out in section 6.2.1, leads to the conclusion that the credit is irrevocable from the moment it is opened:

"it seems to me to be plain enough that the opening of a confirmed letter of credit constitutes a bargain between the banker and the vendor of goods, which imposes upon the banker an absolute obligation to pay, irrespective of any dispute there may be between the parties as to whether the goods are up to contract or not."

I would suggest that this is reading far too much into a statement which is at best unclear, taken from a case where the present issue did not arise. In any case, it simply cannot be correct to say that the contract is concluded when the credit is opened, unless bankers' documentary credits constitute an exception to the usual rules of offer and acceptance: see further below, section 8.1.11.1. What the *dictum* does illustrate, however, is that the seller is relying on the confirmed letter of credit from the moment it is opened.

63. Section 2.3.1.2.

64. See section 2.1.3.

8.1.11 Alternative solutions

8.1.11.1 Relaxation of rules of offer and acceptance

In *The Eurymedon*[65] Lord Wilberforce was prepared to bend the rules of offer and acceptance to suit commercial practice, and in the passage set out in Chapter 7 he specifically alluded to bankers' documentary credits. He must have been referring to the problem considered here, but even on the assumption that these remarks survive the very different approach taken by the Court of Appeal in *The Aramis*,[66] it is impossible to conceive that the courts will construe an offer as being accepted when the seller has done nothing except receive notification of the offer. Whatever views were taken in *The Eurymedon*, therefore, the contract cannot be concluded before the seller has at least started to perform, by acquiring the goods to be shipped, or making other arrangements for shipment, or beginning to manufacture the goods, or whatever. There is no way to avoid this conclusion as long as the relationship between bank and beneficiary is contractual, as it must be in the light of *The American Accord*.

8.1.11.2 Interference with contract

There is another way in which the bank may be bound by the irrevocability of the credit even before the seller has begun to perform, but it is by no means a perfect solution. If the bank revokes, the seller is no longer providing a "reliable and solvent paymaster". The seller can therefore sue the buyer directly for the price. More importantly, by failing to provide a reliable and solvent paymaster, the buyer is thereby put in breach of the contract of sale. This is also a probable consequence of revocation of an irrevocable credit by a bank.[67]

An action against the buyer is no good from the seller's point of view, of course, because the whole point of requiring payment by irrevocable credit is to prevent this necessity arising. By its action, however, the bank by revoking may intentionally have put the buyer in breach of the sale contract, and if so it can itself be sued for the tort of interference with contract.

A difficulty with it is that the liability of the banker may depend on the terms of the contract of sale, which does not accord well with the principle of the autonomy of the credit. The solution may not, in any event, always work, for example if the seller is taken to have waived a requirement for the credit to be confirmed on the principles in the *Panoustos* case,[68] but the bank confirms the credit in any event. If the confirming bank later withdraws its confir-

---

65. [1975] A.C. 154. See further section 7.1.2.1.
66. See section 7.1.2.2.
67. See sections 3.1.5 and 3.2.3.
68. See section 3.1.4.

mation, the buyer is not put in breach of the sale contract, and the bank is probably not liable for interference with contract.[69]

8.2 STANDBY LETTERS OF CREDIT

Standby letters of credit are also called guarantees or performance bonds. They are not true documentary credits, and a book on bankers' documentary credits would be complete without any discussion of guarantees or performance bonds. They are also conceptually quite distinct from a documentary credit, in that they are triggered by default. If payment is guaranteed by a standby letter of credit, for example, the bank simply acts as a guarantor. The primary obligation remains with the buyer, and the seller can sue the buyer for payment, the bank's obligation only arising on his default. By contrast, under a documentary credit the bank comes under a primary liability to pay, and only if the bank fails to pay may the seller proceed against the buyer directly.[70]

Another fundamental difference between a documentary and standby letter of credit is that in the latter the bank is dependent for reimbursement on the personal contract with its customer. It does not obtain the security of a document of title, and hence any security in the goods. A far wider range of documentation can be stipulated under a standby letter of credit than under a traditional documentary credit, and indeed one of the reasons for using the standby letter of credit is precisely because it is difficult or impossible to provide traditional documentation. Indeed, it is possible in theory to operate a standby letter of credit without any documentary requirements at all.

Despite these fundamental differences, standby letters of credit are nevertheless included here for four reasons

1. They are sometimes provided by buyers as a guarantee for payment in circumstances where one might have expected to see a documentary credit, but where for some reason it is difficult to comply with the usual documentary requirements. The use of a standby letter of credit is particularly common for sales of oil cargoes, where it is often impracticable to negotiate the original bill of lading.
2. Standby letters of credit are subject to the U.C.P.[71]
3. Performance bonds are frequently provided by sellers in the same types of transaction as bankers' documentary credits.

---

69. Although the tort is interference with contract, which is not necessarily the same as inducing breach of contract. See, for example, *Torquay Hotel Co. Ltd.* v. *Cousins* [1969] 2 Ch. 106, where a supply contract was not broken because the supplier was able to rely on an exemption clause, but an action (against a strike organiser) for interference with contract succeeded.
70. See section 3.2.
71. See below, section 8.2.5.

4. Much of the law on documentary credits applies equally to performance bonds.

8.2.1 Varieties of guarantee and performance bond provided by seller

The purpose (or at any rate, ostensible purpose), of the guarantee or performance bond provided by the seller is to protect the buyer from unsatisfactory performance by the seller. Sometimes the guarantee protects the buyer only against late delivery of the goods, but sometimes it is triggered by any non-performance, or defective performance, whether actual or alleged, on the part of the seller.

In its simplest form, the buyer retains a percentage of the agreed payment pending his acceptance of the goods as satisfactory. This type of guarantee may be provided for in a commercial credit, where say 90 per cent. of the price is payable on sight and the remaining 10 per cent. at a later date, subject to acceptance of the goods as satisfactory by the buyer.[72] Guarantees of this type give rise to few difficulties, apart from obvious disputes under the sale contract as to whether the goods are in fact satisfactory, in cases where the buyer claims that they are not. In overseas sales it is common for sellers to accept that the final 10 per cent. may never be paid, and to take this into account when quoting the original price.[73]

A more sophisticated variation is where, in the event of an allegation by the buyer of a breach of contract by the seller, the seller is required to pay a sum of money to the buyer. This type is relatively uncommon in English law, since in order for the guarantee to be valid the sum stipulated must represent liquidated damages, and not a penalty. If it is a genuine estimate of the loss that would be caused to the buyer by the seller's breach, it may be regarded as liquidated damages, but if it does not it will be treated as a penalty clause and will be unenforceable under English law.

The performance bond proper is similar to the guarantee described in the previous paragraph, except that here the seller provides a bond whereby, if there is an actual or alleged breach of contract on his part, a sum of money is paid to the buyer by a third party, who will usually be a reputable bank. The performance bond proper appears to avoid the difficulties over penalty clauses, since the seller's obligation to pay derives from the contract it has made with the bank, and not from the contract of sale. As in the documentary credit, the contract between seller and bank is autonomous, and is enforceable on its own terms, regardless of the provisions of the sale contract. In *Comdel Commodities Ltd.* v. *Siporex Trade S.A.*,[74] although the issue did not arise directly, the Court of Appeal appeared to accept that a demand could

---

72. See, e.g., *The Royan*, especially section 6.2.2.2.
73. See, e.g., *Edward Owen Engineering Ltd.* v. *Barclays Bank International Ltd.* [1978] 1 Q.B. 159 (*per* Lord Denning M.R.) at p. 170F.
74. *Comdel Commodities Ltd.* v. *Siporex Trade S.A. (No. 2)* [1990] 1 All E.R. 216; [1989] 2 Lloyd's Rep. 13, affd. on other grounds [1990] 2 All E.R. 552.

validly be made on a performance bond where although there had been a breach of contract by the seller, it had caused the buyer no loss, or at any rate a very much smaller loss than the amount of the bond.[75]

Performance bonds are also commonly used in construction contracts, ostensibly to protect against unsatisfactory performance by the contractor. These are in principle identical to the performance bonds described in the last paragraph.

8.2.2 Standby letter of credit provided by buyer

Although standby letters of credit are usually provided by sellers or contractors to protect the buyer against unsatisfactory performance, they are sometimes also provided by the buyer in order to guarantee payment. Generally speaking, the standby letter of credit has no advantage over the documentary credit proper as a guarantee of payment, except where there are practical difficulties in using documentary credits.

One such situation is the carriage of bulk oil cargoes. As has already been explained, such cargoes are often sold as many as 100 times on the voyage, and if the voyage is of short duration there is no way in which the bill of lading can reach the receiver before the cargo arrives. The cargo is invariably discharged without production of an original bill of lading, subject to an indemnity, and bills of lading are then negotiated at leisure.

Because the bill of lading does not in reality perform the function of being a document of title in such cases, guarantees issued by "first class banks" are sometimes used to secure payment instead of documentary credits. These are essentially the same in principle as the performance bonds considered in the last section, except that they are provided by the buyer to guarantee payment. Typically, the bank is required to pay on demand by the seller, subject to a statement by the seller that the buyer has failed to pay within a stipulated time. The seller may be required to present documents, but usually tender of an original bill of lading will not be required. In The *Delfini*,[76] for example, the guarantee was in the following terms:

"This guarantee is payable at first beneficiary's written request to us in the case of our principals Enichemica S.p.A. fail to pay any amount up to the sum of U.S.$ 6,015,000 within the terms above indicated and against presentation of the following documents:-
    (a) a copy or photocopy of the commercial invoice,
    (b) a copy or photocopy of the bill of lading,
    (c) seller's certificate stating that payment has not been made by Enichemica
       S.p.A. within the due date."

---

75. At least, this appears to be the tentative view of Staughton L.J.: [1990] 1 All E.R. 216, 222b.

76. *Enichem Anic S.p.A.* v. *Ampelos Shipping Co. Ltd., The Delfini* [1990] 1 Lloyd's Rep. 252. See further section 7.1.1.2. The terms of the guarantee are set out at p. 256 (col.1).

In *The Filiatra Legacy*,[77] the sellers were required to certify that the buyer had failed to fulfil its payment obligation within 30 days from the bill of lading date under the contract, and were entitled to tender a letter of indemnity authorising the shipowners to discharge the cargo to the buyers without production of the bills of lading in lieu of original bills of lading.

Standby letters of credit are also used where a bill of lading or other document of title could not be used, for example where there is no carriage element. In *Elder Dempster Lines Ltd.* v. *Ionic Shipping Agency Inc.*,[78] for example, a standby letter of credit was used to guarantee payment for a ship. Obviously a conventional documentary credit would be wholly inappropriate in such a transaction.

No doubt, even where a standby letter of credit is used, the buyer can stipulate tender of documents which provide him with adequate security against the seller's non-performance, and of course the seller can look to a reputable bank for payment. The main difference between this and a commercial credit proper is that the bank does not obtain the security of a document of title, and hence obtains neither special property in, nor constructive possession of the goods. The bank therefore becomes, in effect, an unsecured creditor of the buyer, unless of course, the buyer places it in funds in advance.

8.2.3 The obligation to pay

The law on standby credits and performance bonds is similar to that on documentary credits, in that the relationship between seller and bank (or in the case of a standby credit issued by the buyer, buyer and bank) is governed by the terms of the performance bond or standby credit alone, and not by the contract of sale. Further, as with documentary credits, the banks are not concerned with disputes between the buyer and seller under the sale contract.[79]

This can cause difficulties in particular for sellers, and contractors under construction contracts, when they are required to provide performance bonds which are wide in their scope, or when insufficient conditions are attached. It is often provided that payment is made on demand, in which case the buyer need do no more than allege default for the bond to be triggered. As with documentary credits, the bank is not concerned with the merits of the buyer's allegation, but must enforce the bond unless it can be proven that the buyer is fraudulent.[80]

The leading authority is *Edward Owen Engineering Ltd.* v. *Barclays Bank*

---

77. *Anonima Petroli Italiana S.p.A. and another* v. *Marlucidez Armadora S.A.*, *The Filiatra Legacy* [1990] 1 Lloyd's Rep. 354.

78. Above, f.n. 41.

79. See section 6.2.

80. Note that this is different from the *Comdel Commodities Ltd.* v. *Siporex Trade S.A. (No. 2)* situation considered above, f.n. 74. Here there is an unjustifiable allegation of a default whose consequences may well (had the allegation been well-founded) have exceeded the value of the bond. There there was a clear default, whose consequences were substantially under the value of the bond.

International Ltd.[81] The plaintiffs were English sellers who had contracted with Libyan buyers to erect greenhouses in Libya, and had agreed that a performance guarantee of 10 per cent. of the price (just over £50,000) should be lodged by Barclays Bank with a Libyan bank. Barclays accordingly, on the plaintiffs' behalf, gave a performance bond to the Umma Bank in Libya, which was payable "on demand without proof and conditions."

Under the sale contract the buyers undertook to provide an irrevocable confirmed documentary credit, but no such letter of credit was opened. Accordingly, the sellers repudiated the contract. Unfortunately for them, the bond had already been lodged by then, and indeed it seems that the guarantee was given not only before satisfactory arrangements for payment had been made, but even before the contract of sale had been concluded. The buyer invoked the guarantee from the Umma Bank, and the plaintiffs sought an interlocutory injunction to prevent Barclays Bank from paying the Libyan bank. They failed in the Court of Appeal.

The decision of the Court of Appeal states clearly that "the performance guarantee stands on a similar footing to a letter of credit".[82] The authorities on credits are reviewed,[83] and the conclusion was that Barclays Bank must honour the guarantee it had given to the Umma Bank according to its terms, and was not in the least concerned with relations between seller and buyer. As with documentary credits, the only exception is where fraud on the part of the buyer can be proved, and not only could that not be done in the case itself, but it would be very unlikely for it ever to be proven.

Of course, the sellers could attempt to recoup their loss by suing the buyers for damages under the sale contract, but were not confident of their chances of success, since the sale contract was governed by Libyan law and gave exclusive jurisdiction to the courts of Libya, and it was not practicable for the English sellers to invoke the jurisdiction of the Libyan courts.[84]

8.2.4 Protection of seller (or contractor) and bank

Because the buyer needs to do no more than demand payment under an unconditional performance bond, and the bank is unconcerned with the validity of his claim, performance bonds are potentially far more dangerous for a seller (or contractor) than a documentary credit is to a buyer. At least to claim payment under a documentary credit the beneficiary must obtain and tender the appropriate shipping documents, and it is obviously difficult to do this in the event of total non-performance by him.

The sellers in *Edward Owen Engineering Ltd.* really brought their difficulties upon themselves by agreeing to an unconditional bond in the first place.

---

81. [1978] 1 Q.B. 159; [1977] 3 W.L.R. 764; [1978] 1 All E.R. 976; [1978] 1 Lloyd's Rep. 166.
82. [1978] 1 Q.B. 159, (*per* Lord Denning M.R.) at p. 171A.
83. See section 6.2.
84. [1978] 1 Q.B. 159, (*per* Lord Denning M.R.) at p. 172D.

Since the bond will be enforceable on its own terms independently of the sale contract, it is essential that the bond itself must refer to and depend on the main sale contract. It is also vital that it enumerates the circumstances in which payment becomes due, and preferably that there is some form of independent certification that those circumstances have arisen.

No doubt sellers (or contractors) are concerned that they may lose the contract should they demand that such conditions are imposed on performance bonds. They should be aware, however, that unconditional performance bonds are "virtually promissory notes payable on demand".[85] If the buyer is honest and reputable, or is likely to wish to continue dealing with the seller (or contractor), then that is unlikely to cause problems. Otherwise the seller (or contractor) is almost certain to lose money, and should take this into account in fixing the price.

As noted above,[86] a bank obtains no security under a standby letter of credit, and the same is true for a performance bond. The bank has a personal action only against the seller or contractor, to recoup the amount of the bond. Banks can protect themselves to an extent by taking an assignment of all payments due under the underlying contract, which are paid over to the contractor only in the event of the bond not being called. This protects the bank against default by its customer, but is unlikely to protect it against its bankruptcy, since if the seller or contractor goes into liquidation before the contract is completed, it is unlikely that the buyer will make any payments under the underlying contract. It can still claim against the bank on the performance bond, however.[87]

8.2.5 Application of the U.C.P.

As a result of the 1983 revision, standby letters of credit were brought within the ambit of the U.C.P. Article 1 of the U.C.P. accordingly provides: "These Articles apply to all documentary credits, including, to the extent to which they may be applicable, standby letters of credit, and are binding on all parties thereto unless otherwise agreed . . . " The provisions of the U.C.P. only apply to standby letters of credit, however, "to the extent to which they may be applicable". In *UCP 1974/1983 Revisions Compared and Explained*, Bernard Wheble notes[88]: "The type of documentation . . . gives some indication of 'the extent to which they (UCP) may be applicable' to standby credits. Thus, Articles 23 and 46 would seem likely to apply, whereas many of the Articles dealing with 'Documents' would seem likely not to be applicable."

There is a good argument that standby credits should be governed by their own separate code, and indeed the I.C.C. has published "Uniform Rules for

85. [1978] 1 Q.B. 159 (*per* Lord Denning M.R.) at p. 170H.
86. Section 8.2.1.
87. Banks can also spread their risks by syndication. This is beyond the scope of this book, but see Kronfol, "The Syndication of Risk in Unconditional Bonds" [1984] J.B.L. 13.
88. International Chamber of Commerce Publication No. 411, p. 11.

Guarantees"[89]; which in the long-term may provide the answer to the difficulty. Until the Uniform Rules for Guarantees are universally accepted, however, it is probably better that they remain governed by the U.C.P., although if it is possible to do this, it may be better to state exactly which U.C.P. provisions apply. Unfortunately, it may not be possible, since there are wide differences between individual standby letters of credit.

8.3 PROPER LAW OF THE CONTRACT

8.3.1 Proper law of the four autonomous contracts

In this book I have assumed throughout that all contracts are governed by the law of the United Kingdom, since detailed discussion of the law of other jurisdictions would be beyond the scope of the book. However, the question of whether English law governs the transaction, or whether it is governed by the domestic laws of another jurisdiction is often itself an issue. The jurisdiction whose domestic laws govern the contract is also called the proper law of the contract.

8.3.1.1 Express choice of law clause

Contracts commonly state expressly whose law is to govern, in which case there is unlikely to be any difficulty. Where there is an express choice of law clause, the courts will usually give effect to it, even if neither of the parties has any connection with the country chosen. This is of course unlikely to be the case for a commercial credit, but the eventual parties to a carriage contract may have no connection with the law of the country which governs it, especially if a number of re-sales have taken place, and a bill of lading contract containing an express choice of law clause has been transferred many times under section 1 of the Bills of Lading Act 1855.

Lord Wright in *Vita Food Products Inc.* v. *Unus Shipping Co. Ltd.* thought that the English courts would always give effect to an express choice of law clause[90]: "provided the intention expressed is *bona fide* and legal, and provided there is no reason for avoiding the clause on the ground of public policy."

Probably a proper law clause will be contrary to public policy, or not *bona fide* and legal, only if the intention is to avoid the domestic legislation of the state with the closest connection with the contract. For practical purposes we can assume that the courts will always give effect to an express choice of law clause,[91] except perhaps where the only reason for choosing the law of a

89. International Chamber of Commerce Publication No. 325.
90. [1939] A.C. 277, 290.
91. It is true that some aspects of Lord Wright's speech were criticised by Lord Diplock in *The Hollandia* [1983] 1 A.C. 565, 577G–578A, but this aspect of it is almost certainly still good law.

particular state is to avoid, for example, an order freezing assets in the country with which the transaction has its closest connection.

It is not necessary for the transaction to have a close connection with the country chosen, and indeed in *Vita Food* itself Lord Wright applied English law, though the case had only the most tenuous connection with England, and both parties to the action had pleaded that the proper law of the contract was the law of Newfoundland.

At the time of writing (April 1990), the Contracts (Applicable Law) Bill is proceeding on its passage through Parliament, the purpose of which is to give effect to the Rome Convention on the law applicable to contractual obligations. Assuming the legislation goes through, the Convention will be brought into force when it has been ratified by seven States in the E.C. Currently it has been ratified by six.

The rules on freedom of the parties to choose are set out in article 3 of the Convention. Nothing in this article appears to affect the *Vita Food* position, at any rate for the purposes of documentary credits.

8.3.1.2 No express choice of law clause

As with any expression of intention, this may be inferred from the express wording of the agreement, or can be implied from all the circumstances.

Where the parties do not expressly choose a proper law, the courts will infer an intention. Any factors will be considered, including especially arbitration clauses and choice of forum clauses. If it is impossible even to infer an intention, the courts will apply the law of the state with which the contract has its closest and most real connection. No presumptions are used, and all factors are considered.

If the Rome Convention is adopted, article 4, paragraph 1 will not affect the present position, and the contract will continue to "be governed by the law of the country in which it is most closely connected".

8.3.1.3 Proper law of credit is law of the country in which payment is to be made

Applying the above principles, in general, in the absence of an express choice of law clause, the proper law of a credit is the law of the country in which payment is to be made, because that is the country with which it has the closest connection. In *Power Curber International Ltd.* v. *National Bank of Kuwait S.A.K.*,[92] a c.i.f. contract was made between sellers in North Carolina and buyers in Kuwait, payment by irrevocable but unconfirmed credit, 25 per cent. of the price to be paid against presentation of documents and the remaining 75 per cent. one year after the date of shipment. The credit was issued by the National Bank of Kuwait, to the advising bank (Bank of

---

92. [1981] 1 W.L.R. 1233; [1981] 3 All E.R. 607; [1981] 2 Lloyd's Rep. 394.

America, Florida) through the North Carolina National Bank, which was situated in Charlotte, North Carolina. The National Bank of Kuwait also traded in, and had a registered office in, London.

Twenty-five per cent. of the price was paid under the credit, against presentation of documents, and in accordance with the terms of the credit a usance draft (which is a type of time draft) was drawn by the buyers on the National Bank of Kuwait for the remaining 75 per cent., maturing one year after shipment. Before the draft matured, however, as a result of a dispute between buyers and sellers a provisional attachment order was made in the Kuwaiti courts, the effect of which under Kuwaiti law was to prevent any further payment being made under the credit.

It is interesting to note, in passing, that as regards the remaining 75 per cent., the buyers drew time drafts which they were required to give to the sellers. At first sight this looks very like the early form of credit used in *Re Agra and Masterman's Bank*,[93] but it differs in that the bank also made a direct undertaking in favour of the sellers. Hence, this is indistinguishable conceptually from any other irrevocable but unconfirmed credit.

Power Curber (the sellers) eventually issued a writ in the English High Court against the National Bank of Kuwait in London. Apart from the fact that the National Bank of Kuwait traded in London, the case had no other connection with England. It appeared that the bank wished to honour its obligations to Power Curber, and the question at issue was whether the order of the Kuwaiti courts prevented it from doing so. This depended on whether the credit was governed by Kuwaiti law.

The Court of Appeal held that the proper law of the credit was the law of North Carolina. North Carolina was the country with which the credit had closest connection, because that was where the bank was required, under the terms of the credit, to perform its obligation to pay. Therefore the provisional attachment order of the Kuwaiti courts, which also ran counter to internationally accepted principles that the promise of the issuing bank to pay was wholly independent of any dispute that may arise between buyer and seller, would not be recognised by the English courts.

It follows that in the absence of an express choice of law clause, the proper law of the credit will be governed by the country of the advising or confirming bank, or if there is no advising or confirming bank, then by the country of the issuing bank. *Power Curber* is also in accord with the more general principle applicable to a banker-customer relationship arising from a current or deposit account, that the relationship is governed by the law of the country where the account is kept. This principle was recently restated in the High Court (Queen's Bench Division) in *Libyan Arab Foreign Bank* v. *Bankers Trust Co.*,[94] where the plaintiffs held an account with the defendant American

93. See section 8.1.3.
94. [1989] 1 Q.B. 728; [1989] 3 W.L.R. 314; [1989] 3 All E.R. 252, [1989] 1 Lloyd's Rep. 608, a case which was not reported until more than 2 years after it had been decided.

bank, in London. Staughton J. held that an executive order made by the President of the United States of America freezing all Libyan assets, including those held by overseas branches of American banks, did not apply to the London account, since performance of the defendant bank's obligation to pay was not illegal under English law, although it was of course under the law of the United States. English law applied to the relationship, since the account was held in England, and it was also irrelevant that the defendant bank may have to obtain the necessary funds from the Federal Reserve Bank of New York.

8.3.1.4 Proper law of credit or performance bond independent of proper law of underlying transaction

Because the four contracts within a confirmed irrevocable credit are autonomous, it follows that the proper law of any one will not necessarily be governed by the proper law of any other. Hence, the proper law of a credit or performance bond is independent of the proper law of underlying transaction (the sale contract). In *Power Curber*, in determining the proper law of the credit no account was taken of the proper law of the underlying transaction (which was not determined).

Indeed, the principle that the proper law of the credit or performance bond is the law of the country in which payment is to be made therefore operates even if the underlying contract is expressly governed by a different jurisdiction. In *Attock Cement Co. Ltd.* v. *Romanian Bank for Foreign Trade*,[95] the underlying transaction, which was a contract for the construction of a cement plant by a Romanian company on behalf of the plaintiffs, was made expressly subject to English law. Under the terms of the underlying contract the Romanian contractors were required to furnish a performance bond of 10 per cent. of the contract price, and in pursuance of this the Romanian Bank issued an unconditional and irrevocable bond, undertaking to pay[96]:

"within 30 days from [Attock Cement's] first demand without any other formality of whatever nature or without recourse to the Contractor, such sum or sums as may be demanded by ATTOCK CEMENT LTD. against the simple demand accompanied by its declaration that UZINEXPORTIMPORT (the Contractor) has failed to fulfil any of its obligations . . . "

In other words this was a performance bond payable on demand similar to that considered in the *Edward Owen Engineering* case, above.

Serious disputes arose under the underlying contract, leading the plaintiffs eventually to give notice of termination, and by the use of armed security guards to prevent the contractors' employees from entering their plant. They then made a demand on the performance bond, with which the bank did not comply. The plaintiffs then sought leave under Rules of the Supreme Court,

95. [1989] 1 W.L.R. 1147; [1989] 1 All E.R. 1189.
96. [1989] 1 All E.R. 1189, 1192d.

Order 11, to serve a writ on the bank out of the jurisdiction, and in order to do so had to show a good arguable case that the performance bond was governed by English law.

Their main argument rested on an oral collateral agreement which expressly provided that the performance was subject to English law, but this was rejected on the facts. That being so, the fact that the underlying contract was expressly subject to English law was held by the Court of Appeal to be irrelevant. Applying *Power Curber*, Staughton L.J. held that the proper law was the law of the country where payment was to be made, which was presumably Romania.

8.3.2 Proper law of a Brandt v. Liverpool contract

There is a particular difficulty with a *Brandt* v. *Liverpool* contract,[97] where the courts imply a contract on bill of lading terms between the receiver of the cargo and the carrier. Unlike a statutory Bills of Lading Act contract,[98] the implied contract is entirely separate from the original bill of lading contract. Although it is on bill of lading terms, it is made by different parties to the original carriage contract, at a different place (the port of discharge). Only the carrier himself is necessarily common to both the original bill of lading contract and the *Brandt* v. *Liverpool* contract. Unless there is an express choice of law clause in the bill of lading, it is therefore possible for the *Brandt* v. *Liverpool* contract to be governed by a different system of law to that governing the original contract of carriage.

In *The St. Joseph*,[99] a cargo of French aeroplanes was shipped in Belgium on board a Norwegian vessel by French shippers. Had Belgian law applied the bill of lading should have incorporated the Hague Rules by clause paramount, but no such paramount clause was included in the bill of lading. The cargo was discharged in Guatemala, a contract being implied between carrier and receiver (the Guatemalan Government) on *Brandt* v. *Liverpool* principles. Bateson J. held that the *Brandt* v. *Liverpool* contract was governed by the law of Guatemala. Guatemala had not at that time adopted the Hague Rules, and hence the package limitation of the Hague Rules did not apply to the implied contract. Obviously, the conclusion in *The St. Joseph*, where a different proper law could apply to the *Brandt* v. *Liverpool* contract, could be inconvenient in chain sales, although of course it is circumvented if there is an express choice of law clause in the bill of lading.

In *The Elli 2*,[100] the shipowners applied to serve the defendant receivers out of the jurisdiction, claiming demurrage due under the bill of lading (which incorporated the terms of a charterparty). Under the Rules of the Supreme

97. See section 7.1.2.
98. See section 7.1.1.
99. [1933] P. 119; (1933) 45 Ll.L. Rep. 180.
100. See section 7.1.2.

Court, Order 11, rule 1(1)(f), it was necessary for them to show a good arguable case that their contract with the receiver was governed by English law. English law governed the original bill of lading contract, but counsel for the shipowners conceded that the proper law of the implied contract need not be the same as that of the original contract of carriage. Since the *Brandt* v. *Liverpool* contract was made on discharge in Jeddah, it was arguable that it was governed by Saudi Arabian law. In the event, however, the Court of Appeal thought English law governed the implied contract also, primarily because of the inclusion of a London arbitration clause in the charterparty (whose terms were incorporated into the bill of lading).

The case is different from *The St. Joseph*, because in the earlier case it was by no means clear what was the proper law of the original bill of lading contract. After all, although the cargo was shipped in Belgium, the vessel was Norwegian and the shippers and cargo French. Further, there was no choice of law clause. In *The Elli 2*, the original bill of lading contract was clearly governed by English law. However, the reasoning in *The St. Joseph* is potentially of general application. In the absence of an express choice of law clause in the bill of lading, there is no reason why the implied contract should be governed by the same law as the original bill of lading contract. Indeed, it is clear from the following passage from May L.J.'s judgment in *The Elli 2* that whereas *The St. Joseph* was distinguishable on its facts, in principle the *Brandt* v. *Liverpool* contract can be governed by a proper law different from that governing the original bill of lading contract[101]:

"For the purposes of the instant appeal, Mr. Gross [for the receiver] accepted that . . . it was at the least difficult for him to argue that the proper law of the bills of lading was other than that of England. But Mr. Gross then submitted that it did not necessarily follow that the proper law of the implied contract was the same as the proper law of the bills of lading. In this connection he referred us to the case of *The St. Joseph*. Miss Phelan [for the shipowners] accepted that the two proper laws did have to be considered separately, but she submitted that the facts of *The St. Joseph* were very different from those of the instant case. As the learned Judge pointed out in his judgment below, in *The St. Joseph* there was no direct choice of law in the bill of lading and very little connection between the transaction and the law which was held to be the proper law of the bill of lading. It was therefore understandable that the Court in that case found that a different system of law governed the implied contract . . . "

He continued[102]: "That said, however, on the facts of this case the proper law of the bills of lading was English law . . . "

The Rome Convention, if it is adopted, will in some cases (set out below) determine which jurisdiction applies to the bill of lading contract, in the absence of an express choice of law clause. The criteria will be exactly the same for the *Brandt* v. *Liverpool* contract, so at any rate where the criteria apply, there will no longer be any possibility of it being governed by a different

101. [1985] 1 Lloyd's Rep. 107, 117 (col.1).
102. *Ibid.*, at p. 118 (col.1).

jurisdiction to that governing the original bill of lading contract. Article 4, paragraph 4 provides for a contract of carriage:

" . . . In such a contract if the country in which, at the time the contract is concluded, the carrier has his principal place of business is also the country in which the place of loading or the place of discharge or the principal place of business of the consignor is situated, it shall be presumed that the contract is most closely connected with that country . . . "

However, where the criteria in article 4, paragraph 4 do not apply, the contract shall continue to be governed by the law of the country with which it is most closely connected, and that could continue to be different for the two contracts.

8.4 MISCELLANEOUS PROVISIONS OF THE U.C.P.

The U.C.P contains a number of miscellaneous provisions, which are essentially definitional in nature. These are contained in section E, which comprises articles 43–53. There are also other provisions elsewhere in the U.C.P., which are most conveniently dealt with here, as miscellaneous provisions.

8.4.1 Amendment of credit

The relevant provisions can be found in Articles 13 and 14:

Article 13:

"When a bank is instructed to issue, confirm or advise a credit similar in terms to one previously issued, confirmed or advised (similar credit) and the previous credit has been the subject of amendment(s), it shall be understood that the similar credit will not include any such amendment(s) unless the instructions specify clearly the amendment(s) which is/are to apply to the similar credit. Banks should discourage instructions to issue, confirm or advise a credit in this manner."

Article 14:

"If incomplete or unclear instructions are received to issue, advise or amend a credit, the bank requested to act on such instructions may give preliminary notification to the beneficiary for information only and without responsibility. The credit will be issued, confirmed, advised or amended only when the necessary information has been received and if the bank is then prepared to act on the instructions. Banks should provide the necessary information without delay."

8.4.2 Liabilities and responsibilities

The general exemption clause is contained in Article 19:

"Banks assume no liability or responsibility for the consequences arising out of the interruption of their business by Acts of God, riots, civil commotions, insurrections, wars or any causes beyond their control, or by any strikes, or lockouts. Unless specifically authorized, banks will not, upon resumption of their business, incur a deferred payment undertaking, or effect payment, acceptance or negotiation under credits which expired during such interruption of their business."

There is also a provision (Article 20), the effect of which is to place on the applicant for the credit, rather than the issuing bank, the risk of error by the advising or confirming bank. This affects the relationship between issuing bank and applicant (i.e., contract 2):

"(a) Banks utilizing the services of another bank or other banks for the purpose of giving effect to the instructions of the applicant for the credit do so for the account and at the risk of such applicant.

(b) Banks assume no liability or responsibility should the instructions they transmit not be carried out, even if they have themselves taken the initiative in the choice of such other bank.

(c) The applicant for the credit shall be bound by and be liable to indemnify the banks against all obligations and responsibilities imposed by foreign laws and usages."

8.4.3 Quantity and amount

Article 43 states:

"(a) The words 'about', 'circa' or similar expressions used in connection with the amount of the credit or the quantity or the unit price stated in the credit are to be construed as allowing a difference not to exceed 10% more or 10% less than the amount or the quantity or the unit price to which they refer.

(b) Unless a credit stipulates that the quantity of the goods specified must not be exceeded or reduced, a tolerance of 5% more or 5% less will be permissible, even if partial shipments are not permitted, always provided that the amount of the drawings does not exceed the amount of the credit. This tolerance does not apply when the credit stipulates the quantity in terms of a stated number of packing units or individual items."

The reason for the tolerances in this Article is that for bulk cargoes, it is not always possible in advance to know how much the vessel will be able to load. If the shipper is voyage charterer, he will be under an obligation under the charterparty to load a full and complete cargo, which may be more or less than the amount of the credit. In the case of oil cargoes, there is the additional difficulty that accurate measurements are very difficult to make.

The expressions mentioned in Article 43(a) must qualify the quantity specifically, or the unit price specifically. "About" or "circa" qualifying the quantity will not also qualify unit price, or *vice versa*. The tolerance in Article 43(b) was raised from 3 per cent. to 5 per cent. in 1983.

The Lena[103] concerned the sale of a ship, payment to be by standby letter of credit to which the U.C.P. (1962 revision) applied. The vessel was described in the letter of credit as being of "about 11,250 tons gross register 6,857 tons nett register". The commercial invoices stated the tonnages as 11,123.89 and

---

103. *Kydon Compania Naviera S.A.* v. *National Westminster Bank, The Lena* [1981] 1 Lloyd's Rep. 68.

6,297.41 respectively, and the sellers relied on Article 32 of the 1962 revision, which was in similar terms to Article 43(a) set out above. The discrepancy is clearly under 10 per cent. Parker J. held that the net and gross register tonnages were not quantities, to allow the sellers to take advantage of the 10 per cent. allowance[104]:

"It is contended that net and gross register tonnages come within the expression 'quantity of the goods'. I do not consider that they do, any more than would expressions as to measurement come within the 'quantity' of the goods in such cases as 'about 100 planks of sawn timber about 30 ft. long and about 18 in. wide'."

He also rejected a second argument that the discrepancies in the invoice came within the general meaning of the word "about", quite apart from the particular U.C.P. provision.

The problem with Parker J.'s approach is that if no expressions of measurement are expressions of quantity, that will seriously limit the scope of the Article. Ten thousand tons of bulk oil is a measurement, but if that does not come within the U.C.P. provision then it is difficult to see what does. Surely Parker J.'s test cannot be right. Perhaps a distinction ought to be drawn between the sale of specific items, such as ships, where the 10 per cent. tolerance should not be allowed, and undivided bulk cargoes, where it should. Ideally, of course, the problem should be addressed in a future revision of the U.C.P.

8.4.4 Partial drawings and/or other shipments

Article 44 states:

"(a) Partial drawings and/or shipments are allowed, unless the credit stipulates otherwise.

(b) Shipments by sea, or more than one mode of transport but including carriage by sea, made on the same vessel and for the same voyage, will not be regarded as partial shipments, even if the transport documents indicating loading on board bear different dates of issuance and/or indicate different ports of loading on board.

(c) Shipments made by post will not be regarded as partial shipments if the post receipts or certificates of posting appear to have been stamped or otherwise authenticated in the place from which the credit stipulates the goods are to be dispatched, and on the same date.

(d) Shipments made by modes of transport other than those referred to in paragraphs (b) and (c) of this Article will not be regarded as partial shipments, provided the transport documents are issued by one and the same carrier or his agent and indicate the same date of issuance, the same place of dispatch or taking in charge of the goods, and the same destination."

Paragraphs (c) and (d) were new in 1983, and paragraph (b) modified to cover transport other than port-to-port. This is in line with the general changes to the U.C.P. on transport documents.[105] Partial drawings were also

---

104. [1981] 1 Lloyd's Rep. 68, 76 (col.1).
105. See section 5.1.

covered for the first time in 1983, in paragraph (a), as well as partial shipments, to cater for standby letters of credit.

8.4.5 Drawings and/or shipments by instalments

Article 45 states:

"If drawings and/or shipments by instalments within given periods are stipulated in the credit and any instalment is not drawn and/or shipped within the period allowed for that instalment, the credit ceases to be available for that and any subsequent instalment, unless otherwise stipulated in the credit."

Little comment is required on this provision, the drastic effect of which is obvious, except to note that like Article 44(a), drawings as well as shipments are covered, for the same reason as in 44(a).

8.4.6 Expiry date and presentation

The relevant provisions are contained in Articles 46–49:

Article 46:

"(a) All credits must stipulate an expiry date for presentation of documents for payment, acceptance or negotiation.

(b) Except as provided in Article 48(a), documents must be presented on or before such expiry date.

(c) If an issuing bank states that the credit is to be available 'for one month', 'for six months' or the like, but does not specify the date from which the time is to run, the date of issuance of the credit by the issuing bank will be deemed the first day from which such time is to run. Banks should discourage indication of the expiry date in this manner."

Article 47:

"(a) In addition to stipulating an expiry date for presentation of documents, every credit which calls for transport document(s) should also stipulate a specified period of time after the date of issuance of the transport document(s) during which presentation of documents for payment, acceptance or negotiation must be made. If no such period of time is stipulated, banks will refuse documents presented to them later than 21 days after the date of issuance of the transport document(s). In every case, however, documents must be presented not later than the expiry date of the credit.

(b) For the purposes of these Articles the date of issuance of the transport document(s) will be deemed to be

    (i) in the case of a transport document evidencing dispatch, or taking in charge, or receipt of goods for shipment by a mode of transport other than by air—the date of issuance indicated on the transport document or the date of the reception stamp thereon whichever is the later.

    (ii) in the case of a transport document evidencing carriage by air—the date of issuance indicated on the transport document or, if the credit stipulates that the transport document shall indicate an actual flight date, the actual flight date as indicated on the transport document.

    (iii) in the case of a transport document evidencing loading on board a named vessel—the date of issuance of the transport document or, in the case of an on board notation in accordance with Article 27(b), the date of such notation.

(iv) in cases to which Article 44(b) applies, the date determined as above of the latest transport document issued."

Article 48:

"(a) If the expiry date of the credit and/or the last day of the period of time after the date of issuance of the transport document(s) for presentation of documents stipulated by the credit or applicable by virtue of Article 47 falls on a day on which the bank to which presentation has to be made is closed for reasons other than those referred to in Article 19 the stipulated expiry date and/or the last day of the period of time after the date of issuance of the transport document(s) for presentation of documents, as the case may be, shall be extended to the first following business day on which such bank is open.

(b) The latest date for loading on board, or dispatch, or taking in charge shall not be extended by reason of the extension of the expiry date and/or the period of time after the date of issuance of transport document(s) for presentation of document(s) in accordance with this Article. If no such latest date for shipment is stipulated in the credits or amendments thereto, banks will reject transport documents indicating a date of issuance later than the expiry date stipulated in the credit or amendments thereto.

(c) The bank to which presentation is made on such first following business day must add to the documents its certificate that the documents were presented within the time limits extended in accordance with Article 48(a) of the Uniform Customs and Practice for Documentary Credits, 1983 Revision. I.C.C. Publication No. 400."

Article 49:

"Banks are under no obligation to accept presentation of documents outside their banking hours."

Again, most of these provisions are self-explanatory. However, Article 47 was considerably revised in 1983, mainly because its precursors, Articles 41 and 15, were geared only towards the bill of lading issued for port-to-port shipment, and the new provision is equally appropriate to other types of transport document. The provision does not extend to the standby letter of credit, however, unless a transport document is called for. It is arguable that the 21 day default position in Article 47(a) is too short where multiple re-sales are envisaged,[106] but in that case the parties should stipulate a longer period.

8.4.7 Loading on board, dispatch and taking in charge (shipment)

Article 50 states:

"(a) Unless otherwise stipulated in the credit, the expression 'shipment' used in stipulating an earliest and/or latest shipment date will be understood to include the expressions 'loading on board', 'dispatch', and 'taking in charge'.

(b) The date of issuance of the transport document determined in accordance with Article 47(b) will be taken to be the date of shipment.

(c) Expressions such as 'prompt', 'immediately', 'as soon as possible', and the like should not be used. Banks will interpret them as a stipulation that shipment is to be made within 30 days from the issuance of the credit by the issuing bank.

---

106. F.M. Ventris, *Bankers' Documentary Credits*, first supplement to the second edition (Lloyd's of London Press Ltd. (1985)), p. 38.

(d) If the expression 'on or about' and similar expressions are used, banks will interpret them as a stipulation that shipment is to be made during the period from five days before to five days after the specified date, both end days included."

As with other provisions considered in this section, Article 50(a) was significantly altered in 1983 to cater for transport documents apart from the traditional shipped bill of lading. The previous provision provided for shipment alone, whereas for example a combined transport document will usually be issued earlier.[107]

8.4.8 Date terms

The relevant provisions are contained in Articles 51–53:

Article 51:

"The words 'to', 'until', 'till', 'from' and words of similar import applying to any date term in the credit will be understood to include the date mentioned. The word 'after' will be understood to exclude the date mentioned."

Article 52:

"The terms 'first half', 'second half' of a month shall be construed respectively as the 1st to the 15th, and the 16th to the last day of each month, inclusive.

Article 53:

"The terms 'beginning', 'middle', or 'end' of a month shall be construed respectively as from the 1st to the 10th, the 11th to the 20th, and the 21st to the last day of each month, inclusive."

The problem here is that "from" in Article 51 includes the date mentioned and "after" excludes it. Hence "180 days after sight" is one day later than "180 days from sight". Ideally, perhaps, "from" should be assimilated with "after", so as to exclude the initial date.

---

107. See section 5.3.1.2.

APPENDIX A

UNIFORM CUSTOMS AND PRACTICE ON DOCUMENTARY CREDITS (1983 REVISION) OF THE INTERNATIONAL CHAMBER OF COMMERCE*

A. GENERAL PROVISIONS AND DEFINITIONS

ARTICLE 1

These Articles apply to all documentary credits, including, to the extent to which they may be applicable, standby letters of credit, and are binding on all parties thereto unless otherwise agreed. They shall be incorporated into each documentary credit by wording in the credit indicating that such credit is issued subject to *Uniform Customs and Practice for Documentary Credits*, 1983 Revision. I.C.C. Publication, No. 400.

ARTICLE 2

For the purposes of these Articles, the expressions "documentary credit(s)" and "standby letter(s) of credit" used herein (hereinafter referred to as "credit(s)" means any arrangement, however named and described, whereby a bank (the issuing bank), acting at the request and on the instructions of a customer (the applicant for the credit),

  (i) is to make a payment to or to the order of a third party (the beneficiary), or is to pay or accept bills of exchange (drafts) drawn by the beneficiary, or,
 (ii) authorises another bank to effect such payment, or to pay, accept or negotiate such bills of exchange (drafts), against stipulated documents, provided that the terms and conditions of the credit are complied with.

ARTICLE 3

Credits, by their nature, are separate transactions from the sales or other contract(s) on which they are based and banks are in no way concerned with or bound by such contract(s), even if any reference whatsoever to such contract(s) is included in the credit.

---

* *Uniform Customs & Practice for Documentary Credits* (I.C.C. Publication No. 400), ©️ International Chamber of Commerce 1983. Published by the International Chamber of Commerce and available from I.C.C. United Kingdom, Centre Point, 103 New Oxford Street, London, WC1A 1QB.

ARTICLE 4

In credit operations all parties concerned deal in documents, and not in goods, services and/or other performances to which the documents may relate.

ARTICLE 5

Instructions for the issuance of credits, the credits themselves, instructions for any amendments thereto and the amendments themselves must be complete and precise.

In order to guard against confusion and misunderstanding, banks should discourage any attempt to include excessive detail in the credit or in any amendment thereto.

ARTICLE 6

A beneficiary can in no case avail himself of the contractual relationship existing between the banks or between the applicant for the credit and the issuing bank.

B. FORM AND NOTIFICATION OF CREDITS

ARTICLE 7

(a) Credits may be either (i) revocable or (ii) irrevocable.

(b) All credits, therefore, should clearly indicate whether they are revocable or irrevocable.

(c) In the absence of such indication the credit shall be deemed to be revocable.

ARTICLE 8

A credit may be advised to a beneficiary through another bank (the advising bank) without engagement on the part of the advising bank, but that bank shall take reasonable care to check the apparent authenticity of the credit which it advises.

ARTICLE 9

(a) A revocable credit may be amended or cancelled by the issuing bank at any moment and without prior notice to the beneficiary.

(b) However, the issuing bank is bound to:

(i) reimburse a branch or bank with which a revocable credit has been made available for sight payment, acceptance or negotiation, for any payment, acceptance or negotiation made by such branch or bank prior to receipt by it of notice of amendment or cancellation, against documents which appear on their face to be in accordance with the terms and conditions of the credit;

(ii) reimburse a branch or bank with which a revocable credit has been made available for deferred payment, if such branch or bank has, prior to receipt by it of notice of amendment or cancellation, taken up documents which appear on their face to be in accordance with the terms and conditions of the credit.

ARTICLE 10

(a) An irrevocable credit constitutes a definite undertaking of the issuing bank, provided that the stipulated documents are presented and that the terms and conditions of the credit are complied with:

(i) if the credit provides for sight payment—to pay, or that payment will be made;

(ii) if the credit provides for deferred payment—to pay, or that payment will be made on the date(s) determinable in accordance with the stipulations of the credit;

(iii) if the credit provides for acceptance—to accept drafts drawn by the beneficiary if the credit stipulates that they are to be drawn on the issuing bank, or to be responsible for their acceptance and payment at maturity if the credit stipulates that they are to be drawn on the applicant for the credit or any other drawee stipulated in the credit;

(iv) if the credit provides for negotiation—to pay without recourse to drawers and/or *bona fide* holders, draft(s) drawn by the beneficiary, at sight or at tenor, on the applicant for the credit or on any other drawee stipulated in the credit other than the issuing bank itself, or to provide for negotiation by another bank and to pay, as above, if such negotiation is not effected.

(b) When an issuing bank authorises or requests another bank to confirm its irrevocable credit and the latter has added its confirmation such confirmation constitutes a definite undertaking of such bank (the confirming bank), in addition to that of the issuing bank, provided that the stipulated documents are presented and that the terms and conditions of the credit are complied with:

(i) if the credit provides for sight payment—to pay or that payment will be made;

(ii) if the credit provides for deferred payment—to pay, or that payment will be made on the date(s) determinable in accordance with the stipulations of the credit;

(iii) if the credit provides for acceptance—to accept drafts drawn by the beneficiary if the credit stipulates that they are to be drawn on the confirming bank, or to be responsible for their acceptance and payment at maturity if the credit stipulates that they are to be drawn on the applicant for the credit;

(iv) if the credit provides for negotiation—to negotiate without recourse to drawers and/or *bona fide* holders, draft(s) drawn by the beneficiary, at sight or tenor, on the issuing bank or on the applicant for the credit or on any other drawee stipulated in the credit other than on the confirming bank itself.

(c) If a bank is authorised or requested by the issuing bank to add its confirmation to a credit but is not prepared to do so, it must so inform the issuing bank without delay. Unless the issuing bank specifies otherwise in its confirmation, authorisation or request, the advising bank will advise the credit to the beneficiary without adding its confirmation.

(d) Such undertakings can neither be amended nor cancelled without the agreement of the issuing bank, the confirming bank (if any), and the beneficiary. Partial acceptance of amendments contained in one and the same advice of amendment is not effective without the agreement of all the above-named parties.

ARTICLE 11

(a) All credits must clearly indicate whether they are available by sight payment, deferred payment, by acceptance or by negotiation.

(b) All credits must nominate the bank (nominated bank) which is authorised to pay (paying bank), or to accept drafts (accepting bank), or to negotiate (negotiating bank), unless the credit allows negotiation by any bank (negotiating bank).

(c) Unless the nominated bank is the issuing bank or the confirming bank, its nomination by the issuing bank does not constitute any undertaking by the nominated bank to pay, to accept or to negotiate.

(d) By nominating a bank other than itself, or by allowing for negotiation by any bank, or by authorising or requesting a bank to add its confirmation, the issuing bank authorises such bank to pay, accept or negotiate, as the case may be, against documents which appear on their face to be in accordance with the terms and conditions of the credit and undertakes to reimburse such bank in accordance with the provisions of these articles.

ARTICLE 12

(a) When an issuing bank instructs a bank (advising bank) by any teletransmission to advise a credit or an amendment to a credit and intends the mail confirmation to be the operative credit instrument or the operative amendment, the teletransmission must state "full details to follow" (or words of similar effect), or that the mail confirmation will be the operative instrument or the operative amendment. The issuing bank must forward the operative credit instrument or the operative amendment to such advising bank without delay.

(b) The teletransmission will be deemed to be the operative credit instrument or the operative amendment, and no mail confirmation should be sent, unless the teletransmission states "full details to follow" (or words of similar effect), or that the mail confirmation is to be the operative instrument or the operative amendment.

(c) A teletransmission intended by the issuing bank to be the operative credit instrument should clearly indicate that the credit is issued subject to *Uniform Customs and Practice for Documentary Credits*, 1983 revision, I.C.C. publication No. 400.

(d) If a bank uses the services of another bank or banks (the advising bank) to have the credit advised to the beneficiary, it must also use the services of the same bank(s) for advising any amendments.

(e) Banks shall be responsible for any consequences arising from their failure to follow the procedures set out in the preceding paragraphs.

ARTICLE 13

When a bank is instructed to issue, confirm or advise a credit similar in terms to one previously issued, confirmed or advised (similar credit) and the previous credit has been the subject of amendment(s), it shall be understood that the similar credit will not include any such amendment(s) unless the instructions specify clearly the amendment(s) which is/are to apply to the similar credit. Banks should discourage instructions to issue, confirm or advise a credit in this manner.

ARTICLE 14

If incomplete or unclear instructions are received to issue, advise or amend a credit, the bank requested to act on such instructions may give preliminary notification to the beneficiary for information only and without responsibility. The credit will be issued, confirmed, advised or amended only when the necessary information has been received and if the bank is then prepared to act on the instructions. Banks should provide the necessary information without delay.

C. LIABILITIES AND RESPONSIBILITIES

ARTICLE 15

Banks must examine all documents with reasonable care to ascertain that they appear on their face to be in accordance with the terms and conditions of the credit. Documents which appear on their face to be inconsistent with one another will be considered as not appearing on their face to be in accordance with the terms and conditions of the credit.

ARTICLE 16

(a) If a bank so authorised effects payment, or incurs a deferred payment undertaking, or accepts, or negotiates against documents which appear on their face to be in accordance with the terms and conditions of the credit, the party giving such authority shall be bound to reimburse the bank which has effected payment, or incurred a deferred payment undertaking, or has accepted, or negotiated, and to take up the documents.

(b) If, upon receipt of the documents, the issuing bank considers that they appear on their face not to be in accordance with the terms and conditions of the credit, it must determine, on the basis of the documents alone, whether to take up such documents, or to refuse them and claim that they appear on their face not to be in accordance with the terms and conditions of the credit.

(c) The issuing bank shall have a reasonable time in which to examine the documents and to determine as above whether to take up or to refuse the documents.

(d) If the issuing bank decides to refuse the documents, it must give notice to that effect without delay by telecommunication or, if that is not possible, by other expeditious means, to the bank from which it received the documents (the remitting bank), or to the beneficiary, if it received the documents directly from him. Such notice must state the discrepancies in respect of which the issuing bank refuses the documents and must also state whether it is holding the documents at the disposal of, or is returning them to, the presentor (remitting bank or the beneficiary, as the case may be). The issuing bank shall then be entitled to claim from the remitting bank refund of any reimbursement which may have been made to that bank.

(e) If the issuing bank fails to act in accordance with the provisions of paragraphs (c) and (d) of this article and/or fails to hold the documents at the disposal of, or return them to, the presentor, the issuing bank shall be precluded from claiming that the documents are not in accordance with the terms and conditions of the credit.

(f) If the remitting bank draws the attention of the issuing bank to any discrepancies in the documents or advises the issuing bank that it has paid, incurred a deferred payment undertaking, accepted or negotiated under reserve or against an indemnity in respect of such discrepancies, the issuing bank shall not be thereby relieved from any of its obligations under any provisions of this article. Such reserve or indemnity concerns only the relations between the remitting bank and the party towards whom the reserve was made or from whom, or on whose behalf, the indemnity was obtained.

ARTICLE 17

Banks assume no liability or responsibility for the form, sufficiency, accuracy, genuineness, falsification or legal effect of any documents, or for the general and/or particular conditions stipulated in the documents or superimposed thereon; nor do they assume any liability or responsibility for the description, quantity, weight, quality, condition, packing, delivery, value, or the existence of the goods represented by the documents, or for the good faith or acts and/ or omissions, solvency, performance or standing of the consignor, the carriers, or the insurers of the goods or of any other person whomsoever.

ARTICLE 18

Banks assume no liability or responsibility for the consequences arising out of delay and/or loss in transit of any messages, letters or documents, or for delay, mutilation or other errors arising in the transmission of any telecommunication. Banks assume no liability or responsibility for errors in translation or interpretation of technical terms, and reserve the right to transmit credit terms without translating them.

ARTICLE 19

Banks assume no liability or responsibility for the consequences arising out of the interruption of their business by Acts of God, riots, civil commotions, insurrections, wars or any causes beyond their control, or by any strikes, or lockouts. Unless specifically authorised, banks will not, upon resumption of their business, incur a deferred payment undertaking, or effect payment, acceptance or negotiation under credits which expired during such interruption of their business.

ARTICLE 20

(a) Banks utilising the services of another bank or other banks for the purpose of giving effect to the instructions of the applicant for the credit do so for the account and at the risk of such applicant.

(b) Banks assume no liability or responsibility should the instructions they transmit not be carried out, even if they have themselves taken the initiative in the choice of such other bank.

(c) The applicant for the credit shall be bound by and be liable to indemnify the banks against all obligations and responsibilities imposed by foreign laws and usages.

ARTICLE 21

(a) If an issuing bank intends that the reimbursement to which a paying, accepting or negotiating bank is entitled shall be obtained by such bank claiming on another branch or office of the issuing bank or on a third bank (all hereinafter referred to as the reimbursing bank) it shall provide such reimbursing bank in good time with proper instructions or authorisation to honour such reimbursement claims and without making it a condition that the bank entitled to claim reimbursement must certify compliance with the terms and conditions of the "credit" to the reimbursing bank.

(b) An issuing bank will not be relieved from any of its obligations to provide reimbursement itself if and when reimbursement is not effected by the reimbursing bank.

(c) The issuing bank will be responsible to the paying, accepting or negotiating bank for any loss of interest if reimbursement is not provided on first demand made to the reimbursing bank, or as otherwise specified in the credit or mutually agreed, as the case may be.

D. DOCUMENTS

ARTICLE 22

(a) All instructions for the issuance of credits and the credits themselves and, where applicable, all instructions for amendments thereto and the amendments themselves must state precisely the document(s) against which payment, acceptance or negotiation is to be made.

(b) Terms such as "first class", "well known", "qualified", "independent", "official" and the like shall not be used to describe the issuers of any document to be presented under a credit. If such terms are incorporated in the credit terms, banks will accept the relevant documents as presented, provided that they appear on their face to be in accordance with the other terms and conditions of the credit.

(c) Unless otherwise stipulated in the credit, banks will accept as originals documents produced or appearing to have been produced:
  (i) by reprographic means;
  (ii) by, or as the result of, automated or computerised systems;
  (iii) as carbon copies;
if marked as originals, always provided that where necessary, such documents appear to have been authenticated.

ARTICLE 23

When documents other than transport documents, insurance documents and commercial invoices are called for, the credit should stipulate by whom such documents are to be issued and their wording or data content. If the credit does not so stipulate, banks will accept such documents as presented, provided that their data content makes it possible to relate the goods and/or services referred to therein to those referred to, in the commercial invoice(s) presented, or to those referred to in the credit if the credit does not stipulate presentation of a commercial invoice.

ARTICLE 24

Unless otherwise stipulated in the credit, banks will accept a document bearing a date of issuance prior to that of the credit, subject to such document being presented within the time limits set out in the credit and in these articles.

D.1 Transport Documents (documents indicating loading on board or dispatch or taking in charge)

ARTICLE 25

Unless a credit calling for a transport document stipulates as such document a marine bill of lading (ocean bill of lading or a bill covering carriage by sea), or a post receipt or certificate of posting:

(a) Banks will, unless otherwise stipulated in the credit, accept a transport document which:

 (i) appears on its face to have been issued by a named carrier, or his agent, and

 (ii) indicates dispatch or taking in charge of the goods, or loading on board, as the case may be, and

 (iii) consists of the full set of originals issued to the consignor if issued in more than one original, and

 (iv) meets all the other stipulations of the credit.

(b) Subject to the above, and unless otherwise stipulated in the credit, banks will not reject a transport document which:

 (i) bears a title such as "Combined transport bill of lading", "Combined transport document", "Combined transport bill of lading or port-to-port bill of lading", or a title or a combination of titles of similar intent and effect, and/or

 (ii) indicates some or all of the conditions of carriage by reference to a source of document other than the transport document itself (short form/blank back transport document), and/or

 (iii) indicates a place of taking in charge different from the port of loading and/or place of final destination different from the port of discharge, and/or

 (iv) relates to cargoes such as those in containers or on pallets, and the like, and/or

 (v) contains the indication "intended", or similar in qualification, in relation to the vessel or other means of transport, and/or port of loading and/or the port of discharge.

(c) Unless otherwise stipulated in the credit in the case of carriage by sea or by more than one mode of transport but including carriage by sea, banks will reject a document which:

 (i) indicates that it is subject to a charterparty, and/or

 (ii) indicates that the carrying vessel is propelled by sail only.

(d) Unless otherwise stipulated in the credit, banks will reject a transport document issued by a freight forwarder unless it is the FIATA Combined Transport Bill of Lading approved by the International Chamber of

Commerce or otherwise indicates that it is issued by a freight forwarder acting as carrier or agent of a named carrier.

ARTICLE 26

If a credit calling for a transport document stipulates as such document a marine bill of lading:

(a) Banks will, unless otherwise stipulated in the credit, accept a document which:
- (i) appears on its face to have been issued by a named carrier, or his agent, and
- (ii) indicates that the goods have been loaded on board or shipped on a named vessel, and
- (iii) consists of the full set of originals issued to the consignor if issued in more than one original, and
- (iv) meets all other stipulations of the credit.

(b) Subject to the above, and unless otherwise stipulated in the credit, banks will not reject a document which:
- (i) bears a title such as "Combined transport bill of lading", "Combined transport document", "Combined transport bill of lading or port-to-port bill of lading", or a title or a combination of titles of similar intent and effect, and/or
- (ii) indicates some or all of the conditions of carriage by reference to a source of document other than the transport document itself (short form/blank back transport document), and/or
- (iii) indicates a place of taking in charge different from the port of loading and/or place of final destination different from the port of discharge, and/or
- (iv) relates to cargoes such as those in Containers or on pallets, and the like.

(c) Unless otherwise stipulated in the credit, banks will reject a document which:
- (i) indicates that it is subject to a charterparty, and/or
- (ii) indicates that the carrying vessel is propelled by sail only, and/or
- (iii) contains the indication "intended", or similar in qualification, in relation to:
  the vessel and/or port of loading—unless such document bears an on board notation in accordance with article 27(b) and also indicates the actual port of loading and/or
  the port of discharge—unless the place of final discharge indicated on the document is other than the port of discharge, and/or
- (iv) is issued by a freight forwarder, unless it indicates that it is issued by such freight forwarder acting as a carrier, or as the agent of a named carrier.

ARTICLE 27

(a) Unless a credit specifically calls for an on board transport document, or unless inconsistent with other stipulation(s) in the credit or with article 26, banks will accept a transport document which indicates that goods have been taken in charge or received for shipment.

(b) Loading on board or shipment on a vessel may be evidenced either by a transport document bearing words indicating loading on board a named vessel or shipment on a named vessel, or, in the case of a transport document stating "received for shipment" by means of a notation of loading on board on the transport document signed or initialled and dated by the carrier or his agent, and the date of this notation shall be regarded as the date of loading on board the named vessel or shipment on the named vessel.

ARTICLE 28

(a) In the case of carriage by sea or by more than one mode of transport but including carriage by sea, banks will refuse a transport document stating that the goods are or will be loaded on deck, unless specifically authorised in the credit.

(b) Banks will not refuse a transport document which contains a provision that the goods may be carried on deck, provided it does not specifically state that they are or will be loaded on deck.

ARTICLE 29

(a) For the purpose of this article transhipment means a transfer and reloading during the course of carriage from the port of loading or place of dispatch or taking in charge to the port of discharge or place of destination either from one conveyance or vessel to another conveyance or vessel within the same mode of transport or from one mode of transport to another mode of transport.

(b) Unless transhipment is prohibited by the terms of the credit, banks will accept transport documents which indicate that the goods will be transhipped, provided that the entire carriage is covered by one and the same transport document.

(c) Even if transhipment is prohibited by the terms of the credit, banks will accept transport documents which:

(i) incorporate printed clauses stating that the carrier has the right to tranship, or

(ii) state or indicate that transhipment will or may take place, when the credit stipulates a combined transport document, or indicates carriage from a place of taking in charge to a place of final destination by different modes of transport including a carriage by sea, provided that the entire carriage is covered by the same transport document, or

(iii) state or indicate that the goods are in a container(s), trailer(s),

"LASH" barge(s), and the like and will be carried from the place of taking in charge to the place of final destination in the same container(s), trailer(s), "LASH" barge(s), and the like under one and the same transport document;

(iv) state or indicate the place of receipt and/or of final destination as "C.F.S." (container freight station) or C.Y. (container yard) at, or associated with, the port of loading and/or the port of destination.

ARTICLE 30

If the credit stipulates dispatch of goods by post and calls for a postal receipt or certificate of posting, banks will accept such post receipt or certificate of posting if it appears to have been stamped or otherwise authenticated and dated in the place from which the credit stipulates the goods are to be dispatched.

ARTICLE 31

(a) Unless otherwise stipulated in the credit, or inconsistent with any of the documents presented under the credit, banks will accept transport documents stating that freight or transportation charges (hereinafter referred to as "freight") have still to be paid.

(b) If a credit stipulates that the transport document has to indicate that freight has been paid or prepaid, banks will accept a transport document on which words clearly indicating payment or prepayment of freight appear by stamp or otherwise, or on which payment of freight is indicated by other means.

(c) The words "freight prepayable" or "freight to be prepaid" or words of similar effect, if appearing on transport documents, will not be accepted as constituting evidence of the payment of freight.

(d) Banks will accept transport documents bearing reference by stamp or otherwise to costs additional to the freight charges, such as costs of, or disbursements incurred in connection with loading, unloading, or similar operations, unless the conditions of the credit specifically prohibit such reference.

ARTICLE 32

Unless otherwise stipulated in the credit banks will accept transport documents which bear a clause on the face thereof such as "shippers load and count" or "said by shipper to contain" or words of similar effect.

ARTICLE 33

Unless otherwise stipulated in the credit, banks will accept transport documents indicating as the consignor of the goods a party other than the beneficiary of the credit.

ARTICLE 34

(a) A clean transport document is one which bears no superimposed clause or notation which expressly declares a defective condition of the goods and/or the packaging.

(b) Banks will refuse transport documents bearing such clauses or notations unless the credit expressly stipulates the clauses or notations which may be accepted.

(c) Banks will regard a requirement in a credit for a transport document to bear the clause "clean on board" as complied with if such transport document meets the requirements of this article and article 27(b).

D.2   Insurance Documents

ARTICLE 35

(a) Insurance documents must be as stipulated in the credit, and must be issued and/or signed by insurance companies or underwriters or their agents.

(b) Cover notes issued by brokers will not be accepted, unless specifically authorised by the credit.

ARTICLE 36

Unless otherwise stipulated in the credit, or unless it appears from the insurance document(s) that the cover is effective at the latest from the date of loading on board or taking in charge of the goods, banks will refuse documents which bear a date later than the date of loading on board or dispatch or taking in charge of the goods as indicated by the transport document(s).

ARTICLE 37

(a) Unless otherwise stipulated in the credit, the insurance document must be expressed in the same currency as the credit.

(b) Unless otherwise stipulated in the credit, the minimum amount for which the insurance document must indicate the insurance cover to have been effected is the CIF (cost, insurance and freight . . . "named port of destination") or CIP (freight / carriage and insurance paid to "named port of destination") value of the goods, as the case may be, plus 10 per cent. However, if banks cannot determine the CIF or CIP value, as the case may be, from the documents on their face, they will accept as such minimum amount the amount for which payment, acceptance or negotiation is requested under the credit, or the amount of the commercial invoice whichever is the greater.

ARTICLE 38

(a) Credits should stipulate the type of insurance required and, if any, the additional risks which are to be covered. Imprecise terms such as "usual

229

risks" or "customary risks" should not be used; if they are used, banks will accept insurance documents as presented, without responsibility for any risks not being covered.

(b) Failing specific instructions, banks will accept insurance cover as tendered.

ARTICLE 39

Where a credit stipulates "insurance against all risks", banks will accept an insurance document which contains any "all risks" notation or clause, whether or not bearing the heading "all risks", even if indicating that certain risks are excluded, without responsibility for any risk(s) not being covered.

ARTICLE 40

Banks will accept an insurance document which indicates that the cover is subject to a franchise or an excess (deductible), unless it is specifically stipulated in the credit that the insurance must be issued irrespective of percentage.

D.3 *Commercial Invoice*

ARTICLE 41

(a) Unless otherwise stipulated in the credit, commercial invoices must be made out in the name of the applicant for the credit.

(b) Unless otherwise stipulated in the credit, banks may refuse commercial invoices issued for amounts in excess of the amount permitted by the credit. Nevertheless, if a bank authorised to pay, incur a deferred payment undertaking, accept, or negotiate under a credit accepts such invoices, its decision will be binding on all parties, provided such bank has not paid, incurred a deferred undertaking, accepted or effected negotiation for an amount in excess of that permitted by the credit.

(c) The description of the goods in the commercial invoice must correspond with the description in the credit. In all other documents, the goods may be described in general terms not inconsistent with the description of the goods in the credit.

D.4 *Other Documents*

ARTICLE 42

If a credit calls for an attestation or certification of weight in the case of transport other than by sea, banks will accept a weight stamp or declaration of weight which appears to have been superimposed on the transport document by the carrier or by his agent unless the credit specifically stipulates that the attestation or certification of weight must be by a separate document.

E. MISCELLANEOUS PROVISIONS

Quantity and amount

ARTICLE 43

(a) The words "about", "circa" or similar expressions used in connection with the amount of the credit or the quantity or the unit price stated in the credit are to be construed as allowing a difference not to exceed 10 per cent. more or 10 per cent. less than the amount or the quantity or the unit price to which they refer.

(b) Unless a credit stipulates that the quantity of the goods specified must not be exceeded or reduced, a tolerance of 5 per cent. more or 5 per cent. less will be permissible, even if partial shipments are not permitted, always provided that the amount of the drawings does not exceed the amount of the credit. This tolerance does not apply when the credit stipulates the quantity in terms of a stated number of packing units or individual items.

Partial drawings and/or other shipments

ARTICLE 44

(a) Partial drawings and/or shipments are allowed, unless the credit stipulates otherwise.

(b) Shipments by sea, or more than one mode of transport but including carriage by sea, made on the same vessel and for the same voyage, will not be regarded as partial shipments, even if the transport documents indicating loading on board bear different dates of issuance and/or indicate different ports of loading on board.

(c) Shipments made by post will not be regarded as partial shipments if the post receipts or certificates of posting appear to have been stamped or otherwise authenticated in the place from which the credit stipulates the goods are to be dispatched, and on the same date.

(d) Shipments made by modes of transport other than those referred to in paragraphs (b) and (c) of this article will not be regarded as partial shipments, provided the transport documents are issued by one and the same carrier or his agent and indicate the same date of issuance, the same place of dispatch or taking in charge of the goods, and the same destination.

Drawings and/or shipments by instalments

ARTICLE 45

If drawings and/or shipments by instalments within given periods are stipulated in the credit and any instalment is not drawn and/or shipped within the period allowed for that instalment, the credit ceases to be available for that and any subsequent instalment, unless otherwise stipulated in the credit.

Expiry date and presentation

ARTICLE 46

(a) All credits must stipulate an expiry date for presentation of documents for payment, acceptance or negotiation.

(b) Except as provided in article 48(a), documents must be presented on or before such expiry date.

(c) If an issuing bank states that the credit is to be available "for one month", "for six months" or the like, but does not specify the date from which the time is to run, the date of issuance of the credit by the issuing bank will be deemed the first day from which such time is to run. Banks should discourage indication of the expiry date in this manner.

ARTICLE 47

(a) In addition to stipulating an expiry date for presentation of documents, every credit which calls for transport document(s) should also stipulate a specified period of time after the date of issuance of the transport document(s) during which presentation of documents for payment, acceptance or negotiation must be made. If no such period of time is stipulated, banks will refuse documents presented to them later than 21 days after the date of issuance of the transport document(s). In every case, however, documents must be presented not later than the expiry date of the credit.

(b) For the purposes of these articles the date of issuance of the transport document(s) will be deemed to be:

    (i) in the case of a transport document evidencing dispatch, or taking in charge, or receipt of goods for shipment by a mode of transport other than by air—the date of issuance indicated on the transport document or the date of the reception stamp thereon whichever is the later.

    (ii) in the case of a transport document evidencing carriage by air—the date of issuance indicated on the transport document or, if the credit stipulates that the transport document shall indicate an actual flight date, the actual flight date as indicated on the transport document.

    (iii) in the case of a transport document evidencing loading on board a named vessel—the date of issuance of the transport document or, in the case of an on board notation in accordance with article 27(b), the date of such notation.

    (iv) in cases to which article 44(b) applies, the date determined as above of the latest transport document issued.

ARTICLE 48

(a) If the expiry date of the credit and/or the last day of the period of time after the date of issuance of the transport document(s) for presentation of documents stipulated by the credit or applicable by virtue of article 47 falls on a day on which the bank to which presentation has to be made is closed for reasons other than those referred to in article 19 the stipulated expiry date and/or the last day of the period of time after the date of issuance of the transport document(s) for presentation of documents, as the case may be, shall be extended to the first following business day on which such bank is open.

(b) The latest date for loading on board, or dispatch, or taking in charge shall not be extended by reason of the extension of the expiry date and/or the period of time after the date of issuance of transport document(s) for presentation of document(s) in accordance with this article. If no such latest date for shipment is stipulated in the credits or amendments thereto, banks will reject transport documents indicating a date of issuance later than the expiry date stipulated in the credit or amendments thereto.

(c) The bank to which presentation is made on such first following business day must add to the documents its certificate that the documents were presented within the time limits extended in accordance with article 48(a) of the *Uniform Customs and Practice for Documentary Credits*, 1983 revision. I.C.C. publication No. 400.

ARTICLE 49
Banks are under no obligation to accept presentation of documents outside their banking hours.

Loading on board, dispatch and taking in charge (shipment)

ARTICLE 50
(a) Unless otherwise stipulated in the credit, the expression "shipment" used in stipulating an earliest and/or latest shipment date will be understood to include the expressions "loading on board", "dispatch", and "taking in charge".

(b) The date of issuance of the transport document determined in accordance with article 47(b) will be taken to be the date of shipment.

(c) Expressions such as "prompt", "immediately", "as soon as possible", and the like should not be used. Banks will interpret them as a stipulation that shipment is to be made within 30 days from the issuance of the credit by the issuing bank.

(d) If the expression "on or about" and similar expressions are used, banks will interpret them as a stipulation that shipment is to be made during the period from five days before to five days after the specified date, both end days included.

Date terms

ARTICLE 51
The words "to", "until", "till", "from" and words of similar import applying to any date term in the credit will be understood to include the date mentioned. The word "after" will be understood to exclude the date mentioned.

ARTICLE 52

The terms "first half", "second half" of a month shall be construed respectively as 1 to 15, and 16 to the last day of each month, inclusive.

ARTICLE 53

The terms "beginning", "middle", or "end" of a month shall be construed respectively as from 1 to 10, 11 to 20,and 21 to the last day of each month, inclusive.

F. TRANSFER

ARTICLE 54

(a) A transferable credit is a credit under which the beneficiary has the right to request the bank called upon to effect payment or acceptance or any bank entitled to effect negotiation to make the credit available in whole or in part to one or more other parties (second beneficiaries).

(b) A credit can be transferred only if it is expressly designated as "transferable" by the issuing bank. Terms such as "divisible", "fractionable","assignable", and "transmissible" add nothing to the meaning of the term "transferable" and shall not be used.

(c) The bank requested to effect the transfer (transferring bank) shall be under no obligation to effect such transfer except to the extent and in the manner expressly consented to by such bank.

(d) Bank charges in respect of transfers are payable by the first beneficiary unless otherwise specified. The transferring bank shall be under no obligation to effect the transfer until such charges are paid.

(e) A transferable credit can be transferred once only. Fractions of a transferable credit (not exceeding in the aggregate the amount of the credit) can be transferred separately, provided partial shipments are not prohibited, and the aggregate of such transfers will be considered as constituting only one transfer of the credit. The credit can be transferred only on the terms and conditions specified in the original credit, with the exception of the amount of the credit, of any unit prices stated therein, of the period of validity, of the last date for presentation of documents in accordance with article 47 and the period for shipment, any or all of which may be reduced or curtailed, or the percentage for which insurance cover must be effected, which may be increased in such a way as to provide the amount of cover stipulated in the original credit, or these articles. Additionally, the name of the first beneficiary can be substituted for that of the applicant for the credit, but if the name of the applicant for the credit is specifically required by the original credit to appear in any document other than the invoice, such requirement must be fulfilled.

(f) The first beneficiary has the right to substitute his own invoices (and drafts if the credit stipulates that drafts are to be drawn on the applicant for the credit) in exchange for those of the second beneficiary, for amounts not in excess of the original amount stipulated in the credit and for the original unit prices if stipulated in the credit, and upon such substitution of invoices (and drafts) the first beneficiary can draw under the credit for the difference, if any, between his invoices and the second beneficiary's invoices.

When a credit has been transferred and the first beneficiary is to supply his own invoices (and drafts) in exchange for the second beneficiary's invoices (and drafts) but fails to do so on demand, the paying, accepting or negotiating bank has the right to deliver to the issuing bank the documents received under the credit, including the second beneficiary's invoices (and drafts) without further responsibility to the first beneficiary.

(g) Unless otherwise stipulated in the credit, the first beneficiary of a transferable credit may request that the credit be transferred to a second beneficiary in the same country, or in another country. Further, unless otherwise stipulated in the credit, the first beneficiary shall have the right to request that payment or negotiation be effected to the second beneficiary at the place to which the credit has been transferred, up to and including the expiry date of the original credit, and without prejudice to the first beneficiary's right subsequently to substitute his own invoices and drafts (if any) for those of the second beneficiary and to claim any difference due to him.

ARTICLE 55

The fact that a credit is not stated to be transferable shall not affect the beneficiary's right to assign any proceeds to which he may be, or may become, entitled under such credit, in accordance with the provisions of the applicable law.

BILLS OF LADING ACT 1855

(Chapter 111)

An Act to amend the Law relating to Bills of Lading.   [14 August 1855]

Preamble

Whereas, by the custom of merchants, a bill of lading of goods being transferable by endorsement, the property in the goods may thereby pass to the indorsee, but nevertheless all rights in respect of the contract contained in the bill of lading continue in the original shipper or owner; and it is expedient that such rights should pass with the property: And whereas it frequently happens that the goods in respect of which bills of lading purport to be signed have not been laden on board, and it is proper that such bills of lading in the hands of a *bona fide* holder for value should not be questioned by the master or other person signing the same on the ground of the goods not having been laden as aforesaid:

Consignees, and indorsees of bills of lading empowered to sue

1. Every consignee of goods named in a bill of lading, and every indorsee of a bill of lading to whom property in the goods therein mentioned shall pass upon or by reason of such consignment or indorsement shall have transferred to and vested in him all rights of suit, and be subject to the same liabilities in respect of such goods as if the contract contained in the bill of lading had been made with himself.

Saving as to stoppage in transitu, and claims for freight, etc

2. Nothing herein contained shall prejudice or affect any right of stoppage *in transitu*, or any right to claim freight against the original shipper or owner, or any liability of the consignee or indorsee by reason or in consequence of his being such consignee or indorsee, or of his receipt of the goods by reason or in consequence of such consignment or indorsement.

Bill of lading in hands of consignee, etc., conclusive evidence of shipment as against master, etc.

3. Every bill of lading in the hands of a consignee or indorsee for valuable consideration, representing goods to have been shipped, shall be conclusive evidence of such shipment as against the master or other person signing the same, notwithstanding that such goods or some part thereof may not have been so shipped, unless such holder of the bill of lading shall have had actual notice at the time of receiving the same that the goods had not in fact been laden on board: Provided, that the master or other person so signing may exonerate himself in respect of such misrepresentation by showing that it was caused without any default on his part, and wholly by the fraud of the shipper, or of the holder, or some person under whom the holder claims.

INDEX

References are to section numbers
*Section numbers in **bold** type indicate the main discussion*